WITHDRAWN

JUAN DE MARIANA AND EARLY MODERN SPANISH POLITICAL THOUGHT

Juan de Mariana
and Early Modern Spanish
Political Thought

HARALD E. BRAUN
University of Liverpool, UK

ASHGATE

BIRKBECK LIBRARY COLLEGE

© Harald E. Braun 2007

All rights reserved. No part of this publication may be reproduced, stored in a retrieval system or transmitted in any form or by any means, electronic, mechanical, photocopying, recording or otherwise without the prior permission of the publisher.

Harald E. Braun has asserted his moral right under the Copyright, Designs and Patents Act, 1988, to be identified as the author of this work.

Published by
Ashgate Publishing Limited
Gower House
Croft Road
Aldershot
Hampshire GU11 3HR
England

Ashgate Publishing Company
Suite 420
101 Cherry Street
Burlington, VT 05401-4405
USA

Ashgate website: http://www.ashgate.com

British Library Cataloguing in Publication Data
Braun, Harald (Harald Ernst)
  Juan de Mariana and early modern Spanish political thought.
  – (Catholic Christendom, 1300–1700)
  1.Mariana, Juan de, 1535–1624 – Political and social views
  2.Mariana, Juan de, 1535–1624. De rege 3.Policy sciences –
  Spain – History –16th century
  I.Title
  320'.092

Library of Congress Cataloging-in-Publication Data
Braun, Harald (Harald Ernst)
  Juan de Mariana and early modern Spanish political thought / Harald E. Braun.
      p. cm. – (Catholic christendom, 1300–1700)
  Includes bibliographical references and index.
  1. Mariana, Juan de, 1535–1624. 2. Political science– Spain– History. I. Title.

JA84.S7B73 2007
320.092– dc22

2006018489

ISBN 978-0-7546-3962-6

Printed and bound in Great Britain by Antony Rowe Ltd, Chippenham, Wiltshire

Contents

Acknowledgements

This book evolved from my Oxford D.Phil. thesis. I would like to thank the British Academy, the Carlyle Scholarship Committee and St. Edmund Hall, Oxford, for supporting my doctoral research. The advice and the time so generously offered by many friends and scholars helped turn the dissertation into a book. Fernando Cervantes, George Garnett, Andrew Hegarty, Alistair Malcolm, Tom Mayer, Mia Rodríguez-Salgado, Joan-Pau Rubiés, Martin Stone and the anonymous reader each made suggestions and corrections that proved invaluable. I am particularly indebted to Sir John Elliott for his critical readership, encouragement and ongoing support. Whatever the mistakes and shortcomings of this book, they are entirely my own responsibility.

Writing your first monograph can be a pretty arduous exercise at times. This book owes more to my wife's patience, wisdom and good counsel than I can express in words. It is dedicated to her, Rebecca Joanne, with all my love.

Series Editor's Preface

The still-usual emphasis on medieval (or Catholic) and reformation (or Protestant) religious history has meant neglect of the middle ground, both chronological and ideological. As a result, continuities between the middle ages and early modern Europe have been overlooked in favour of emphasis on radical discontinuities. Further, especially in the later period, the identification of 'reformation' with various kinds of Protestantism means that the vitality and creativity of the established church, whether in its Roman or local manifestations, has been left out of account. In the last few years, an upsurge of interest in the history of traditional (or Catholic) religion makes these inadequacies in received scholarship even more glaring and in need of systematic correction. The series will attempt this by covering all varieties of religious behaviour, broadly interpreted, not just (or even especially) traditional institutional and doctrinal church history. It will to the maximum degree possible be interdisciplinary, comparative and global, as well as non-confessional. The goal is to understand religion, primarily of the 'Catholic' variety, as a broadly human phenomenon, rather than as a privileged mode of access to superhuman realms, even implicitly.

The period covered, 1300–1700, embraces the moment which saw an almost complete transformation of the place of religion in the life of Europeans, whether considered as a system of beliefs, as an institution, or as a set of social and cultural practices. In 1300, vast numbers of Europeans, from the Pope down, fully expected Jesus' return and the beginning of His reign on earth. By 1700, very few Europeans, of whatever level of education, would have subscribed to such chiliastic beliefs. Pierre Bayle's notorious sarcasms about signs and portents are not idiosyncratic. Likewise, in 1300 the vast majority of Europeans probably regarded the pope as their spiritual head; the institution he headed was probably the most tightly integrated and effective bureaucracy in Europe. Most Europeans were at least nominally Christian, and the Pope had at least nominal knowledge of that fact. The papacy, as an institution, played a central role in high politics, and the clergy in general formed an integral part of most governments, whether central or local. By 1700, Europe was divided into a myriad of different religious allegiances, and even those areas officially subordinate to the pope were both more nominally Catholic in belief (despite colossal efforts at imposing uniformity) and also in allegiance than they had been four hundred years earlier. The Pope had become only one political factor, and not one of the first rank. The clergy, for its part, had virtually disappeared from secular governments as well as losing much of its local authority. The stage was set for the Enlightenment.

Thomas F. Mayer,
Augustana College

Preface

This study aims to reassess the political thinking of Juan de Mariana SJ (1535-1624). It focuses on his treatise on the education of the prince: *De rege et regis institutione libri tres*. Mariana enjoyed a reputation of excellence both as a theologian and a historian of his native Spain when he published this book in 1599. It was to change his reputation profoundly, lastingly, and in a way unforeseen by its author. The treatise was written at the behest of García de Loaysa, archbishop of Toledo, tutor to the future king of Spain, and one of Philip II's most influential clerical counsellors during the later years of his reign. Published soon after Philip II's death in 1598, the treatise was meant to remind his son and heir Philip III of the principles of good kingship and of the rightful place of the clergy of Castile in the government of the *monarquía española*. Soon, however, the work became infamous for the radical doctrines it allegedly contained. The majority of readers outside Spain took *De rege* as further evidence that the Society of Jesus actively encouraged the killing of legitimate rulers whom it deemed enemies of the Catholic faith. Modern interpreters in turn tended to regard the book as a singularly daring, albeit not entirely coherent exploration of medieval notions of popular sovereignty and individual right of resistance. Mariana is said to have pushed notions of medieval scholastic constitutionalism to their radical conclusion, bestowing upon the private individual the right to kill a legitimate prince whose abuse of power had clearly marked him out as a tyrant. It was noted that he had failed to develop his theories with proper attention to juridical detail and procedure. Though commissioned by the former tutor of Philip III of Spain and dedicated to his pupil, *De rege* was read as a violent indictment of Habsburg absolutism conceived and written in the terms of scholastic juridical tradition.

Revisiting what Mariana actually wrote and what meaning he meant to convey is overdue. Recent research has done much to change our views of the cultural, institutional and political contexts within which early modern Spanish political thinking evolved. For instance, the notion of Spanish Habsburg absolutism has been thoroughly revised. John Elliott, José Fortea Pérez, Charles Jago and I.A.A. Thompson have shown that the government of Spain was far from being 'centralized' in the modern sense of the word, and that the fortunes of the cortes of Castile and Aragon revived during the reigns of Philip II and Philip III.[1] José Fernández-Santamaria,

---

1   See, for instance, J.H. Elliott (1988), 'Foreign Policy and Domestic Crisis: Spain 1598-1659', in K. Repgen (ed.), *Krieg und Politik, 1618-1648* (Schriften des Historischen Kollegs, Kolloquien; Vol. 8), Munich, pp. 185-202 [reprinted ibid., (1989), *Spain and its World, 1500-1700*, Yale University Press, New Haven and London, pp. 114-36]. For revisionist angles on Castilian parliamentarism see J.L. Fortea Pérez (1991), 'The Cortes of Castile and Philip II's Fiscal Policy', in *Parliaments, Estates and Representation*, Vol. 11, pp. 117-38; C. Jago (1981), 'Habsburg Absolutism and the Cortes of Castile', *American Historical Review*, Vol. 86, pp. 307-26; and id. (1995), 'Taxation and Political Culture in Castile, 1590-1640', in R.L. Kagan and G. Parker (eds), *Spain, Europe and the Atlantic World*, Essays in honour of John H. Elliott, Cambridge University

Joan-Pau Rubiés and Xavier Gil have taken great strides to bring together the theory and practice of Spanish reason of state.[2] Mariana himself enjoys renewed interest in his life and thought. *De rege* is now available in Luis Sánchez Agesta's scholarly translation into the Spanish vernacular.[3] Ronald Truman in his book on Spanish mirrors-of-princes includes Mariana among the leading Spanish political thinkers of his time, and Harro Höpfl in his excellent study *Jesuit Political Thought* compares Mariana's handling of seminal issues of early modern statecraft to that of prominent fellow Jesuit theologians.[4] Yet even the most recent discussions of Mariana's political thinking still tend to consider him primarily as a 'humanist precursor to modern constitutionalism'.[5] Höpfl and Truman are to my knowledge the first to cast tentative doubts on his standing as a (proto-) constitutionalist thinker. The treatise still needs to be read and taken seriously as a whole rather than have its content and value judged, ultimately, on the basis of the few passages apparently offering a radical early modern perspective on tyrannicide and sovereignty.

This study argues that *De rege* is anything but a Jesuit's exercise in early modern scholastic constitutionalism. Mariana is a thinker resigned rather than radical in his approach to issues of resistance and sovereignty. His resignation is the result of an altogether pessimistic, Augustinian view of the *conditio humana*. This rather depressing assessment of the moral and intellectual capabilities of monarchs and subjects alike causes him to be uncommonly disillusioned with conventional juridical theorems concerning the rights of princes and subjects. At the same time, Mariana is acutely aware of the transformation of European political discourse in the wake of the reception of Machiavelli's *Il Principe*. He responds by integrating topics and terminologies familiar from juridical and theological texts and debates into a discourse of political prudence. Not infrequently, Mariana indulges in deliberately

---

Press, Cambridge, pp. 48-72. Also I.A.A. Thompson (1994), 'Castile: Polity, Fiscality and Fiscal Crisis'; in P.T. Hoffmann and K. Norberg (eds), *Fiscal Crises, Liberty and Representative Government, 1450-1789*, Stanford University Press, Stanford, pp. 140-80. A critical review of revisionist standpoints (concerning the crown of Aragon) is offered by X. Gil, (1993), 'Crown and Cortes in Early Modern Aragon: Reassessing Revisionism', *Parliaments, Estates and Representation*, Vol. 13, pp. 109-22.

2   J.A. Fernández-Santamaria (1983), *Reason of State and Statecraft in Spanish Political Thought*, University Press of America, Lanham, Md.; J.-P. Rubiés (1995), 'Reason of State and Constitutional Thought in the Crown of Aragon, 1580-1640', *Historical Journal*, Vol. 38, pp. 1-28; X. Gil (2000), 'La razón de estado en la España de la Contrarreforma. Usos y razones de la política', in S. Rus Rufino et al. (eds), *La razón de estado en la España moderna*, Real Sociedad Económica de Amigos del País, Valencia, pp. 37-58.

3   Juan de Mariana (1981), *La dignidad real y la educación del rey (De rege et regis institutione)*, ed. L. Sanchez-Agesta, Centro de Estudios Constitucionales, Madrid.

4   R. Truman (1999), *Spanish Treatises on Government, Society and Religion in the Time of Philip II, The 'de regimine principum' and associated Traditions*, Brill, Leiden; H. Höpfl (2004), *Jesuit Political Thought. The Society of Jesus and the State, c. 1540-1630* (Ideas in Context), Cambridge University Press, Cambridge.

5   Sanchez-Agesta, *La dignidad real y la educación del rey*, introduction: *El P. Juan de Mariana, un humanista precursor del constitucionalismo*, especially pp. xxii-xxiv.

ornate paraphrase and inversion of themes, concepts and terminologies drawn from scholastic and classical sources. He freely chooses and uses traditions at least as much as he is 'influenced' by them.[6] The result is a unique mix of terminologies and discourses that borders on constituting a political language in its own right.

Mariana is innovative in further respects. The final chapters of each of the three books of his treatise are dedicated to matters of religion. In many respects, the discussion in these chapters follows conventional lines of contemporary prudential discourse on religious toleration or the relationship between Church and monarchy. It culminates, however, in a comprehensive, indeed grandiose assault on one of the very pillars of royal power in Habsburg Castile: the power over the Church. *De rege* is the work of a partisan of a post-Tridentine Castilian secular clergy keen to preserve and, indeed, dramatically enhance its hold on political power. Mariana exposes himself as truly worthy of his longstanding notoriety - though not in the manner which his many detractors and admirers suggested.

---

6   On the problem of 'influences' in the study of early modern political thought, see F. Oakley (1996), '"Anxieties of Influence": Skinner, Figgis, Conciliarism and Early Modern Constitutionalism', *Past and Present*, Vol. 151, pp. 60-110; and H. Höpfl and M.P. Thompson (1979), 'The History of Contract as a Motif in Political Thought', *The American Historical Review*, Vol. 84, pp. 919-44; see also the introduction to T.F. Mayer (1989), *Thomas Starkey and the Commonweal: Humanist Politics and Religion in the Reign of Henry VIII*, Cambridge University Press, Cambridge. The debate was spurred by Q. Skinner's article (1969), 'Meaning and Understanding in the History of Ideas', *History and Theory*, Vol. 8, pp. 3-53. A useful introduction to the debate is provided by the contributions in J. Tully (ed.) (1987), *Meaning and Context: Quentin Skinner and his Critics*, Polity Press, Cambridge.

Revisiting *De rege*

When Juan de Mariana SJ published *De rege et regis institutione* in 1599, he was already known as a distinguished Jesuit theologian and, more widely yet, as the foremost historian of his native Spain.[1] *De rege* had been commissioned by none other than the former tutor to the heir to the throne and archbishop of Toledo, García de Loaysa. It was dedicated to Loaysa's former pupil, King Philip III of Spain. The treatise was to use historical examples to draw out the Christian principles of statecraft by which the young king was to abide.[2] Mariana's task was not an easy one. The death of Philip II after a reign of more than forty years had opened the vent for animated and divisive debate over the future course of the monarchy. The regime of the royal favourite, Don Francisco Gómez de Sandoval y Rojas, latterly Duke of Lerma, had not yet channelled and curtailed public discussion. At the same time, Machiavelli and his alleged decoy Tacitus had made it eminently more difficult for orthodox Catholic writers to lay down the moral laws of politics. In a Europe torn apart by confessional war, writing a mirror-of-princes could be a hazardous business. Outside Spain, *De rege* was soon denounced for its 'corrosive and destructive' doctrine, and its author branded a regicidal poison-pen. Yet, arguably, the primate of Spain could not have chosen a better man than Mariana.

Historian of Spain and Teacher of Political Wisdom

It is easy to see why García de Loaysa turned to Mariana. By the time he was asked to write *De rege*, Mariana had made his mark as a humanist and theologian. Born in Talavera de la Reina in 1535, the natural son of a local canon joined the Society of Jesus in 1554.[3] After studying theology at the University of Álcala de Henares, he went on to teach at Jesuit seminaries in Loreto, Sicily and Paris.[4] Two years after bearing witness to the 'miserable spectacle' of the Saint Bartholomew's

---

1   Juan de Mariana (1599), *De rege et regis institutione libri III*, Pedro Rodríguez, Toledo [further Latin editions with varying pagination: Mayence in 1605 and 1611]. Modern translation into Spanish: Juan de Mariana (1981), *La dignidad real y la educación del rey (De rege et regis institutione)*, ed. L. Sanchez-Agesta, Centro de Estudios Constitucionales, Madrid. All references are to the 1599 edition. I have slightly updated the original spelling and punctuation.

2   *De rege*, preface.

3   Hardly anything is known about the education Mariana received before he took holy orders. See G. Cirot (1904), 'La famille de Juan de Mariana', *Bulletin Hispanique*, Vol. 6, pp. 309-31, and ibid. (1936), 'Mariana jesuite: la jeunesse', *Bulletin Hispanique*, Vol. 38, pp. 295-352.

4   On his career as a teacher of divinity see F. Asensio SJ (1953), 'El profesorado de Juan de Mariana y su influjo en la vida del escritor', *Hispania*, Vol. 31, pp. 581-639.

Day Massacre,[5] Mariana returned to his native Spain, semi-retiring to the house of the Society of Jesus in Toledo. Soon after his return, he used his theological and philological expertise to defend the Polyglot Bible produced under the direction of Benito Arias Montano (1572) against the suspicion of heresy.[6] His standing was such that the Inquisitor General Gaspar de Quiroga consulted him on the Spanish Index of prohibited and expurgated books issued in 1583 and 1584.[7] In 1592, he further enhanced his standing as a man of letters by providing the Spanish and European public with the first history of Spain. Meriting numerous editions and translations, the *Historiae de rebus Hispaniae* would remain the standard work on Spanish history up to the eighteenth century.[8]

Some countrymen soon linked the Jesuit's fame to the fact that he had produced not only the first great history of Spain, but also one with a distinct and very contemporary edge.[9] The Toledan ecclesiastical historian and political writer Eugenio Narbona explains what kind of edge that was. He makes extensive reference to the *History of Spain* and *De rege* in particular in the preface to his *Doctrina política civil* (1604). Narbona calls Mariana not just the Livy of Spain, but also her Thucydides and Tacitus.[10] The *Historiae* does not merely report events in lucid chronological order and with admirable objectivity, but includes analyses of the mechanisms of princely power. Mariana offers historiography with the added value of political wisdom nurtured on clear-eyed observation of the uses and abuses of power. In Narbona's view, that would already suffice to make him a Spanish Tacitus.[11] *De rege*,

---

5   Juan de Mariana (1605), *Historiae de rebus Hispaniae libri XXV* [XX], Balthasar Lipp, Mayence, *Sumario*, anno 1572.

6   The *censura* was produced in 1577. See Juan de Mariana (1609), *Pro editione Vulgata*, in *Tractatus VII*, Anton Hierat, Cologne.

7   F. Asensio SJ (1972), 'Juan de Mariana ante el Indice quiroguiano de 1583-84', *Estudios Bíblicos*, Vol. 31, pp. 135-78, p. 178, suggests that it should be called the 'Indice de Mariana'.

8   Juan de Mariana (1592), *Historiae de rebus Hispaniae libri XXV*, Pedro Rodríguez, Toledo. On Mariana's historiographical work see the masterly study by G. Cirot (1905), *Études sur l'historiographie espagnole: Mariana historien* (Bibliothèque de la Fondazion Thiers; Vol. 8), Feret et Fils, Bordeaux.

9   The *Historiae* was very positively received. A critique was offered by the faultfinding Pedro Mantuano (1611), *Advertencias a la historia del Padre Juan de Mariana de la Compania de Iesus*, n.p., Milan. The dispute is reconstructed by Cirot, *Mariana historien*, pp. 191-97. On historiographical controversies in early modern Spain see P. Linehan (1993), *History and the Historians of Medieval Spain*, Clarendon Press, Oxford.

10   Eugenio Narbona (1621), *Doctrina política civil, escrita en aphorismos: sacados de la doctrina de los Sabios, y exemplos de la experiencia*, n.p., Toledo, *Advertencias al Lector* [unpaginated]. This is the slightly expurgated version of a treatise first published in 1604. The changes demanded are insubstantial. See J. Vilar (1968), 'Intellectuels et Noblesse: Le *Docteur* Eugenio de Narbona (Une admiration politique de Lope de Vega)', *Études Iberique*, Vol. 3, pp. 7-28.

11   A similar statement in N. Antonio (1788), *Bibliotheca hispana nova: sive Hispanorum scriptorum qui ab anno MD. ad MDCLXXXIV floruere notitia*, J. de Ibarra, Madrid, Vol. 1, p. 732.

however, complements and augments the narrative of the *Historiae* in that prudent *sententiae* illuminate historical *exempla*. Narbona goes on to call himself a proud 'disciple of Mariana'. Having awarded himself this accolade, he certainly seems to have felt entitled to lift long passages from the treatise. This was not the only time authors marshalled, and, in some cases misrepresented Mariana in order to boost the authority of their own argument.

Mariana himself repeatedly alerts readers to the fact that he sees a close connection between his historiographical work and the treatise on the education of the prince. The preface to his own vernacular translation of the *Historiae* (1601) reminds Philip III that he was not long ago presented with 'a book that comprised the virtues that befit a good king'.[12] *De rege*, he says, discusses in a theoretical manner (*especulativamente*) all the 'precepts, counsels and the rules' that ought to govern the life of a prince. Historical *exempla* enliven the abstract discussion. The many volumes of his history of Spain further illustrate these principles of statecraft and 'show how they are put into practice' by means of even more examples drawn from ancient, and especially from Spanish, history. *De rege* promises to furnish Philip with nothing less than an integrated history, ethics and theory of government sufficiently comprehensive and complex to inform the kind of decisions expected from a king of Spain.

The *Historiae*, clearly, was not conceived to be followed up with a treatise on political prudence. The reader consulting the two works in tandem more often than not will have to read between the lines to find shared meaning. Yet artful and imaginative reading between the lines is exactly what the reader of *De rege* is required to do. Many of the historical examples lined up seemingly in support of the argument in fact subvert or differentiate its meaning. Some of Mariana's pronouncements on deception as a means of politics are of the kind Catholic theologians would stomach only in an author of whose Christian orthodoxy they were fully assured. Other *exempla* illustrate Mariana's topical conviction that the prince reading the works of select historians will listen 'to mute teachers (…) who advise often what is salutary and condemn in others the vices of the reader'.[13] In this vein, the Roman historian Tacitus and his own history of Spain supply some of the most powerful references for the abuse of the law and the depravity of peoples as well as princes and their courtiers.

The categorical condemnation of the royal favourite or *privado* is a particularly striking example of Mariana's use of Tacitean history as a 'mute teacher'. The treatise is sprinkled with pithy references to Sejanus and his Spanish equivalent Don Alvaro de Luna, the favourite of John II of Castile (1406-54). The duke of Lerma is never identified by name, though contemporary readers could hardly miss

---

12   Juan de Mariana (1601), *Historia general de Espana, Compuesta primero en Latin, despues buelta en Castellano por Iuan de Mariana*, Pedro Rodriguez, Toledo, I, preface, p. 3.

13   *De rege*, pp. 389-90. Translations are my own unless stated otherwise. I have consulted the English translation by G.A. Moore (1948), *The King and the Education of the King*, The Country Dollar Press, Chevy Chase.

the parallel between Don Francisco and those 'courtiers and fawners' who crowd the courts and confuse princes. Yet, while comparing Lerma more or less explicitly to Sejanus and Alvaro de Luna might easily have earned Mariana the enmity of a powerful man, it did not represent the kind of Tacitism (that is, Machiavellianism at one remove) likely to disturb theologians and political moralists.

There is evidence to suggest that Mariana had been involved in the education of Prince Philip some years before the publication of *De rege*. In 1594, the papal nuncio reports that García de Loaysa was reading to his pupil a treatise entitled *De institutione principis*.[14] While the term is merely generic, Mariana suggests in the preface of *De rege* that Loaysa had urged him to bring into publishable form ideas on the education of the prince he had drafted some years previously. When Mariana informed the archbishop that the publication of *De rege* was imminent, the latter quickly responded expressing his hope that *De rege* would help further the interest of the Church at the court in Madrid.[15] The treatise was commissioned not least to outline Church-friendly views and policies the new government was expected to adopt. García de Loaysa appears to have been content with the result.[16]

De rege is replete with instances of prescient and daring critique of the ills of Spanish government and society. The repetitive denunciation of the *privado* already mentioned is just one example. Another one is that Mariana impresses upon Philip III the expediency of military disengagement as well as the need to seek a fairer distribution of the burden of war among the component parts of the monarchy.[17] The count-duke of Olivares would refer to his proposals when developing his ill-fated plans for the Union of Arms.[18] Olivares would note, too, Mariana's outright indictment of the corrosive effect of the *limpieza de sangre* statutes. His words on the matter are yet another example of Mariana's aptitude for lucid and coolly rational scrutiny. His argument is cast exclusively in terms of language of political prudence. Divine providence, and certainly Christian dogma are noticeably absent

---

14   In a letter to cardinal Aldobrandini dated 27 April 1594, Camillo Borghese (later Paul V) describes the education of the future Philip III, and remarks that 'Don García de Loaysa le ha leido una parte de los *Comentarios* de César y ahora le lee un tratado *De Institutione Principum*'; R. de Hinojosa (1896), *Los despachos de la diplomacia pontificia en España*, Vol. 1, B.A. de la Fuente, Madrid, p. 380 (the original is in the *Archivio Secreto de la Santa Sede, Archivio Borghese*, Cod. III, 94ᶜ).

15   British Library Egerton Manuscripts, 1875, p. 19 (printed: Juan de Mariana (1783), *Historia general de España*, B. Monfort, Valencia, Vol. 1, xcviii).

16   On García de Loaysa's ideas concerning the relationship between prince and Church in post-Tridentine Spain see H.E. Braun (2004), 'Conscience, Counsel and Theocracy at the Spanish Habsburg Court', in H.E. Braun and E. Vallance (eds), *Contexts of Conscience in Early Modern Europe, 1500-1700*, Palgrave-Macmillan, Basingstoke, pp. 56-66.

17   See *De rege*, pp. 295-98.

18   See J.H. Elliott and J.F. de la Pena (eds) (1980), *Memoriales y cartas del conde duque de Olivares*, Tomo II: *Política interior: 1628 a 1645*, Ediciones Alfaguara, Madrid, pp. 145-46. See also J.H. Elliott (1963), *The Revolt of the Catalans: a Study in the Decline of Spain*, Cambridge University Press, Cambridge, especially pp. 204-208, pp. 514-15.

from his consideration. Mariana is prepared to infuse Spanish political thinking with a healthy dose of pragmatism. His fierce patriotic feelings towards Castile as well as the Church of Toledo would continue to permeate his writing.

In this respect, the objective of *De rege* is very similar to those of other treatises published during the period of transition of power after the death of Philip II. One of the most influential and in many ways paradigmatic writers is Baltasar Álamos de Barrientos. Álamos de Barrientos is as keen as Mariana to provide an inexpert and untried heir to the throne with pragmatic advice. His *Discurso político al rey Felipe III al comienzo de su reinado* (1598) shows the mind of a seasoned courtier, politician and administrator at work.[19] The *Discurso* provides a systematic survey of those issues specific to the various realms which constituted the *monarquía española*. Separate chapters highlight some of the general predicaments faced by rulers of early modern composite monarchies.[20] Álamos de Barrientos's central concern is with Castile. Though 'doubtlessly the head of this monarchy', she can no longer be expected to carry almost on her own the burden of defending the Spanish Habsburg monarchy against her many enemies.[21] The new regime will have to reduce military and political commitments in order to save Spain's power and possessions. Álamos de Barrientos is also one of the Spanish sixteenth-century authors explicit about the need to combine political reform with a new ethics of politics sourced from Tacitus. He would soon follow up his *Discurso* with what turned out to be his most widely read work, namely his epigrammatic 'translation' of Tacitus.[22]

Mariana's choice of terminology and the issues raised in *De rege* show that he wishes to join a specific debate. The treatise was meant to be read in comparison or competition with prudential literature of the kind produced by Álamos de Barrientos and Narbona. Like the latter, Mariana seeks to enhance the status of political prudence as a vehicle for the preservation of the Habsburg monarchy. Theologians like his fellow Jesuit and friend Pedro de Ribadeneira, on the other hand, wish to demarcate tight boundaries for political pragmatism in Habsburg Spain. Ribadeneira's prime concern is to preserve the ideological purity of Spanish Christian political thinking. Providence is to remain the handmaiden of divine providence. Somewhere between Ribadeneira's profoundly providential perspective

---

19 I use the modern edition: (1990), *Discurso político al rey Felipe III al comienzo de su reinado*, ed. M. Santos (Textos y Documentos; Vol. 7), Anthropos, Madrid.

20 J.H. Elliott (1992), 'A Europe of Composite Monarchies', *Past and Present*, Vol. 137, pp. 48-71.

21 *Discurso*, cap. 'Castilla', p. 26.

22 Baltasar Álamos de Barrientos (1614), *Tácito español, ilustrado con aforismos*, Luis Sa[n]chez, Madrid. On Álamos de Barrientos, the strategies he employed in his adaptation of Tacitist themes see C. Davies (2001), 'Baltasar Álamos de Barrientos and the Nature of Spanish Tacitism', in N. Griffin, C. Griffin, E. Southworth and C. Thompson (eds), *Culture and Society in Habsburg Spain*, Tamesis, London, pp. 57-78. On the many facets of Spanish Tacitism see also the relevant chapters in J.A. Maravall (1975), *Estudios de historia del pensamiento español*, Vol. 3: *siglo XVII*, 2nd edn, Ediciones Cultura Hispanica, Madrid; and the valuable contributions in Rus Rufino, 'La razón de estado' [see Preface, p. xxi. Footnote 2].

and Álamos de Barrientos's more secular outlook, Mariana carves out his own discriminating stance on where the Castilian political mind should turn.

Drawing on a variety of European political discourses, these authors sought to produce political manuals tailored specifically to fit the needs of the Spanish Habsburgs and their domains. Despite the clear emphasis in terms of issue and outlook, *De rege* has yet to be recognized as a contribution to this specific debate about the future course of the Spanish monarchy in the late 1590s. Much of the blame has to be apportioned to the way in which the treatise was received outside Spain. It is useful, therefore, to make a brief detour and touch upon the way in which the treatise was read before I outline the purpose of this study in more detail.

The Making of Mariana's Notoriety

By the time Mariana thought it expedient to remind Philip III of the existence of *De rege*, his patron had died in disgrace, and his book had started to cause a commotion of unforeseeable nature and dimension. In Chapter six of Book one of *De rege*, Mariana appeared to praise Henry III's assassin Jacques Clément as the 'eternal glory of France'.[23] More worryingly still, he seemed to combine a doctrine of popular sovereignty with a defence of the right of the private individual to kill not only the usurper of the throne but also the *tyrannus ex parte exercitii* (a legitimate ruler whose exercise of power marked her or him out as a tyrant).[24] Mariana, indeed, repeatedly assures readers that 'there is no doubt that royal power has its source in the *respublica* which may call the king before the law in specific circumstances, and, if necessary, even deprive him of his *principate*'.[25] The treatise helped corroborate suspicions about the regicidal attitudes and machinations so widely ascribed to the Society of Jesus. Catholic and Calvinist *politiques* in France were particularly quick to take issue with Mariana's 'pernicious doctrines'.[26]

De rege was identified as a Jesuit reworking of doctrines of popular sovereignty and popular resistance already expounded in the treatises of the so-called

---

23   *De rege*, pp. 68-69.

24   The literature on early modern conceptions of tyrannicide and the debate on what does and what does not constitute legitimate resistance is boundless. For a general survey see M. D'Addio (1987), 'Il Tirannicidio', in L. Firpo (ed.), *Storia delle idee politiche, economiche e sociali*, Vol. 3: *Umanesimo e Rinascimento*, Turin, pp. 511-610 (on Mariana, pp. 581-84); and M. Turchetti (2001), *Tyrannie et tyrannicide de l'antiquité à nos jours*, Presses Universitaires de France, Paris.

25   *De rege*, p. 72; see also p. 76, p. 79, p. 81.

26   See, for instance, the scholarly refutations of *De rege* and defence of the divine right of kings by Antoine Leclerc (1610), *La defense des puissances de la terre*, n.p., Paris; and Michel Roussel (1610), *Antimariana ou refutation des propositions de Mariana*, n.p., Paris. Roussel's treatise was published twice in 1610. A good example of the vitriolic polemics triggered by *De rege* is the anonymous *Anticoton ou refutation de la lettre declaratoire du Père Coton* published in 1610.

'Monarchomachs'. The latter term refers to the group of French Catholic writers who provided much of the ideological backbone of the Catholic League.[27] Authors like Jean Boucher or William Reynolds drew on their Calvinist contemporaries and adapted arguments developed by sixteenth-century conciliarists such as Jacques Almain and John Mair.[28] Though by no means homogeneous in experience and outlook, the Monarchomachs agreed that some form of supreme and inalienable political authority was lodged in the *populus* as a corporate whole. The people, not the violent mob but rather a 'prudent multitude assembled by law', had the power to depose and kill a king who abused the authority and trust bestowed upon him.[29] Though the composition of that 'prudent multitude' was never really specified, it was evident that it would comprise all those who thought that Henry IV should share the fate of Henry III. Royalist writers in turn tried to smother the French penchant for fratricide. William Barclay is paradigmatic in that he sought to impose the image of a king who is subject only to God, acting 'ex certa scientia, supra ius, contra ius et extra ius'.[30]

After the assassination of Henry IV (May 1610), *De rege* was widely denounced as blatant Jesuit agitation to kill Henry and deliver France into the hands of Philip III, and the Gallican Church into those of the Pope. Mariana's 'contagious and corrosive' doctrines were alleged to have directly inspired the final attempt on the life of the 'good king Henry'.[31] *De rege* was publicly burnt by the hangman of Paris

---

27   See Jean Boucher (1589), *De iusta Henrici Tertii abdicatione*, n.p., Paris; or William Reynolds (1592) [Gulielmus Rossaeus], *De justa reipublicae Christianae in reges impios et haereticos authoritate*, Johannes Kerbergius, Antwerp. For a succinct introduction to sixteenth-century Catholic and Protestant theories of resistance see J.H.M. Salmon (1991), 'Catholic Resistance Theory, Ultramontanism, and the Royalist Response, 1580-1620', in J.H. Burns (ed.), *Cambridge History of Political Thought 1450-1700*, [from here on: *CHPTh*], Cambridge University Press, Cambridge pp. 219-53.

28   The conciliarist legacy of Almain and Mair is the subject of lively scholarly debate. See, for instance, the work of F. Oakley and J.H. Burns. Oakley's seminal articles are collected in (1984), *Natural Law, Conciliarism and Consent in the Late Middle Ages*, Ashgate, London. See also his (2003), *The Conciliarist Tradition, Constitutionalism in the Catholic Church, 1300-1870*, OUP, Oxford, especially pp. 111-40. Among Burns' contributions are (1991), 'Conciliarism, Papalism, and Power, 1511-1518', in D. Wood (ed.), *The Church and Sovereignty, c.590-1918*, Essays in Honour of Michael Wilks, Basil Blackwell, Oxford, pp. 409-28; and his (1992), *Lordship, Kingship, and Empire: The Idea of Monarchy, 1400-1525*, Clarendon Press, Oxford.

29   Boucher, *De iusta (...) abdicatione*, 1, 9, p. 19.

30   William Barclay (1600), *De regno et regali potestate aduersusBuchananum, Brutum, Boucherium et reliquos Monarchomachos libri VI*, Guillelmus Chaudiere, Paris, III, 14, p. 193. See also Leclerq, *Puissance*, especially pp. 23-27; and Roussel, *Antimariana*, especially chapter 20, pp. 114-21.

31   The assassin, François Ravaillac, was questioned under torture as to whether Mariana's treatise had induced him to commit the murder. Ravaillac denied any acquaintance with the book. See the printed edition of the protocol of the interrogation, Louis I [de Bourbon, Prince de Condé] (1743), *Mémoires de Condé ou Recueil pour servir à l'histoire de France (...) où l'on trouvera des preuves de l'histoire de M. de Thou*, Vol. 6, n.p., The Hague, pp. 217-44 [*Procés examen (...) du (...) parricide F. Ravaillac*]. For a thorough discussion of Ravaillac's motives

at the request of the Sorbonne and by order of the *parlement* of Paris.[32] Every attempt made by the Jesuit superior general to stem the tide of abuse against the Society in general and Mariana in particular failed.[33] Though he required Jesuits not to write in defence of *De rege*, Claudio Aquaviva neither publicly condemned or punished Mariana, nor did he manage to clarify the 'Jesuit position' on tyrannicide in a way that could have satisfied its detractors.[34] It is doubtful that he could have done anything to appease the critics of the Society. The one thing he may have succeeded in is preventing a discussion in which either the author himself or others on his behalf would have been able to defend and clarify the seemingly contentious ideas contained in *De rege*. The work of a Spanish Jesuit, *De rege* simply had to be a regicidal pamphlet.[35] Mariana became a liability to the Society and the reputation of Catholic political thought.[36]

Anti-Marianan writers commonly ignored the fact that the least Mariana does is to distinguish between the right to slay a tyrant and the authority to decide whether or not a king actually must be considered a tyrant. Even Barclay concedes that a king who seeks to devastate his kingdom deprives himself of all lordship and *de*

---

as well as the repercussions of his action for the Society in France see R. Mousnier (1964), *L'assassinat d'Henri IV, 14 mai 1610 (Trente journées qui ont fait la France;* Vol. 13), Gallimard, Paris, especially Part VII; and now also E. Nelson (2005), *The Jesuits and the Monarchy, Catholic Reform and Political Authority in France (1590-1615)*, Ashgate, Aldershot, pp. 147-207.

32   Anonymous (1610), *Arrest de la cour du Parlement ensemble la censure de la Sorbonne contre le livre de Jean Mariana intitulé de Regis & Rege institutione* (…), n.p., Paris.

33   A copy of Aquaviva's decree sent to the upper-Rhenish provinces is printed in M. Pachtler SJ (1887-94), *Ratio studiorum et institutiones scholasticae Societas Jesu per Germaniam (…)* (Monumenta Germaniae pedagogica), A. Hofmann, Berlin, Vol. 9, p. 48. Aquaviva's orders, however, were not attended to as faithfully as he wished. See, for instance, the tract of J. Gretser SJ (1610*), De imperatorum, regum ac principum Christianorum in Sedem Apostolicam munificentia*, Adam Sartorius, Ingolstadt. Gretser, a German Jesuit teaching at the University of Ingolstadt, participated with a number of pamphlets and treatises in the oath of allegiance controversy. He crudely misrepresents Mariana's argument on tyrannicide, suggesting that he gives the Pope the right to excommunicate and depose rulers.

34   The text of the decree in J. Jouvancy SJ (1710), *Historia Societatis Jesu pars quinta*, Vol. 2: 1515-1616, San Marco, Rome, p. 124.

35   Particularly offensive to Gallican sympathies are Mariana's ideas on the fiscal immunity of the clergy. See, for instance, Anonymous (1610), *Aphorismes ou Sommaires de la Doctrine des Iesuites, & de quelques autres leurs Docteurs*, n.p., Paris, pp. 15-17.

36   Jesuits in France expressed concerns about the *De rege* as soon as it was published. A treatise by a Spanish Jesuit which appeared to defend the right of the people or the private individual to depose or even slay a legitimate prince was bound to cause trouble. The first request to suppress the book was duly put forward by the provincial synod of the Society of Jesus in France in the very year of its publication. The provincial congregations of Paris and Lyons duly repeated their calls for the suppression of the treatise immediately after *De rege* was republished in Mayence in 1605. Excerpts from both requests in B. Duhr SJ (1921), *Geschichte der Jesuiten in den Ländern deutscher Zunge*, Vol. 3, G.J. Manz, Munich and Regensburg, pp. 738-39.

facto if not *de iure* ceases to be king. The example is Nero, and the scenario Barclay describes is hardly different to the one offered in *De rege*.[37] The allegation that Mariana was an advocate of regicide itself was based largely on a few, frequently distorted citations, and on biased conjecture that drew solely from select pages from Chapter six of Book one of *De rege*. Michel Roussel is exemplary in that he uses about five brief citations from Chapter six as a peg on which to hang his theory of truly absolute kingship.[38] Like many contemporary and subsequent readers, Roussel takes the allegedly regicidal slogans of the text as indication of its sole purpose. He simply assumes that Mariana wished to join his debate.

Anti-Jesuit conjecture would continue to distort the arguments of *De rege*. In England, for instance, *De rege* became enmeshed in the paranoia stimulated by the Gunpowder Plot of 1605 and the subsequent Oath of Allegiance controversy.[39] Together with his former pupil cardinal Bellarmine, Mariana was one of the prime targets of Protestant suspicion. Addressing parliament in 1616, James I denounced the author of *De rege* for his blatant violation of the theory of the divine right of kings. Keen to turn Mariana into a papalist, and in a less than subtle manner, the king asks:

> why, if the Pope doth not approve and not like the practice of king-killing, wherefore hath not his Holiness imposed severe censure upon the booke of Mariana the Jesuite (by whom parricide are highly commended, nay, highly extolled) when his Holiness hath been pleased the pains to censure and call in some of Mariana's other books?[40]

None of Mariana's 'other books' were ever 'called in' by the papacy. Yet what actually happened to work and author had very little to do with what was said about it. Outside his native Spain, and despite being rather unlikely candidates, Mariana and his treatise for more than 300 years became inseparably connected with radical notions of popular sovereignty and the arbitrary murder of kings.

Fame instead of Notoriety: Mariana the 'Humanist Precursor' of Modern Democracy

At first, Mariana and *De rege* did not fare much better in times less passionate about the murder of kings and increasingly more enlightened about the countless conspiracy theories revolving around the Society of Jesus. Leopold von Ranke considered the book the most reckless contemporary discussion of popular sovereignty and regicide. Despite the lack of evidence, he felt bound to confirm that Mariana's 'doctrines had unquestionably kindled the fanaticism of the assassin

---

37 Barclay, *De regno*, III, 8, p. 159.

38 Roussel *Antimariana*, pp. 374-80.

39 For a concise summary of the debate see Salmon, 'Catholic Resistance Theory', pp. 236-44, pp. 247-53.

40 *The Political Works of James I*, ed. C.H. McIlwain (Cambridge, Mass., 1918), p. 247.

[of Henri IV]'.[41] Even within the Society of Jesus, Mariana's reputation recovered only gradually. John Laures SJ, the first to investigate Mariana's economic theory in some detail (1928), first of all apologizes for the 'one false and fatal doctrine that had sufficed to condemn him'. He goes on to plead with the readers that Mariana's other 'much more useful works' should not be ignored because of that mistake. Yet, at the same time, perhaps in order to increase Mariana's appeal to a modern readership, Laures confirms that the author of *De rege* 'hated tyranny more than anything else', and 'made important contributions to the development of democracy'.[42] Laures's remarks already indicate the interpretative turn in the study of Mariana's political thinking. His radical advocacy of popular sovereignty coupled with what was taken to be an unabashed defence of tyrannicide came to distinguish him in the view of modern, liberal students of intellectual history.

Historians of political ideas inherited from the early modern theologians and pamphletists the tendency to focus on the doctrine of individual resistance and popular sovereignty. They interpreted the argument of *De rege* in the predominantly juridical terms of late medieval scholastic constitutionalism, identifying Mariana as a passionate enemy of absolutism. For J.N. Figgis, *De rege* plays a major role in 'the embryology of modern politics'. According to Figgis, 'Mariana planted, Althusius watered, and Robespierre reaped the increase'.[43] In the view of Guenter Lewy, Mariana has the stature of a man who proposed 'for Spain the same rejuvenation of medieval constitutional ideas and practices which John Locke [would] undertake a hundred years later in England'.[44] Spanish history of political thought shares this view of Mariana. Luis Abellán finds in Mariana the kind of social contract that would later be developed and advanced by Hobbes and Rousseau, and calls him an 'outright defender of socialist attitudes'.[45] Luis Sánchez Agesta, finally, the editor of the modern Spanish translation of *De rege*, calls him 'a humanist precursor of constitutionalism'.[46] All in all, *De rege* is seen as representing a significant step forward on the long and arduous road towards the conceptualization of modern

41   L. von Ranke (1923), *Die römischen Päpste in den letzten vier Jahrhunderten*, 12th. ed., Duncker und Humblot, Munich, p. 379. A. Astraín, SJ (1923), *Historia de la Compañia de Jesús en la asistencia de España*, Vol. 3, Razón y Fe, Madrid, p. 558, finds praise for Mariana's integrity, scholarliness and literary style, but blames the conception of *De rege* on its author's eccentricity and a deeply cynical attitude.

42   J. Laures SJ (1928), *The Political Economy of Juan de Mariana*, Fordham University Press, New York, vii. See also the entry 'Juan de Mariana' in: A. de Backer (1890-1932), *Bibliotèque de la Compagnie de Jésus*, ed. C. Sommervogel, 12 vols., Schepens, Brussels, p. 1547.

43   J.N. Figgis (1907), *Studies in Political Thought from Gerson to Grotius: 1414-1625*, 2nd. ed., Cambridge University Press, Cambridge, p. 34.

44   G. Lewy (1960), *Constitutionalism and Statecraft during the Golden Age of Spain, A Study of the Philosophy of Juan de Mariana, S.J.* (Travaux d'Humanisme et Renaissance), E. Droz, Geneva, p. 51.

45   L. Abellán (1979), *Historia crítica del pensamiento español*, Vol. 2, Espasa-Calpe, Madrid, p. 586.

46   Juan de Mariana, *La dignidad real*, introduction, pp. xxii-xxiv.

parliamentary democracy. Mariana's place in this retrospective teleology of political theory is still that of the Spanish brother of the Monarchomachs.[47]

Yet modern authors increasingly acknowledge both the conceptual sagacity of the author as well as the richly woven texture of his treatise. Sánchez Agesta remarks upon the humanist way of political thinking that distinguishes Mariana from his neo-Thomist contemporaries. Gerhard Oestreich highlights some of the neo-Stoic themes that invite a comparison between *De rege* and the works of Justus Lipsius.[48] Quentin Skinner makes out predominantly anti-Machiavellian and anti-Tacitist attitudes in *De rege*, whilst Richard Tuck is struck by that 'unusual Jesuit's determinedly 'imperialist-Tacitist' language and conceptualization of politics.[49] Both are well within their rights identifying 'Tacitist' as well as 'anti-Tacitist' themes and elements in *De rege*. With equal justification, Joan Pau Rubiés admires in Mariana a courageous critic of Habsburg policies in late sixteenth-century Spain.[50] Like the spirited Mateo Lisón de Bedma, *procurador* for Granada, Mariana invokes some of the ideals and the languages of classical republicanism and medieval contractualism. This clash of interpretive angles is not easily reconciled. Its implicit contradictions make it difficult to identify Mariana as either 'Tacitist', 'anti-Tacitist', or as a clear-cut defender of 'constitucionalismo castellano'. At the same time, the very fact that *De rege* inspired such a multiplicity of interpretations offers first clues as to its distinct traits and meaning.

The Purpose of this Study: Towards a fuller Understanding of *De rege*

The rich and somewhat confusing tapestry of interpretation enveloping *De rege* is not least the author's own responsibility. Mariana tackles some of the most controversial issues of his day. The subject matters of tyrannicide, the royal *privado* and the *limpieza de sangre* statutes have already been mentioned. Yet he does not expound his doctrines and proposals in the systematic and detailed manner of a scholastic theologian or expert Roman lawyer. He prefers the flexibility and flourish of humanist rhetoric to the principles of scholastic juridical and theological discourse.

---

47 See, for instance, R.W. Carlyle and A.J. Carlyle (1936), *A History of Medieval Political Theory in the West*, Vol. 6: *Political Theory from 1300 to 1600*, Blackwood, Edinburgh and London, pp. 369-70 (Boucher and Mariana); or R. Dessens (1995), *La pensée politique de Juan de Mariana dans le mouvement monarchomaque catholique*, unpublished PhD thesis, Paris; also Q. Skinner (1978), *The Foundations of Modern Political Thought*, 2 vols., Cambridge University Press, Cambridge, Vol. 2, pp. 345-46.

48 *La dignidad real*, introduction, p. xv; G. Oestreich (1989), *Antiker Geist und moderner Staat bei Justus Lipsius (1547-1606), Der Neustoizismus als politische Bewegung*, ed. N. Mout (Schriftenreihe der Historischen Kommission bei der Bayerischen Akademie der Wissenschaften;Vol. 38), Vandenhoeck und Ruprecht, Göttingen, pp. 202-203,

49 Skinner, *Foundations*, Vol. 2, p. 172; R. Tuck (1993), *Philosophy and Government, 1572-1651*, Cambridge University Press, Cambridge, pp. 79-81.

50 J.-P. Rubiés (1996), 'La idea del gobierno mixto y su significado en la crisis de la monarquía hispanica', *Historia Social*, Vol. 24, pp. 57-81, pp. 68-69.

In this sense, *De rege* is non-systematic or untechnical in nature. Especially with regard to the topic of tyrannicide (or regicide), the way in which Mariana puts forward his argument is prone to invite multiple interpretations.

Yet the elegant flow of humanist Latin more than compensates for what may be perceived as lack of philosophical rigidity. In fact, the way in which *De rege* is constructed is as salient to our understanding of its meaning and place in history as the doctrine it contains.[51] Political wisdom is presented mainly in the condensed form of the commonplace. Pithy pearls of sombre truth permeate and indeed connect the various and diverse themes discussed in this comprehensive work. Mariana is thus able both to interlace the more theoretical with the more practical parts of his argument, and to ensure the most prominent themes are approached from various angles. Not dissimilar to Tacitus, Mariana's *sententiae* illuminate as much as they obscure the multi-layered historical examples served up to his readers. Many often carefully construed ambiguities give the audience ample opportunity to make up their own minds.[52] Wittingly or unwittingly, *De rege* empowers its readers. Mariana's style is dictated not least by his keen desire to involve readers outside the academic forum. This, again, is characteristic not just of *De rege*, but of the works of 'Tacitist' contemporaries like Álamos de Barrientos and Justus Lipsius. The way in which he writes may have invited varying interpretations. This does not, however, lessen the substance and value of what the treatise tells us about the multilayered, theoretical as well as practical ways of contemporary political thinking.

The relevance of *De rege* as a source of knowledge about early modern Spanish political thinking is confirmed by two of its particularly notable features. Both have consistently been ignored due to the focus on the allegedly radical constitutionalist nature of Mariana's argument. The first is the point of departure of his enquiry. Unlike Álamos de Barrientos, Lipsius, or Ribadeneira, *De rege* sets off with a speculative and in several respects unparalleled enquiry into the origins and nature of monarchical power (Book one). Mariana's profoundly pessimistic assessment of human nature puts him firmly into the Augustinian wing of contemporary Catholic

---

51   For a sceptical view of *De rege* as a work of 'political theory' see R. Truman (1999), *Spanish Treatises on Government, Society and Religion in the Time of Philip II, The 'de regimine principum' and associated Traditions*, Brill, Leiden. Truman's extremely learned book recovers a number of eminent Spanish political thinkers from undeserved obscurity. He considers *De rege* one of those Spanish treatises on government which 'are not primarily or predominantly works of political theory (…)', and therefore decides to exclude Book one of *De rege* (dealing with the origins and scope of political authority, including the issue of tyrannicide) from his analysis. Yet early modern political theory comes in many literary and conceptual shapes and forms. The 'values and attitudes of (...) authors concerning a broad range of matters relating to the individual and to society at large' which Truman so skilfully elucidates, invariably betray their authors political agenda as well as the high degree to which they reflect upon and participate in contemporary debates on the origin, nature and exercise of political authority.

52   D. Ferraro (1989), *Tradizione e Ragione in Juan de Mariana* (Filosofia e scienza nel Cinquecento e nel Seicento; Serie I, Studi; Vol. 32), F. Angeli, Milan, sheds some light on the way in which rhetorical twists and turns either sidetrack or inspire the readers of *De rege*.

thought. It also inspires a refusal to put much trust in either princes or peoples or the laws they give themselves. The implications of this have yet to be accorded their due attention. His deeply sceptical view of laws and legal thinking obliges Mariana to condense juridical and theological discourse into the kind of humanist 'prudent sentences' Narbona singled out as so appealing. This *de facto* rhetoricization of familiar legal-theological discourses is one of the most curious, yet at the same time completely neglected aspects of Mariana's book.

The second distinct and hitherto ignored characteristic of Mariana's argument is the altogether clerical perspective of the treatise. Books two and three expand the scope of discussion to include almost every practical aspect of early modern government. At the same time, the argument as a whole is held together by the concluding chapters of the three books of the treatise. Each one deals with the role of religion and the position of the secular clergy in the government of Habsburg Spain. The fact that Mariana expounds religion as the only operable civic ideology is hardly surprising. The extent to which he appears to exclude genuinely theological consideration, however, is worth mentioning. Even among Jesuits generally prepared to judge the means according to the ends, Mariana stands out for his altogether secular political ethics. More notable, and, indeed, much more problematic are the practical demands that result from his view of the Church as sole defender of the *civilis societas*. His proposals for a theocratic reform of Habsburg government are more radical than anything his contemporaries are prepared to argue. This study is the first to explore them.

Spanish contemporaries did not perceive Mariana as a regicide. The death of Philip II produced a welter of treatises outlining proposals for reform. Mariana is one of these authors, who are commonly referred to as *arbitristas*. Yet he is an *arbitrista* with a difference. He writes on behalf of the secular clergy of Castile rather than a prince. His surprising foresight and fierce patriotism unite his breathtakingly independent stance on the political role of the Castilian clergy with more mainstream contemporary discourse. The context within which Mariana wanted to be read is that of the relationship between Church and state in Castile at the turn of the sixteenth century. This study is the first to place *De rege* within this context. It focuses on the way in which Mariana makes ingenious use of elements from Roman and canon law, scholastic theology and the classical humanist tradition to construe his very own and in many respects quite original take on Church, state and society in early modern Spain.

CHAPTER ONE

Human Nature, the Origins of Civil Society, and the Power of Princes

Mariana begins his treatise on the education of the prince with a detailed discourse on the nature of man and the origins of civil society and government.[1] Examining how human nature relates to the transition from pre-civil to civil society is not the ordinary point of departure for the author of an early modern mirror-of-princes. Desiderius Erasmus, for instance, launches straight into the early education of the prince, then moves on to tangible topics like the preservation of peace or the imposition of taxes.[2] Treatises concerned with the 'art' of government as such commonly ignore the issue. Giovanni Botero, Pedro de Ribadeneira or the Flemish humanist Justus Lipsius immediately set out to provide a doctrine of statecraft just as practicable, though morally less offensive than the one found in Machiavelli's *Il Principe*.[3] Mariana clearly intends to do his readers a similar service. Yet he enters the debate on the scope and limit of Christian statecraft from a very different angle. He is perhaps the only Jesuit author to root the transfer from pre-civil to civil society in a 'state of nature' *after* the Fall and *before* the conception of civil society.[4]

At first glance, Mariana's account reads like a humanist melange of diverse motifs, lines and passages. Tenets from a wide variety of medieval and classical texts are woven into a flow of elegant and difficult Latin. Cicero's *De inventione*, Virgil's *Georgica*, Machiavelli's *Discorsi*, as well as the works of Seneca and Saint Thomas Aquinas feature prominently. Mariana risks confusing readers who expect to enter a discourse on practical matters pertaining to the education of the prince and the conduct of government. Yet the complex, occasionally jumbled texture of his introductory chapters provides the foundation for much of what is to follow.

---

1   *De rege*, I.1, 'Homo natura est animal sociabile', especially pp. 16-22.

2   *Institutio principis Christiani* (1516), Johann Froben, Basle.

3   Giovanni Botero (1589), *Della ragion di stato*, Gioliti, Venice; Pedro de Ribadeneira (1597), *Tratado de la religion y virtudes que deve tener el principe christiano, para governar y conservar sus estados, contra lo que Nicolas Machiavelo y los politicos deste tiempo enseñan*, Plantin-Moret, Antwerp Justus Lipsius (1589), *Politicorum sive civilis doctrinae libri sex*, Plantin, Leiden.

4   With the possible exception of Luis de Molina. See Q. Skinner (1978), *The Foundations of Modern Political Thought*, 2 vols., Cambridge University Press, Cambridge, Vol. 2, p. 155. Skinner contends that 'Thomist' writers 'possess the concept of the state of nature even when they do not possess the phrase, and that they already recognise the heuristic value of employing it as a device for elucidating the relationship between positive laws and the theorems of natural justice.' For a different view see H. Höpfl, *Jesuit Political Thought*, pp. 224-62, especially pp. 231-32. My point is that Mariana exposes the deeply problematic nature of the heuristic use of this concept.

The themes and contradictions that emerge from his intricate narrative go a long way to explain how and why he arrived at some of his surprising conclusions.

Human Nature

Initially, Mariana's account of human nature reads like a paraphrase of well known passages from the treatise *De regimine principum* jointly attributed to Saint Thomas Aquinas and Bartholomew (Ptolemy) of Lucca.[5] Man is the *animal sociabile*. Though humans and animals share the desire to live communally, the former did not receive the physical characteristics, strength and helpful instincts which help animals survive. Yet human beings are amply compensated for these deficiencies. God endowed them with the power of speech. Individuals able to communicate can decide to combine their skills and resources. Experience thus gathered and skills honed over the course of generations enable humanity to overcome many of the illnesses and dangers that would have cut short their ancestors' lives. At this point, Mariana seems upbeat about the nature and capabilities of humankind. His observations echo the confident belief in the moral and intellectual qualities of man familiar from the work of early sixteenth-century humanists like Erasmus or his Spanish follower Juan Luis Vives.[6]

This buoyant voice quickly dies away. Despite their undoubted ability to pool skills and resources, Mariana says, men will always be in desperate 'need of many things', and will always remain painfully aware of 'the frailty of the human body'.[7] Those who believe that human success in the arts, medicine and war will improve their lot sadly deceive themselves. The things purporting to 'distinguish, enlighten and adorn human life' are nothing but the result of man's vain struggle to escape death and alleviate the endless misery of this life. *De rege* is not the only instance where Mariana elaborates on the theme of human destitution. Not long after the publication of his treatise on the education of the prince, he drafted a little humanist treatise clearly fashioned on Seneca's *De morte et mortalitate*, even borrowing its title from Nero's tutor.[8] The work only ever lifts the most pessimistic and disillusioning traits from Seneca's writings, especially the many variations on the theme of life as permanent death and misery.[9]

---

5   *De rege*, pp. 16-17. Compare *De Regimine Principum*, I, 1.

6   See, for instance, Erasmus's *Enchiridion militis Christiani*; and Juan Luis Vives's *Fabula de homine*. On Vives's anthropology see J.-A. Fernández-Santamaría (1998), *The Theater of Man: J.L. Vives on Society* (Transactions of the American Philosophical Society; Vol. 88/2), American Philosophical Society, Philadelphia. Still the most comprehensive account is M. Bataillon's (1991), *Érasme et l'Espagne, Nouvelle édition en trois volumes, Texte établi par D. Devoto*, Droz, Geneva [first edition: (1937), Droz, Paris].

7   *De rege*, pp. 18-21.

8   Juan de Mariana (1609), *De morte et mortalitate*, in *Tractatus VII*, Anton Hierat, Cologne, pp. 355-444. On the reception of Seneca's *De morte et mortalitate* in early modern Spain see K.A. Blüher (1969), *Seneca in Spanien, Untersuchungen zur Geschichte der Seneca-Rezeption in Spanien vom 13. bis 17. Jahrhundert*, Francke, Munich, especially pp. 273-77.

9   Mariana, *De morte*, 1.3, 'Quotidie morimur' (also paraphrasing Seneca, *Ad Lucilium epistulae morales*, 24.20), and 1.6: 'Multis diu vixisse nocuit' (also paraphrasing Seneca, *Ad*

Positive reflections on human life, like the Stoic appreciation of heroism as a virtue are completely ignored.[10] Seneca is the source of many of the themes of Mariana's tale of despair and deprivation, helping Mariana to sum up his sobering disquisition on human nature in *De rege*. Thus he provides the adage that man enters into life shedding tears, and never ceases to do so until the day he dies.[11] The reader is assured that there is very little reason to rejoice in life.

Mariana goes on to present a dark and powerful explanation for the origin of society. Paraphrasing Aquinas again, he is now keen to emphasize the Augustinian strand in the latter's writing. It is worth quoting his words in full:

> If man really had the strength and robustness to repulse dangers, and did not require the assistance of others, what sort of society would there be? Would men respect one another? Would there be any order to life? Would there be any mutual trust? Any love of humanity? (…) What could there be more monstrous and more savage than man unrestrained by law and the fear of judgement? Could any beast cause such carnage?[12]

Man's baseness and malice are without bounds. Indeed, the mere thought of self-sufficient man is terrifying. Such a 'cruel beast' would focus all his energies on inflicting unspeakable misery on his fellow man. Mariana takes the opportunity to criticize the kind of ancient scepticism increasingly current among educated Spaniards.[13] He disparages those who contend that 'nature is a stepmother, not a mother of the human race, who has instructed dumb animals in all good things, but has cast man needy and feeble into the pursuit of this life (…)'.[14] It is foolish to accuse God of putting man in permanent fear of his life. Such a line of reasoning 'smacks of impiety'.[15] Men have every reason to thank God for having created them utterly

---

Marciam de consolatione, 22.3).

10 *De morte* incurred the mild suspicion of the Inquisition, mainly because Mariana points the finger at Saint Augustine as bearing quite some responsibility for the emergence of a Reformed doctrine of grace and predestination. *De morte*, especially pp. 429-31; and A. de Sotomayor, (1640), *Novissimus librorum prohibitorum et purgatorum index*, Diaz, Madrid, p. 718, col. 2.

11 *De rege*, p. 18. Clearly paraphrasing Seneca, *Ad Polybium de consolatione*, 4.3.

12 Ibid., p. 22; see also p. 21. Compare this to the view of man offered in Aristotle, *Politics*, 1253a.

13 See, for instance, Francisco Sánches (1581), *Quod nihil scitur*, Antonius Gryphius, Lyons [Engl. transl.: (1988), *That nothing is known = quod nihil scitur*, ed. E. Limbrick and D.F.S. Thompson, Cambridge University Press, Cambridge]. On the influence of classical scepticism on early modern political thought, see C.B. Schmitt (1983), 'The Rediscovery of Ancient Skepticism in Modern Times', in M. Burnyeat (ed.), *The Skeptical Tradition*, University of California Press, Berkeley and Los Angeles, pp. 225-51; and R. Popkin (1979), *The History of Scepticism from Erasmus to Spinoza*, University of California Press, Berkeley, especially pp. 37-41.

14 *De rege*, p. 21. See also ibid., pp. 17-18, pp. 22-23. Mariana draws on the discussion of man as the stepchild of nature in Pliny, *Naturalis Historia*, VII; prooemium, pp. 1-5.

15 *De rege*, p. 21.

.

weak and dependent on their fellow men. It is their flawed nature which forced men to 'live in one place, under the same laws and associated into a multitude' in the first instance.[16] It is their very frailty which encouraged men to discover Christian charity and friendship. Physical weakness and resultant mutual dependence are a supreme expression of divine grace. The notion that man ignorant of law, justice and virtue is like a beast pervades classical, medieval and early modern literatures.[17] Yet even among authors united in their pessimistic stance on human nature, Mariana stands out for the way in which he links such pessimism with rational proof for God's love of His creation.

The transition from pre-civil to civil society

The sombre treatment of human affairs continues. Mariana omits any reference to the Fall and the status of man before the Fall. Instead, he focuses on the condition of man immediately after the Fall. Though he never actually refers to ages of gold, silver, bronze and iron, his account is clearly inspired by ancient stories of a 'Golden Age' and subsequent decline of the human condition.[18] He uses pertinent themes and motifs from a range of classical authors in order to describe the situation of post-lapsarian man as one that is changed for the worse by the progress of 'time and the wickedness of men'. In doing so, Mariana in fact historicizes the transition from pre-civil to civil society.

For an unspecified period of time after the Fall, Mariana says, men lived a life of Arcadian innocence. Paraphrasing a Ciceronian *locus classicus*, he describes these 'first men' as being completely ignorant of laws, civil authority and private ownership (*dominium*).[19] Whatever earth yielded, they used in common. Peaceful hunters and gatherers roamed the woods and plains. This Arcadian interval yet to be disturbed by the consequences of the Fall is epitomized in elegant verse lifted from Virgil's *Georgica*:

> Even to mark the land with private bounds
> Was wrong: men worked for the common store, and earth
> Herself, unbidden, yielded all the more fully.[20]

---

16   Ibid., p. 17.

17   It can be traced to Aristotle, who links it to the idea that only what is perfectly self-sufficient (a deity, for instance) can live outside society.

18   Compare Hesiod, *Works and Days*, I; Polybius, *Histories*, VI, 5; Cicero, *De inventione*, 1.2.2; Seneca, especially *Ad Luc*, 90; and Virgil (see below).

19   *De rege*, 16-17. Paraphrasing mainly Cicero, *De inventione*, 1.2.2; see also Cicero, *De officiis*, 3.6.23; and Seneca, *Ad Lucilium*, 90, especially 3-4. Salmon, 'Catholic Resistance Theory', pp. 240-41, acknowledges that Mariana describes a state of nature preceding civil society. However, he presents Mariana as thinking in purely Ciceronian terms, and as conceiving of the transition from bestiality to civic life as a change for the better.

20   Ibid., p. 17. Virgil, *Georgica*, 1, 125-28 (quoted from Virgil (1982), *Georgics*, transl. L.P. Wilkinson, Penguin, London, p. 61). In the same context quoted by Seneca, *Ad Luc*, 90, 37.

Men and women co-habited, and started setting up families. These small familial groups soon formed larger units. They were now much more able to satisfy their many needs, and to protect themselves against wild animals.[21] Sons and grandsons went on to set up house close to the seats of the patriarch of the family until a cluster of families came to constitute a new and distinct form of community, the 'sib' or 'clan' (*pagus*). At some point, many *pagi* joined together, thus establishing yet another community, the barbarian 'tribe' (*gens* or *natio*). *Pagus*, then, denoted an ethnically defined community that was distinguished from *gens*, *natio* or *populus* by its lesser degree of political consciousness and organization.[22] The fact that Mariana prefers *pagus* to the more common humanist translation of the relevant Aristotelian term (*vicus*) is likely to be more than just a matter of stylistic variation. By using *pagus* rather than *vicus*, he stresses the pre-political, yet already ethnical rather than purely familial nature of the sib or clan as a stage in the development of the *civilis societas*.

Eventually, with further procreation and dispersion of families, more and more clans established themselves. Mariana admits that these primeval men, pure and innocent though they were, could not have existed without 'some sort of government'. 'Natural instinct and impulse' (*naturae instinctus et impulsus*), he says, advised them to submit willingly and unconsciously to the counsel and guidance of their elders.[23] No one man was more powerful than his neighbour, and violence among men unheard of. The picture is one of nomadic clans emerging from the dawn of mythical time still utterly ignorant of avarice, violence and deceit.[24] Their life bore all the hallmarks of the ancients' Golden Age.

In the following, Mariana infuses his account with his ever more prevalent theme of decline and corruption. Though he does not mention the Fall of Adam, he depicts a post-lapsarian mankind increasingly beset by vice. Developing his theme of a post-lapsarian state of nature, Mariana is increasingly out of tune with Thomist-Aristotelian conceptualizations of how society came into being. He does not, for instance, allow for a natural (in the Aristotelian sense) progression from this imagined state of nature to civil society. Civil society is not merely a complex and much more accomplished extension of family and clan. Civil society is the product of a period of transition characterised by the creeping progress of human corruption.

At some point after the Fall, powerful men became aware of their ability to terrorize and exploit their neighbours.[25] Organizing themselves into vagrant bands of robbers, they set out to deprive their fellow men of their lives and goods. These

---

Concerning the use of *fas* as a synonym for *lex*, Mariana probably draws on Cicero, *De officiis*, 3.6.23, and *De oratore*, 1.28; also possible is Aquinas, *ST*, I.I., Qu. 57, art. 1.

21   Ibid., p. 16. Compare Aristotle, *Politics*, 1252b15. See also *De rege*, p. 19.

22   See F. Gschnitzer (1992), 'Volk, Nation, Nationalismus, Masse', II.1: 'Völker als politische Verbände', in O. Brunner, W. Conze and R. Koselleck (eds), *Geschichtliche Grundbegriffe, Historisches Lexikon der politisch-sozialen Sprache in Deutschland*, Vol. 7, Klett-Cotta, Stuttgart, pp. 151-55 [from here on: *GG*].

23   *De rege*, p. 16.

24   Ibid., p. 17.

25   Ibid., p. 20.

bands of murderers and thieves are the first associations to transgress and transcend the primeval *pagus* (the 'instinctive', still family-based community). Mariana calls them *populus* or *societas*. Yet to him they represent merely a preliminary stage of societal organization. These *populi* are nothing but rudimentarily organized mobs, held together by no more than the prospect of pillage and plunder. They existed without civic leaders as opposed to leaders of murderous gangs, and did not organize themselves on the basis of positive law. Yet they instigated the establishment of civil society. Under threat of being overwhelmed by ferocious *potentiores*, 'some men' came to recognize the need 'to bind themselves with others in a mutual covenant of society (*mutuum foedus societatis*)'. Placing themselves under the authority of a *rector*, they formed the first civil societies. It was not the hostility of their natural environs that induced men to enter into a compact. Only a situation of escalating internecine strife forced them to abandon the primeval patriarchal community.

Mariana thus identifies a serious discontinuity between the formation of *familia* and *pagus* on the one hand, and that of *civilis societas* on the other. He readily acknowledges that family and clan are natural to man. *Familia* and *pagus*, after all, are the result of a 'natural instinct and impulse' that is 'written in the hearts of men'. However, he vigorously denies that civil society is founded upon the same 'natural law' or 'natural instinct and impulse' leading to the formation of family and clan. The *pagus*, Mariana says, based upon the authority of parents or grandparents as it was, 'may have appeared to resemble the future *populus*'.[26] It may even have resembled civil society's short-lived predecessor, the proto-*civitas* made up of thieves and murderers. Yet he explicitly states that clan and family must be confused neither with the latter nor with civil society itself.

Mariana's conviction that *familia* and *pagus* cannot be regarded as initial stages in a natural process culminating with the Aristotelian *civitas perfecta* is further borne out by his definition of *ius naturale*.[27] The 'natural law' which had post-lapsarian men gather around their elders, according to Mariana, is merely 'the law that is shared by man and beast'.[28] It is akin to 'natural instinct'. Patriarchal authority exercised among the 'first men', therefore, cannot be understood as being derived from the same law of nature upon which the *societas civilis* would be based. The definition itself is borrowed from Roman law. It introduces readers to the notion that *familia* and *pagus* are institutions rooted in a law of nature that does not include development towards the Aristotelian *civitas perfecta*. This is a conception of natural law as sufficient to instigate pre-lapsarian order, but altogether too primitive (and therefore shared by animals) to help men advance towards more complex forms

---

26   Mariana's terminology tends to lack clarity. He frequently denotes both the proto-*civitas* and the fully fledged *civilis societas* as *populus*.

27   For Aristotle's teleological conception of the formation of the *civitas* see *Politics*, especially 1252b27.

28   *De rege*, p. 21. He paraphrases Ulpian, *Dig.* 1.1.1.: 'Ius naturale est, quod natura omnia animalia docuit'. Roman law did not lend itself easily to an understanding of natural law as divine law intelligible to human natural reason independent of revelation.

of societal organization. Civil society and political authority, in turn, are clearly earmarked as institutions that have to evolve from positive human law.

Discontinuity is accentuated by Mariana's identification of two distinct states of man after the Fall. There is the peaceful state immediately after the Fall, and there is, towards the end of the unspecified period of transition that follows on from it, the chaotic state of internecine strife. Family and clan clearly belong to the former, *civilis societas* is the result of the latter. Accordingly, primeval patriarchal authority differs from transitional proto-*civitas* and fully developed *civitas* in two respects. First in that family and clan were altogether ignorant of laws and individual property as well as blissfully oblivious of any authority other than the moral guidance offered by their elders. Secondly, primeval patriarchal authority is exercised over uncorrupted men and without recourse to courts, magistrates and princes. *Familia* and *pagus*, *populus* and *civilis societas* are distinguished by the very different degree to which the corruption of pre-lapsarian order has set in.

Mariana introduces an element of historicity not found in any other Jesuit or Dominican account of the lineage of civil society.[29] With the possible exception of Molina, none of the authors generally included in the 'School of Salamanca' operates the notion of a post-lapsarian state of nature.[30] His sustained emphasis on civil society as the result and continual manifestation of human viciousness and misery further sets him apart from more sanguine interpretations prevalent among the theologians within whose orbit he is often placed.[31] Francisco de Vitoria, Domingo de Soto, Luis de Molina and Francisco Suárez are commonly referred to as the 'second Scholastic' or 'School of Salamanca'.[32] Highly versatile and complex thinkers whose views and terminologies could differ significantly, they nonetheless

---

29 See Skinner, *Foundations*, Vol. 2, especially pp. 148-66; and Höpfl, *Jesuit Political Thought*, pp. 224-63. See ibid., pp. 239-48 for Höpfl 's highly commendable account of government, compact and state of nature in Mariana. Höpfl, however, underplays the strong element of historicity in Mariana's thinking, and fails to put enough store by the fact that Mariana's Augustinian pessimism drives his argument to an extent and towards conclusions that distinguish him from his fellow Jesuits.

30 Skinner, *Foundations*, Vol. 2, p. 155. Mariana's account is similar to that of the *doctor utriusque iuris* Ferdinand Vázquez de Menchaca; see A. Brett (1997), *Liberty, Right and Nature. Individual Rights in Later Scholastic Thought*, Cambridge University Press, Cambridge, pp. 165-204.

31 On the appreciation of creation demonstrated by the majority of Jesuit theologians see J.W. O'Malley (1993), *The First Jesuits*, Harvard University Press, Harvard, especially pp. 250-53. On diversity, differentiation and controversy in sixteenth-century Jesuit theology see V. Beltrán de Heredia (1971-73), *Miscelánea Beltrán de Heredia: colección de artículos sobre historia de teología española* (Biblioteca de teólogos españoles; Vols 25-28), 4 Vols, n.p., Salamanca,Vol. 2, chapter 35: 'La enseñanza de S. Tomas en la compañia de Jesus', pp. 309-42, especially pp. 309-29.

32 For a comprehensive history of the theology and theologians commonly subsumed under the epithet 'School of Salamanca' or 'second scholastic' see J. Belda Plans (2000), *La Escuela de Salamanca y la renovación de la teología en el siglo XVI* (Biblioteca de autores cristianos maior; Vol. 63), Biblioteca de Autores Cristianos, Madrid. Belda Plans, ibid., p. 856, places Mariana within the sphere of Salamancan Thomist thought.

agreed on essential characteristics of civil society and secular authority. Developing the ideas of Saint Thomas Aquinas, they held that civil society, and with it legitimate monarchical authority sprang from the dictate of *prima praecepta* of natural law. God had implanted these 'first precepts', a body of universal, rationally recognizable and immediately self-evident principles deep 'in the hearts of men'. They had been left almost untouched by Adam's fall from grace, and could therefore never be abrogated. Nor, as a result, could legitimate power so firmly based on them ever be abolished. In formulating these views, Vitoria and those who followed his lead had been mainly concerned with protecting the authority of secular princes against the implications of Reformed theology with its emphasis on divine grace and human will rather than natural law. If secular authority was dependent on grace, any community or individual could lawfully cease to obey a ruler whom they considered a heretic. A strong emphasis on the invariable nature of the relationship between ruler and subject was intended to reject any such suggestion.

Mariana's account of the origin of society strongly contrasts with the Salamancan consensus on secular authority as rooted in precepts of the law of nature. He in fact denies that natural law and hence *civilis societas* were left fairly unscathed by the Fall. He also contradicts the Stoic account in that he identifies both *humanitas* and *civilis societas* as upshots of the suppression of human bestiality. This is Augustinian lore. It quickly becomes clear that the author of *De rege* deliberately latches on to the weaker points in the Thomist defence of monarchy as rooted in universal precepts of the law of nature.[33] Why should post-lapsarian political order be regarded as relatively unaffected by the Fall? And, if so, why did men have to abandon their primeval freedom in the first instance? Mariana's answer refers to the contemporary scholastic debate on whether or not *dominium* (in the sense of private ownership as well as political power) existed before the Fall.

A multi-layered term, *dominium* denotes both ownership of private property and power over men.[34] Many scholastic theologians offered their views on this matter within the confines of a particular genre, the *Summa de casibus conscientiae*, and, within that genre, in the context of discussing a particular topic, namely the sacrament of penance. Peter Lombard's treatment of the question whether or not restitution

---

33   For a long view of the problems intrinsic to Thomist natural law theory see P.C. Westerman (1997), *The Disintegration of Natural Law Theory. Aquinas to Finnis* (Brill's Studies in Intellectual History; Vol. 84), Brill, Leiden.

34   Brief surveys of the conceptual development of *dominium* during the late medieval and early modern period are provided by P. Moraw (1982), 'Herrschaft [*dominium*]', II.1: 'Herrschaft im Mittelalter', in *GG*, Vol. 3, pp. 5-13; H. Günther (1982), III.1: 'Herrschaft von der frühen Neuzeit bis zur Französischen Revolution', ibid., pp. 14-33; J. Coleman 1988). 'Property and Poverty', in *The Cambridge History of Medieval Political Thought, c.350-1450*, ed. J.H. Burns, Cambridge University Press, Cambridge, pp. 607-48; and J.H. Burns (1991), 'Scholasticism: Survival and Revival', in *CHPTh*, pp. 132-55, pp. 140-46. See also R. Tuck (1979-81), *Natural Rights Theories: Their Origins and Development*, Cambridge University Press, Cambridge. Very illuminating, in particular regarding the conceptual relationship between *dominium* and *ius* is Brett, *Liberty*.

of unjustly possessed goods is part of satisfaction in Book IV, Distinction 15 of his *Sententiae* is a common starting point. Whether or not restitution is satisfactory depends, according to Lombard, on how *dominium* in the sense of private ownership came into the world in the first instance. Did private ownership exist before the Fall, and thereby have a basis in natural law, or was it established by acts of positive law after the Fall? The implications for political theory were momentous. Theologians were quick to expand on the question of the origin of *dominium*. If *dominium* was rooted in natural law, so were civic society and political authority. If it was not, and if civic society and political authority, too, were deemed to have originated in positive law, this opened up a whole host of possibilities for contractual interpretation and limitation of political authority. Viewing political power as having been established by an act of positive rather than of natural law, for instance, would commonly lead to a more tolerant treatment of the rights of a community or an individual to challenge or resist legitimate authority.

In this matter, followers of Saint Thomas Aquinas were commonly pitched against those of the Franciscan John Duns Scotus.[35] Thomists would generally hold that *dominium* together with civil society and political authority as its corollaries were brought into being by the law of nature. Of course, Thomist thinkers had to explain whether, and to what extent, the precepts of the law of nature had survived the Fall. Saint Thomas, pursuing a course chosen by Saint Anselm of Canterbury in the eleventh century and Alexander of Hales and Saint Albert the Great in the thirteenth, had tried to resolve this problem by introducing the seminal distinction of a twofold state of Adam before the Fall.[36] The differentiation was one between the 'pure nature' (*pura natura*) of man and the supernatural gifts of divine grace or original justice that had perfected it before the Fall. The latter were not to be recognized as intrinsic to human nature as such, but as *donum superadditum*, a special divine gift transcending the nature of man. The resultant proposition was that original sin consisted in the loss only of sanctifying grace or original justice, that is, in the loss of those privileges of divine grace that had directed innocent man to his supernatural end and enabled him to keep his inferior powers in complete submission to natural reason. Saint Thomas at least implied that the precepts of natural law relevant to the condition of man as *animal sociale* remained part of *pura natura* – a point upon which his many followers elaborated. From this angle, original

---

35   I seek to outline and highlight contrasting themes and traditions, but I do not mean to divide up differentiated and highly complex scholastic political theology into monolithic, easily discernible Thomist and Scotist 'schools'.

36   Saint Thomas Aquinas, *ST*, I.II, Qu. 100, art.1 and art. 3. On *pura natura* also I.II, Qu. 17, art. 9 ad 3; Qu.81, art.3 ad 3. For a brief introduction to Aquinas's understanding of original sin, natural law and the emergence of *dominium* see P.E. Sigmund (1993), 'Law and Politics', in N. Kretzmann and E. Stump (eds), *The Cambridge Companion to Aquinas*, Cambridge University Press, Cambridge, pp. 217-31. A succinct analysis of pre-Reformation theological doctrine of original sin and justification is provided by H.M. Köster (1979), *Urstand, Fall und Erbsünde: in der Scholastik* (Handbuch der Dogmengeschichte; Bd.2, Faszikel 3b), Herder, Freiburg.

sin did not change the substance of human nature. Man as a social animal was weakened, but not too dramatically affected by original sin.

Aquinas's concept of the twofold nature of man was widely applied to secular commonwealth and secular authority: the laws of nature relevant to the conception of civil society and political authority were seen as not defiled and perverted by the Fall of Man. His position was in effect adopted and restated by the Council of Trent (1545-63). The Fathers followed Augustine's teachings only in as much as they accepted the existence and transmission of a corrupted nature from Adam to his descendants, whereas both the nature of that transmission and the nature of original sin were mitigated in deliberate contrast to Reformed doctrine. [37]

Those inclined to think with Scotus, on the other hand, held that *dominium* and civil society originated in human or positive law.[38] In his Oxford commentary on Book IV, Distinction 15 of Lombard's *Sententiae*, Scotus distinguishes between a pre-lapsarian state of man when individual possession of particular objects was unknown and a post-lapsarian state when it constitutes the norm. He states that originally everything was held in common by the law of nature or divine law, each man occupying only what he needed for his preservation and sustenance.[39] But, he continues, 'the precept of the law of nature about having everything in common was revoked after the Fall (…) and with reason.'[40] The reason was that the strong began to oppress the weak merely to satisfy their avarice. Scotus concludes that:

> after the revocation of that precept (…) and the consequent concession of a licence to appropriate and separate out common things, the actual distinction did not happen through the law of nature nor the divine law (…). It follows that the first division of *dominia* came about by some positive law.[41]

---

37   See *Decrees of the Ecumenical Councils, Reprinted with an English Translation* (1990), ed. N.P. Tanner, 2 Vols, Georgetown University Press, London and Washington, Vol. 2, Decree on original sin (Session 5, 17 June 1546), pp. 665-67; Decree on justification and merit (Session 6, 13 January 1547), pp. 671-83. On the soteriology of Saint Augustine, see L. Panier (1996), *Le péché originel: naissance de l'homme sauvé*, Éditions du Cerf, Paris; and H. Rondet (1967), *Le Péché originel dans la tradition patristique et théologique*, Fayard, Paris. See Köster, *Urstand*, pp. 47-54, pp. 55-56, for a brief discussion of why the Council's determination to advance a safe and straight Thomist argument prevented further clarification of the doctrine of the nature of original sin.

38   With regard to Scotus's conceptualization of the origin of *dominium*, I am very much indebted to Brett, *Liberty*, especially pp. 29-34. See also H. Möhle (2003), 'Scotus' Theory of Natural Law', in T. Williams (ed.), *The Cambridge Companion to Duns Scotus*, Cambridge University Press, Cambridge, pp. 312-33; and H.P.F. Mercken (1998), 'Necessity and the Moral Order: Scotus's Interpretation of the *Lex Naturae* in the Perspective of Western Philosophical Ethics', in E.P. Bos (ed), *John Duns Scotus (1265/6-1308): Renewal of Philosophy*, Rodopi, Amsterdam, pp. 171-82.

39   John Duns Scotus (1497), *Quaestiones in quattuor libros Sententiarum*, Bonetus Locatellus for Octavianus Scotus, Venice, Dist. 15, Q. 2, p. 76v, col. 2.

40   Ibid., p. 77r, col. 1.

41   Ibid.

Because the part of the law of nature relevant to *dominium* was revoked after the Fall, not only private property but communities too came into being by acts of positive law.[42] This is the point at which Scotus radically parts company with Aquinas and Thomist thinking. Though Scotus goes on to divide legitimate authority into paternal and political just like theologians of Thomist inclination, he is also quick to stress, very much unlike Thomist thinkers, that only paternal authority is legitimate because it is a precept of the natural law that has never been revoked. Political authority, on the other hand, is legitimate not because it originated in the expansion of that law of nature, but because it proceeded from the consent of the people constituting a community in an act of positive law.[43]

Scotus introduces a dynamic of decline affecting human nature and society after the Fall. He argues that human law did not immediately complement and succeed the law of nature. Rather there were two disjunctive states of *dominium* after the Fall, one of collective *dominium* resembling the pre-lapsarian state and existing under the law of nature; and another of separate *dominia* under positive law. Between these two states existed 'a fluid situation of *de facto* appropriation'.[44] It was during this period fraught with danger and misery especially for the meek and weak that human agency came to establish civil society. This sense of time and historical dynamic which Scotus brings to bear on his interpretation of the immediate post-lapsarian period, distinguishes him, again, from Thomist treatments of the same. Scotus's conclusions on the origins of *dominium* can be held to have broken the spell of that Aristotelian teleology of natural law and civil society so ingeniously upheld by Aquinas. Annabel Brett argues convincingly that Scotus's treatment of restitution constitutes a complex of ideas that can be called neo-Augustinian.[45] Like other medieval and early modern European thinkers debating in various contexts, Mariana found that he, too, could put Scotist figures of thought to good use.

Without getting involved in unravelling the complex conceptual relationship between *ius* and *dominium*, Mariana uses *dominium* in the neo-Augustinian sense to refer to post-lapsarian private ownership and political power rooted in positive law.[46] Particularly striking is the way in which he adopts the idea of a partial revocation of the law of nature after the Fall as well as that of a period of transition during which positive law gradually came to take its place. He transposes these tenets of scholastic theology into a humanist idiom by borrowing references relevant to a pre-

---

42   Ibid., pp. 76v, col. 2–77r, col.1.

43   Ibid., p. 77r, col. 1.

44   Brett, *Liberty*, p. 31.

45   Ibid. On features of early modern Catholic-Augustinian thinking see also W.J. Bouwsma (1975), 'The Two Faces of Humanism: Stoicism and Augustinianism in Renaissance Thought', in H.A. Oberman and T.A. Brady (eds), *Itinerarium Italicum: The Profile of the Italian Renaissance in the Mirror of its European Transformations*, Brill Publishers, Leiden, pp. 3-60; and A.D. Wright (2005), *The Counter-Reformation. Catholic Europe and the Non-Christian World*, Ashgate, Aldershot, especially chapters one and six.

46   Equating *ius* with *dominium*, the neo-Augustinian approach to political authority is mainly concerned with the just assignation of *dominia distincta*. See Brett, *Liberty*, pp. 30-31.

social stage in human development from a number of classical authors. Stoic motifs illustrating primeval mankind as primitive but innocent are particularly prominent. Again, the title of the first chapter of Book one asserting that 'man is by nature a sociable animal' is misleading.[47] Any suspicion that the reader might be presented with a mere reproduction of fairly orthodox Thomist-Aristotelian doctrine is quickly dispelled. Mariana offers a sharply contrasting argument in which he manipulates Thomist-Aristotelian terminology by describing man's natural sociability in a manner at once provocative and ingenious.

Monarchy

In his opening chapters, Mariana seizes upon one of the weakest and at the same time most crucial building stones of neo-Thomist explication of the origin of society and political authority. He undermines and finally abandons the notion that pre-lapsarian precepts of the law of nature determined the emergence of secular society and authority. Mellifluent humanist Latin cloaks a savage critique of civil society and political authority as corollaries of the Fall of man. Stoic themes are brought into play to contrast the primitive but still peaceful life of the first post-lapsarian race of men with a conflict-ridden existence in the *civilis societas*. Mariana deploys his armoury of civilian and classical topoi within a chronology of post-lapsarian decline provided by theorems on the origins of private ownership and political authority (*dominium*) first conceived in thirteenth-century Franciscan theology. Merging these themes and traditions, Mariana transforms the Fall of man from a single moment in eschatological time to a gradual process in mytho-historical time. However, his assault on the Thomist consensus does not stop here. He has merely laid the foundations for the further historicization and disintegration of mainstream Thomist ideas on society, secular authority and natural law. Mariana goes on to develop and extend his theme of post-lapsarian gradual decline over the course of secular history.

To explain the motives of primeval men, the disposition of the first rulers and the invention and nature of the first laws, Mariana reworks a passage in Cicero's *De officiis*.[48] He emphasizes much more strongly than Cicero that the transgressions of rulers impelled men to create laws. When men first agreed to form a *societas civilis*, they were unreasonably confident that they would be able to preserve essential features of their previous Arcadian life. Surrounded by pillaging, raping and plundering hordes, they could still find among their number men 'outstanding in prudence and moral integrity' and worthy to be entrusted with the protection of the community.[49] According to Mariana, the rule of the first *rectores* still closely resembled that of the pre-lapsarian *paterfamilias*.[50] His terminology reflects his

---

47   *De rege*, p. 16; see Aristotle, *Politics*, 1253 a1; 1253a7, and *NE*, 1.7.
48   *De officiis*, 2.12-14, and especially 2.41-42.
49   *De rege*, p. 20.
50   Ibid., p. 23.

postulate. The first rulers (*rectores*), Mariana suggests, lead by means of *auctoritas* rather than *potestas*. Their fellow men intuitively recognized exemplary virtue and sense of justice, and preferred to be led by example rather than pressure to obey. The institution of these first *rectores* marks the beginnings of royal office. Yet their style of rulership, he says, had better be described as *regia maiestas* rather than *regia potestas*. Mariana uses the term *maiestas* only to describe the early period of the rule of the *rectores*. Following Aristotle, his intention seems to have been to put the emphasis on the dignity and reputation of the incumbent rather than the coercive force attached to the office.[51] The moral integrity of these first rulers and the high esteem in which they were held by their 'subjects' meant that they did not need to surround themselves with the *principatus apparatus*. That is to say, they did not yet deploy the trappings of a princely court and the terror of courts of law to prop up their rule.[52] Their good judgement and benevolence was enough to settle 'all public and private conflicts' and to restrain 'the high, middle and low strata of society' in a rule of equity.[53] Organizing defence against enemies from within and without, they could depend entirely on the goodwill of the community. Most importantly, the primeval *rectores* did not try to browbeat their fellow men into submission. The latter, in turn, did not need to delineate clearly the limits of their authority and 'hedge them about with laws'.[54]

This is the most strongly emphasized feature of early single rule in *De rege*. It already indicates the paradox that informs Mariana's treatment of secular authority as a whole. On the one hand, the authority of the mythical first rulers is not to be comprehended in terms of coercive power or jurisdiction. On the other hand, it is difficult to imagine a more powerful, more divine and more absolute ruler than this final near-incarnation of pre-lapsarian patriarchal authority. Mariana posits that single rule is 'closest to the true (pre-lapsarian) nature of things' if it is understood and exercised in terms of authority that is moral rather than juridical in nature. The declared purpose of *De rege* is to draw attention to the origins of royal office and to encourage the heir to the throne to imitate the rule of the primordial *rector* as much as human weakness will allow.

Somewhat paradoxically, Mariana uses terms lifted from Roman law in order to develop his notion of the a-juridical nature of primordial rule (especially the term *rector*). He will continue to use legal terminology to build up his vision of primordial government as one characterized by individual virtue rather than law and coercive force. The first *rectores*, he says, acted *quasi multitudinis custos*. Even a reader not too deeply steeped in legal jargon would associate the term *custos* with the concept of

---

51   The assumption that the dignity of the royal office issues from the outstanding example of individual kings to whom people voluntarily submitted themselves underlies Book five of the *Nicomachean Ethics*.

52   *De rege*, p. 23.

53   Ibid.

54   Ibid., p. 20, p. 23.

custodia prominent in Roman private law.[55] The concept described the liability of a guardian (*custos, curator* or *tutor*) for the infringement of the rights and interests of another person or institution. The guardian could, for instance, be liable to protect the rights and interests of a person or institution as a party to a commercial contract. The actual form of that liability depended on the specific nature and content of the agreement between the guardian and his tutee.[56] Describing the exercise of political power as an exercise of *custodia*, then, Mariana seems intent on confirming that a ruler could or should be considered liable and held legally responsible if he ignored his duties. He does not, however, go on to develop this element from Roman private law into a full blown contractual theory defining the respective rights of ruler and subject.

Mariana's reasoning is that only the first, mythical rulers can be said to have truly acted *quasi custodes multitudinis*, that is, acted as if they were guardians of the people.[57] *Custos* only denotes the *rector* 'not yet hedged about with laws'. *Custos* describes a primeval and ideal but, unfortunately, transient historical reality. Only at the very beginning of historical time did rulers identify themselves as *multitudinis custos*.[58] As a result, once Mariana comes to talk in later chapters of his book about the degenerate

---

55   See, for instance: *Cod.* 5.37 ['De Administratione Tutorum et Curatorum']; and Ulp. 303 (18), 302 (42). On *custodia* in Roman law of obligations see J.A.C. Thomas (1975), *The Institutes of Justinian, Text, Translation and Commentary*, North-Holland Publishing Company, Amsterdam and Oxford, p. 204, p. 266; P. van Warmelo (1976), *An Introduction to the Principles of Roman Civil Law*, Juta, Cape Town, especially p. 646; and W.W. Buckland (1963), *A Textbook of Roman Law from Augustus to Justinian*, 3rd edn, rev. by P. Stein, Cambridge University Press, Cambridge, pp. 560-61. *Custos* is also the term Franciscans preferred to refer to the heads of their convents.

56   See, for instance, the Roman law concepts of *custos provinciae* or *civitatis* and *custos ecclesiae*. The former refers to military officials instituted by the late Roman emperors to defend a province or city, the latter to bishops preventing infringements on the rights and property of their churches; see *Cod.* 1.27.2, 4-4b ['De officio praefaecti']; 1.2.21 ['De episcopis']; and 2.13.1, 1 [R 'Ne Liceat Potentioribus Patrocinium Litigantibus Praestare vel Actiones in se Transferre'].

57   *De rege*, especially p. 23, 'Adiuncta est regia maiestas quasi multitudinis custos, uno praelato de quo magna erat suscepta animis opinio probitatis & prudentiae.'

58   Ibid., p. 23. Another term only used to describe primordial forms of community is *coetus* or *coetus urbanus*. Ibid., p. 20, 'Hinc urbani coetus primum regiaque; maiestas orta est. Quae non divitiis & ambitu, sed moderatione, innocentia, perspectaque, virtute olim obtinebatur.' The term *coetus* is found in classical authors, but rarely used by humanists as a synonym for *societas civilis*; see Cicero, *De re publica*, 1.25.39; Seneca, *Ad Luc.*, 95, 52. A notion of a gradation of forms of social organization akin to that of Mariana is found in Reynolds, p. 6, 'Natura (...) hominum coetus et communiones induxit, natura civitates fabricavit, natura reipublices instituit'. *Coetus* and *communio* are synonymous denominations for a first, deficient 'proto-populus' preceding *civitas* and *societas civilis*. Other authors use it as a strict synonym for *societas civilis* or *civitas*; see Samuel Pufendorf (1688), *De iure naturae et gentium libri octo*, n.p., Amsterdam, 7, 2, 8: '(...) ille, vel illi, in quem vel quos regimen coetus confertur'; and Thomas Hobbes (1670), *Leviathan sive de materia, forma, & potestate civitatis*

forms of monarchical government that eventually arose with the progress of time, *custos* mainly recurs either in combination with modal verbs or with verbs in the subjunctive mood. *Custos* is employed as a term to remind the prince of what he ought to do or ought to have done. It is not used as a term describing actual juridical and political reality. The legal figure of guardianship may serve as a pedagogical tool, may serve to remind a prince of how he should conceive of his office, but it simply cannot grasp the historical reality of kingship.

This same polarity between the nature and purpose of primeval, ideal rulership and its subsequent actualizations in history informs the *mutuum foedus societatis*, the original compact with which single rule was established. The combination of terms in *mutuum foedus societatis* calls to mind both the Biblical *foedus duplex* (two one-sided agreements between the people and God, and the prince and the people) and the Roman law-based concept of *mutua obligatio* (a reciprocal bond between two parties in a contract).[59] God, however, has no part whatsoever in the original *foedus* as described in *De rege*. The Biblical allusion is not developed. The clue to Mariana's understanding of the *mutuum foedus societatis* lies in the concept of *mutua obligatio*. In Roman private law, *mutua obligatio* specifies a unilateral contract. If this concept is applied to the *mutuum foedus societatis*, the respective positions of *rector* and *populus* can be defined as that of promissory party (*rector*) and stipulating party (*populus*). The people as the party that makes the stipulation have no duties, only rights. The *rector* as promissory party has no rights, only duties. Quite in tune with this figure lifted from Roman private law, Mariana gives no indication whatsoever that he wishes *mutuum foedus societatis* to refer to anything more than an agreement among free men to accept the leadership of one individual able to lead them in war and settle their disputes by virtue of his moral integrity. The primordial contractual relationship is one of a mutual obligation among free men acting as a corporate body.[60]

---

ecclesiasticae et civilis, n.p., Amsterdam, 2, 31: '(…) summa potestate unius hominis vel coetus, vocabulum (…)'.

59   For concise definitions of the biblical and legal terms of compact see *Vindiciae contra tyrannos* (1994), ed. and transl. by G. Garnett, Cambridge University Press, Cambridge, glossary: lxxviii [*foedus*], lxxxii [*stipulatio*]; and the discussion of the argument of the *Vindiciae*, especially xxiii-xxiv. On the legal fiction of the *foedus duplex* in early modern political thought see also G. Oestreich (1982), *Neostoicism and the Early-Modern State*, ed. B. Oestreich and H.G. Koenigsberger, transl. D. McLintock, Cambridge University Press, Cambridge, pp. 135-54 [a translation of G. Oestreich (1969), *Geist und Gestalt des frühmodernen Staates, Ausgewählte Aufsätze*, Duncker and Humblot, Berlin].

60   Mariana uses the terms *universitas, universus populus, universa reipublica* as well as *cives universos*. The *universitas* or corporate whole is not a real person, but a person by fiction of law. It can act only through the men in their corporate aspect that make it up (the *universi*), or the magistrates which represent them and act in their stead. The *universi* or in their corporate aspect are quite distinct from private individuals (*singuli*) who cannot exercise political rights. Mariana glosses over various distinctions defining the *cives* or *subditus* entitled to political activity as *universus*. See ibid., p. 23, 'Ut dum singuli metuebant supplicia, sese facilius universi a flagitio continerent [on the function of the first laws];' ibid., p. 55: '(…) respublica in proprio nomine dicitur, tum existit, cum universi populares imperii participes sunt'; ibid., p.

Again, however, Mariana does not develop these terms and concepts derived from the Roman law of private contracts so as to define a contractual relationship apt to reform existing, invariably corrupted forms of government. Only the compact as agreed immediately after the Fall can be understood to have worked in terms of promissory and stipulating parties. The 'first race of men' living immediately after the Fall had been far superior to their descendants in terms of their physical, moral as well as intellectual stature. Still 'close to the true nature of things', they had yet to become aware of the fact that the order of society was thoroughly tainted by the consequences of original sin. They were far too confident in expecting moral integrity in subsequent *rectores*. Their descendants, however, would soon find themselves betrayed both by the promissory party as well as their own indolence. Before long, the development of the *mutuum foedus societatis* would reflect the general decline affecting post-lapsarian society.

At first, rulers were indeed much more concerned with defending the borders of their communities (*urbs* or *populus*) than with expanding their territories.[61] With the progress of time and moral degeneration, however, their attitude changed. This pattern of decline is adapted from Seneca, *Ad Lucilium*.[62] *'Some kings', Mariana observes, 'either impelled by greed for more possessions, or incited by ambition for praise and glory, sometimes* [my emphasis] *even exasperated by wrongs'*, began to subjugate free people (*gens libera*, *civitas libera*) in their neighbourhood and went on to found the first empires (*imperia*).[63] Numerous free city-states under rulers less and less

---

102, 'Atque iis legibus non mode oboedire Princeps debet, sed neque eas mutare licebit, nisi universitatis consensu certaque sententia (on the fundamental laws the prince cannot change without the consent of the *universi*)'; see also ibid., pp. 89-90, pp. 101-102 (the people act as *universus populus* or *universa reipublica*). The fact that Mariana excludes the *singuli* from political responsibility has significant implications for his theory of resistance.

61   *De rege*, pp. 23-24, 'Deinde [for a period of time after the institution of the first kings; H.B.] Reges tuendis finibus magis quam proferendis intenti, cuique urbi aut populo suus, tot numero censebantur quantus erat numerus civitatum.'

62   Seneca, *Ad Luc.*, 90, here 3-6, 'Sed primi mortalium quique ex his geniti naturam incorrupti sequebantur, *eundem habebant et ducem et legem* [my emphasis], commissi melioris arbitrio. (…) Illo ergo saeculo quod aureum perhibent, penes sapientes fuisse regnum (…). Hi continebant manus et infirmiorem a validioribus tuebantur, suadebant dissuadebantque et utilia atque inutilia monstrabant. Horum prudentia ne quid deesset suis providebat, fortitudo pericula arcebat, beneficentia augebat ornabatque subiectos. Officium erat imperare, non regnum. Nemo quantum posset adversus eos experiebatur per quos coeperat posse, nec erat cuiquam aut animus in iniuriam aut causa, cum bene imperanti bene pareretur nihilque rex maius minari male parentibus posset quam ut abiret e regno. Sed postquam subrepentibus vitiis in tyrannidem regna conversa sunt, opus esse legibus coepit, (…).' Whereas Seneca has ancient sages issue the first laws, Mariana identifies the corporate body of the people as the first lawgiver.

63   *De rege*, p. 24, 'Progrediente vero tempore sive plura habiendi cupiditate impulsi, sive laudis & gloriae ambitione incitati, nonnunquam etiam iniuriis lacessiti, gentes liberas subiugare, cupiditatem imperandi causam belli habere, Reges caeteros ditionibus pellere, & in omnium fortunis soli coeperunt dominari.' See also ibid., p. 26, pp. 35-38.

prepared to act as unselfish *custodes* of their people gradually yielded to expanding empires ruled by kings finally and fully succumbing to human lust for power. Mariana reduces the *civitas libera* of the classical and medieval Bartolist tradition to a passing moment in the generic development of monarchical government.[64] The founders of empires, Ninus, Cyrus, Alexander and Caesar, regardless of the praise and glory that countless eulogists may have heaped upon them, were nothing but 'thorough plunderers'. However much 'vulgar opinion' admires them, they are not the legitimate princes of the people they conquered, but usurpers and cruel tyrants.[65] Monarchy and empire are presented not as the products of a law of nature virtually unimpaired by original sin, but as the result of persistent and ruthless obliteration of man's natural liberty and happiness.[66] Having originated in a 'race' and a period before the full onset of the process of deterioration, the *mutuum foedus societatis* is a historical and contingent phenomenon nonetheless. It can be expected to be a malleable matter in the hands of cunning princes. The gruesome history of the decline of the primordial compact continues.

The process of decline began with the introduction of single rulers, and continued with empires being erected on the ruins of *civitates liberae*. It finds its culmination in the establishment of hereditary kingship. This is the fate not only of the more immediate descendants of the 'first race of men'. It is the pattern that describes the development of communities throughout secular history. Each nation (*natio* or *gens*) will initially establish themselves as a *civitas libera*. Each will suffer a gradual decline of original freedom. Initiating the process by instituting single rulers, each *natio* will eventually mark the loss of all or much of its primeval liberty by introducing hereditary kingship. History affords Mariana many examples, though the paradigm is provided by Scripture: the 'commonwealth of the Jews' (*respublica Iudaeorum*).[67] Initially, judges (*iudices*) selected from all the tribes and with no power to alter the laws or customs of their nation ruled the people of Israel.

---

64 On the concept of the *civitas libera* in medieval political thought, see M. Ryan (2000), 'Bartolus of Sassoferrato and Free Cities (The Alexander Prize Lecture)', *Transactions of the Royal Historical Society*, Vol. 10 (Sixth Series), pp. 65-90; and J. Canning (1987), *The political thought of Baldus de Ubaldis* (Cambridge Studies in Medieval Life and Thought; 4th ser.; 6), Cambridge University Press, Cambridge, especially chapter three, pp. 93-131.

65 *De rege*, p. 24, '(…) Ninus, Cyrus, Alexander, & Caesar, qui magna constituerunt primi & fundarunt imperia, non legitimos fuisse Reges, non monstra domuisse sublata per terras tyrannide, non vitia ut videri volebant depulisse, sed praedatoriam exercuisse videantur, tametsi vulgi opinione immensis laudibus celebrentur & gloria.'

66 Mariana acknowledges only self-defence and the oppression of tyrants as legitimate reasons for expansion. The spreading of Christianity is conspicuously absent; see Ibid., p. 24, p. 25.

67 *De rege*, pp. 30-31, p. 31, 'Regiam potestatem in eam gentem [Israel] tempus invexit, & malitia atque improbitate Heli primum, deinde Samuelis filiorum irritati populares Regem sibi dari extorserunt, multum quamvis reclamante Samuele, atque imminentes ex eo calamitates severa denunciatione praedicente: foreque ut accepta potestate Reges abuterentur ad tyrannidem.'

Led astray by the misdemeanours of Eli and the sons of Samuel, however, the Israelites acted against better advice and demanded that Samuel anoint Saul as their king. After the introduction of kingship, the liberties and fortunes of the people of Israel inevitably declined. The glories of David's and Salomon's rule are passed over in silence.

This is a pattern that is to recur in the history of Rome as well as the history of the Iberian peoples. Mariana briefly refers to the gradual loss of *libertas* the Roman people suffered from the early republic to the principate of Augustus. His emphasis is firmly on Spain. At the mythical beginning of peninsular history, the inhabitants of free cities cultivated the soil. These *civitates* were suppressed by the expanding empire of the Carthaginians, who were followed by the Romans and later the Visigoths. Finally, after the destruction of the Visigoths during the Muslim invasion, the process of moral and constitutional degeneration entered its final stage: kingship became hereditary.[68] During the otherwise glorious period of the *reconquista*, a corrupted people that preferred to grovel rather than defend its liberties helped to consolidate the 'excessive power of kings and hereditary rule' in Spain.[69] Mariana has particularly caustic remarks for the 'learned men' involved in this process. These *viri prudentes* were only too willing to help Visigothic kings persuade their people that hereditary kingship was fully in consonance with law and natural equity

The phrase epitomizing this dynamic of decline befalling the people of Israel, and every people thereafter, is *tempus invexit*. 'Time', Mariana says, 'introduced kingship to the people of Israel'. 'Time and the wickedness of men' assured that the pattern of decline revealed in Scripture would return to visit the histories of Rome and the Spanish peninsula.[70] The foolish acts of flawed individuals ensure that the consequences of the Fall manifest themselves over and again in historical time. The phrase *tempus invexit* encapsulates the idea of a recurrent historical dynamic extending from the early mythical beginnings of mankind into recorded history. Time and human corruption have been linked and elevated to the position of historical agent. 'Time and the wickedness of man' replace legal order of any kind as the prime factor determining the life of monarchies.

Unsurprisingly, Mariana's pitiless pessimism and corresponding analysis of all-pervasive and recurrent decline does not stop short of hereditary rule and the process of dynastic change.[71] Corruption and decline are intrinsic to the dynastic system. Again, his main example is taken from Spanish history: the rise and decline of the House of Trastámara. The Trastámaras introduced themselves as Castile's

---

68   Ibid., p. 3,: 'In Hispania tandiu Principes omnibus imperaturi ex omnibus eligebatur, quandiu in ea Gotthorum imperium stetit: imperio & legibus commutatis haereditariam successionem tempus invexit. Nimia Regum potentia, populisque Principum voluntati blandientibus haereditaria successio invecta est.'

69   Ibid., p. 36, p. 37.

70   Ibid., p. 31, pp. 36-38, pp. 42-43.

71   For the following, see ibid., I.3, 'Num principatus haereditarius esse debeat', pp. 35-47; and I.4, 'De iure regiae successionis inter agnatos', pp. 48-55.

royal family in a less than upright manner: by means of an act of fratricide, no less. Mariana, both in his history of Spain and in *De rege* remains noticeably ambiguous as to whether or not Peter I († 1369) of Castile deserved the epithet 'the Cruel', and whether his half-brother Henry of Trastámara (Henry II, † 1379) killed him and seized the throne in order to satisfy his ambition rather than defend the common good.[72] He simply observes that, whatever the political, moral or legal implications of Henry's seizure of the throne of Castile, he justified his actions by being a determined and able ruler. Not all of Henry's descendants, however, could live up to his example. Already in his grandson and great-grandson, John I and Henry III, the glory of Henry II's reign 'waned, and, indeed, was turned into a joke.'[73] When Isabella of Castile († 1504) succeeded to the throne, an exhausted bloodline gave way to the 'industry and good quality' of another branch of the dynasty. Although Mariana does not propose a linear pattern of dynastic decline, he does call attention to the intrinsic fragility of dynastic systems. Too much depends on the personality and qualities of the individual monarch, and 'often enough sons are unlike their parents in intellect, nature and morals'.[74]

These observations relate not just to contemporary concerns about dynastic politics in general, but the state of the Spanish monarchy in particular. The decline of the House of Trastámara indicates the imminent decline of the Habsburgs. The new king of Spain, Philip III, did not distinguish himself by willpower, intellect or diligence. His own father seems to have thought of him as a monarch more likely to be ruled by rather than rule over his courtiers. An ailing child and a shy prince, piety was considered young Philip's highest virtue. His father had struggled to produce healthy issue, and Philip III had yet to produce an heir to the throne. The same logic that brought Henry II to power could induce a transfer of power from the Habsburgs to another, foreign dynasty. More likely than not, a transfer of power caused by a king unable to produce issue was likely to go along with civil war and foreign invasion. The fortune of dynasties is best comprehended in terms of a cycle of ascendancy, corruption, decline and eventual substitution by a more vigorous family. Questions of legitimacy find themselves subordinated to the dynamics and demands of *realpolitik*. 'Time and the wickedness of man' define and sanction the world of dynastic politics as one of inevitable, ceaseless, callous struggle among families competing for the royal title. They make sure that monarchies cannot escape from the general pattern of decline and corruption so conspicuous in human history.

With dynasties certain to succumb to corruption, the question arises as to whether hereditary monarchy can still be deemed a viable form of government. Mariana acknowledges that the corrupted state of monarchy after the Fall caused 'some of the greatest philosophical minds' to doubt whether single rule should indeed be preferred to the rule of the many or the rule of the few. Adopting the

---

72 Ibid., pp. 41-42, pp. 43-44.

73 Ibid., 42.

74 Ibid.

scholastic argumentative mode of thesis, antithesis and synthesis, Mariana responds to what he concedes are legitimate reservations with a thorough enquiry into the respective merits of hereditary monarchy, elective monarchy and alternative, non-monarchical forms of government. Aristotle is one of those 'greatest minds', and it is the vexing awareness of post-lapsarian decline that compels Mariana to revisit the *Politics* and *Nicomachean Ethics*.[75] He reviews and revises elementary features of the Aristotelian theory of government, making sure they reflect the reality of recurrent decay and corruption in Spanish government as he sees it.

According to Aristotle, the form of government assumed by the individual *civitas* could be shaped by a variety of factors.[76] Mariana starts off his argument by effectively reducing them to a single one: that of the moral corruption of man over time. He does so by focusing on one of the more enigmatic passages of the *Politics*, where Aristotle himself suggests that a single individual outstanding in virtue may be awarded permanent and all-powerful kingship, that is, kingship above the law.[77] In concession to his teacher Plato, Aristotle discusses the possibility that such a ruler might not cease to remain wholly virtuous while in power, and that such virtue might even survive in his descendants. Honing in on what is a largely hypothetical reflection in Aristotle, Mariana makes it fit his general scheme of decline and corruption.

Single rule (*unius principatus*) is the best form of government (*genus principatuus*), albeit only theoretically. Mariana praises *unius principatus* in wholly Aristotelian terms as the form of government 'especially consonant with the laws of nature', suggesting that single rule is inherent to 'spiritual and material creation'.[78] Again, however, its ideal form was only ever actualized at the beginning of time, immediately after the Fall.[79] Only there and then did the ideal man exist 'who surpasses all other

---

75   See ibid., I.2, 'Unum reipublicae praeesse, quam plures praestantius est', pp. 22-34, pp. 22-23. See Books three and four of Aristotle's *Politics*.

76   See, for instance, *Politics*, 1259a; 1289b35; 1327-31. Aristotle forged an alliance between the concept of degeneration and the idea of material progress already present in Thucydides. He has no theory of progress, but the emphasis is still on notions of progress. In *Politics*, 1265a17 and 1325b38, he insists that the ideal state is possible. He praises the past, but also exposes its faults. The past is by no means the embodiment of the ideal; see R. Weil (1977), 'Aristotle's View of History', in J. Barnes, M. Schofield and R. Sorabji (eds), *Articles on Aristotle*, Vol. 2, *Ethics and Politics*, Duckworth, London, pp. 202-17.

77   See *De rege*, p. 35, for a paraphrase of *Politics*, 1288a15.

78   Ibid., pp. 25-26, 'Primum enim caeteris principatuum generibus regium esse praestantius declarat, quod naturae legibus maxime consentaneum est, universitatis, caelique regimen ad unum caput revocantis: quod in caeteris naturae partibus observamus a corde animantis vitam spiritumque diffundi in omnia membra. (…) Quae gubernandi ratio non solum mundi rectioni consentanea est, sed cum suis partibus congruens domo una, pago, civitate: quae ab uno regi amant, multa capita auersantur.' Mariana paraphrases and comments on Aristotle, *Nicomachean Ethics*, 8:10, 1160ª31-1161ª10, and *Politics*, 3:5, 1279ª32-9.

79   Ibid., p. 26, '(…) Quod Aristoteles fatetur multis locis, ab unius principatu ad alias imperii formas ventum esse. Et est verisimile, uti antea dictum est, multitudinem initio ab iis oppressam qui maiores opes habebant, societate cum aliis inita, unum aliquem sibi prefecisse

citizens in prudence, honesty and love of justice', the man in whom 'the *bonum* and the *unum* are so integrated with each other, that one follows the other as a logical consequence'.[80] This man still belonged to the 'primeval and better race' that 'perceived more easily the true nature of things' subsequently obscured by original sin.[81] Only the first race of men, acting out its memory of a nature unimpaired by the Fall, was right to identify the *unius principatus* as the *genus* 'closest to the true nature of things'.

Mariana employs figures of thought reminiscent of Plato's Fable of the Cave to describe the subsequent process of decline. It is one during which the ideal form of kingship increasingly became a mere shadow and vague resemblance of its original self. The historical record of *unius principatus regius*, accordingly, is one of the varying, and ever lesser degrees to which individual princes came to represent the primordial actualization of *rector* and *unius principatus*. The rate of success is dispiriting. The prophet Samuel was only too right when he warned the people of Israel that 'after kings got the power they would abuse it to the point of tyranny'.[82] The ruler who 'uniquely surpasses all his countrymen in his wealth of honesty and prudence' is an unlikely or at least incredibly rare phenomenon. The historical actualizations of the *unius principatus* clearly reflect the impact of the Fall. Once the ideal of monarchical government was actual historical reality. Now it survives only in the form of a philosophical construct, as a principle of social organization in the animal world, and, as we will see, in the collective memory of peoples. It is preserved in tales of mythical, often deified heroes, a hazy reference to a distant past.[83] Terms and citations lifted from Aristotle's words are integrated into the conceptual opposition between the primeval, mytho-historical ideal and the subsequent historical actualization of monarchy. Aristotle's (largely hypothetical) virtuous ruler is re-defined as a transient moment in the post-lapsarian beginning of human history.

Could elective monarchy remedy or mitigate the impact of human corruption on single rule? Would it afford a better protection of the laws people put into effect to protect their interests and well-being against the ambition of their rulers?

---

ducem, qui iniurias hostium praehiberet, & vindicaret. Alias principatuum formas tempus invexit.'

80   Ibid., p. 28, p. 35.

81   Ibid., p. 26, 'Primi homines considerantes, qui propius aberant a prima & meliori progenie, eoque facilius rerum naturam intuebantur, unius imperium amplexi sunt.'

82   Ibid., p. 31, 'Regiam potestatem in eam gentem tempus invexit, & malitia atque improbitate Heli primum, deinde Samuelis filiorum irritati populares Regem sibi dari extorserunt, multum quamvis reclamante Samuele, atque imminentes ex eo calamitates severa denunciatione praedicente: foreque ut accepta potestate Reges abuterentur ad tyrannidem.'

83   Ibid., p. 52, 'Praeclare cum rebus humanis ageretur, si ut in gregibus & inter apes contingit, a praeside utraque regi naturae praestantioris: ita rector populi conditione mortali maior esset Heros aliquis, uti primis temporibus factum memorant.'

Mariana firmly denies this.[84] History simply affords no proof that elective monarchy produces better rulers. In fact, the examination of historical examples demonstrates that the opposite is the case. Monarchs 'obtained by selection rather than hereditary succession' have been equally worthless, 'equally base in their morals, and no less numerous', to say the least.[85] What is more, the 'dregs and monstrosities' of the Roman empire as well as the inadequate leaders chosen by the Visigoths more than strongly suggest that 'when the princes were selected from all (*ex omnibus*), they were much worse kings than [hereditary kings] in later times'.[86] Mariana further illustrates this point by means of reference to the history of medieval Spanish feudalism. The example he has in mind is an institution called *behetría de villas y ciudades*.[87]

The term *behetría* is a thirteenth-century vernacular derivative of the Latin *beneficium*. A corporate body, the *behetría* entered into feudal relations with a lord (*señor*). The vassals (*hombres de behetría*) had the right to select their *señor* either from the members of a particular family (*behetría de linaje*) or from anywhere in the Christian parts of the Spanish peninsula (*behetría de mar a mar*).[88] In the case of serious misdemeanour, the vassals had the right to remove the *señor* from his lordship and replace him. The feudal bond was dissolved with the death of the *señor*. In this respect, the position of the *señor de behetría* differed profoundly from that of other peninsular feudal lords. During the thirteenth and in particular the late fourteenth century, the *señores* of the perhaps six-hundred *behetrías* still existing

---

84   Ibid., p. 31, 'Quo argumento efficitur, aut regiam potestatem civili praestantiorem non esse, aut illius certe populi moribus, atque eo praesertim tempore non satis fuisse accomodatam. Quod enim in aliis rerum generibus contingit, ut quae praestantiora sunt & elegantiora non omnibus conveniant, vestes, calcei, domicilia: idem in reipublicae forma contingere arbitror, ut quae praestantissima sit, eam non omnium populorum mores & instituta recipiant. In non dispari enim argumentorum pondere, & ea sententiarum varietate animus inclinabat ut credere, ac vero pro certo ponerem, unius principatum caeteris omnibus reipublicae formis esse praeferendum.'

85   Ibid., pp. 41-42.

86   Ibid., p. 42.

87   Ibid., pp. 38-39. For the *behetría* in Spanish law, see *Las siete partidas*, IV, 12, 3; *Fuero viejo*, VIII; and *Ordenamiento de Alcalá*, XXXII. The importance of the *behetría* in Spanish constitutional and political history is generally acknowledged. Despite the studious efforts of Sánchez-Albornoz, however, little research has so far been done. On the *behetría* as a phenomenon of the feudalization of the peninsula during the High Middle Ages, see C. Sánchez-Albornoz (1924), 'Las Behetrías. La encomendación en Asturias, León y Castilla', *Anuario de historia del derecho español*, Vol. 1, pp. 158-336; and the brief summary remarks in L.G. de Valdeavellano (1968), *Curso de historia de las instituciones españolas, De los orígenes al final de la Edad Media*, Alianza Editorial, Madrid, pp. 341-43, pp. 511-14.

88   Mariana's rendition of the distinction between *behetría de linaje* and *behetría de mar a mar* is characteristic for his preference of letters over precise legal definition; see, for instance, *De rege*, p. 38, 'Quaedam ex universa gente eum Principem iubebant, quem suis rationibus opportunum maxime iudicarent, alia es una tantum familia.'

in Old Castile and León gradually deprived the corporate bodies of their privileges or *libertates*.[89]

The fact that the *behetría*, an Iberian incarnation of the *civitas libera*, falls prey to nobles lusting for nothing but power, however, does not count as a great loss in Mariana's eyes. The *behetría* as a form of government had clearly outlived its usefulness. Corruption had long set in. According to Mariana, the right to elect and depose *señores de behetría* had led to a situation of permanent political confusion and strife already by the end of the thirteenth century.[90] Noble families as well as members of the same family vied with one another for *señoríos de behetría*. Political and constitutional change came to be semantically reflected in that the word *behetría* changed from a constitutional term describing an ancient privilege and institution into a catchphrase for a permanent situation of political confusion and unrest.[91] A mocking, pejorative proverb is the only trace left of the last free medieval corporate bodies in Spanish language and political consciousness.

Mariana's discussion of the *behetría* highlights his comparison between electoral and hereditary kingship. Hereditary kingship is the lesser of two evils simply because it responds much better than electoral monarchy to self-interest and weakness as principal features of the human mind and character. A single ruler will look after the *res communes* much more conscientiously and determinedly if his direct descendant is to inherit his power.[92] What is more, both nobility and multitude are much more likely to defer to a dynasty that has been in place for a long time than to elected princes with a much less established claim to power.[93] *Interregna*, for instance, are thus more easily avoided.[94] Even if a son is noticeably less able than his father, his rule will still be supported out of respect for the dynasty. Succession clearly ordered along the principle of heredity is also the form of government most likely to stifle noble factionalism and thus most likely to prevent civil war arising from a

---

89   A development encapsulated in royal legislation at the Cortes of Toro (1371), where Henry II of Castile, apparently in order to obtain the support of the Castilian nobility during the civil war, sanctioned the transformation of *señores de behetría* into *señores naturales* (hereditary feudal lordships).

90   On urbanization and state-building in medieval and early modern Spain, see P. Fernández Albaladejo (1994), 'Cities and the State in Spain', in C. Tilly and W.P. Blockmans (eds), *Cities & the Rise of States in Europe, 1000-1800*, Westview Press, Boulder, Col., pp. 168-83.

91   His reference to the pejorative proverbial meaning of the term *behetría* is confirmed by the entries under 'behetría' in contemporary dictionaries of the Castilian language. See, for instance, Sebastián de Covarrubias (1611), *Tesoro de la Lengua Castellana o Española*, Luis Sánchez, Madrid, pp. 203-4; and *Diccionario de Autoridades* (1726), ed. Real Academia Española, Gredos, Madrid, p. 588; see also Mariana, *Historiae*, XVI, 17.

92   *De rege*, p. 40.

93   Ibid., p. 39, 'Reverentiam exhiberi maiorem iis, qui ex Regibus avis atque atavis nati sunt, non a civibus modo sed a externis ipsisque publicis hostibus. Imperii majestas quid aliud quam salutis tutela reipublicae salus est? (…) nobilitas enim instar lucis est, multitudinis sed & procerum oculos perstringentis fraenantisque temeritatem.'

94   Ibid., p. 40.

succession crisis.[95] These are arguments altogether familiar from Machiavelli's brief but potent outline of the unbeatable advantages of hereditary rule.[96]

Similar reasons permit Mariana to discard 'the rule of the few or the many' as viable alternatives to hereditary monarchy. They must be considered worse manifestations of post-lapsarian moral and epistemological degeneration than hereditary rule.[97] 'The rule of the few or the many' is a mere product of historical time does not even count as a very poor reflection of the pre-lapsarian order. The opinion 'that it is better to be governed by several' is itself based on contingent historical experience. It is found especially among those who were born in one of the few remaining independent city-states, *civitates liberae* like Venice or Geneva.[98] Governed by oligarchies rather than the virtuous *rector* of primordial times, their citizens now suffer even more from the defects affecting hereditary monarchy. By far the most powerful argument against 'the rule of the few or the many' is that greed, the most vicious of all vices, and the one particularly corrupting to justice, 'is less in one prince than in the many'.[99] It is less in a prince, simply because it is easier to suppress, curb and control it from early on in his life. If ignorance, avarice and reckless ambition that bring disaster to many communities are to be curtailed effectively, *potestas* must be concentrated in one person rather than distributed among the few or the many.[100]

According to Mariana, this is particularly evident if we come to look into how political decisions are made. If more than one person is involved in the actual making of decisions, paralysing controversies and constant dissent will slow down the process of deliberation and resolution. The more people are involved, the more likely it is that vile, corrupt, and dishonest individuals will take advantage of political office. According to Mariana,

---

95   Ibid., p. 43.

96   Machiavelli, *Il principe*, chapter two.

97   *De rege*, p. 26, 'Quod Aristoteles fatetur multis locis, ab unius principatu ad alias imperii formas ventum esse. Et est verisimile, uti antea dictum est, multitudinem initio ab iis oppressam qui maiores opes habebant, societate cum aliis inita, unum aliquem sibi prefecisse ducem, qui iniurias hostium prohiberet, & vindicaret. Alias principatuum formas tempus invexit.'

98   Ibid., p. 30, 'His argumentis victi quidam manus dant eruditione praestanti viri, praesertim ex eorum numero qui in liberis civitatibus nati sunt. Et est insitum natura, ut assuetis stare homines malint, nisi quae usus manifeste arguit. Neque periculo vacabat patria instituta movere, contraria quamvis sentientes.'

99   Ibid., p. 26, 'Pravae cupiditatis, per quam mens excaecatur, iustitia corrumpitur, res publicae & privatae perturbantur, minus in uno Principe & quam in pluribus est, sive rerum copia fastidium faciente, seu quia unum quam multos praestare facilius est. imminuta cupiditate maior iustitiae locus erit, maior libertati.'

100 Ibid., p. 26, pp. 26-27, 'Postremo cum principatus potestasque imperandi vana sine viribus sit: eae vires in uno homine coniunctae validiores sunt, maioresque; impetus dant, quam cum pluribus participatae, sive illae opes sint, sive auctoritas imperandi, sive populi studia in unum coniuncta, plura maioraque efficiunt quam divisa inter multos.'

in every part of the people there is a number of dishonest subjects who are by far the most numerous; the *sanior pars* will be beaten in every deliberation by the *peior pars* if the governing power is in the hands of more than one. For the votes will not be weighed but counted. It cannot be otherwise.[101]

The celebrated *maior* or *sanior pars* of the medieval constitutionalist tradition is merely another sad illusion conjured up to obscure the seriousness of Adam's Fall from grace. Mariana's conclusion flies in the face of French Huguenot and Catholic League theorists of resistance who, drawing on conciliarist sources, identified magistrates as the *maior* or *sanior pars populi*.[102] Again, it is Mariana's view of human nature, bearing even heavier on the rule of the few or the many than on that of the single man, that determines his judgement.

For all its flaws, then, hereditary monarchy compares well with its competitors. Denying that hereditary kingship is the comparatively best form of government counts as a foolish act of idealizing the past coupled with an equally inexcusable ignorance of the human condition:

> We appraise affairs in a silly and foolish manner; we blame others for their faults and prefer not to consider what difficulties they shouldered and contended with in times past under a different set of circumstances. We shrink from the corruption we behold, thinking that the past was better than the present, and that only the future brings the recurrent cycle of evil. Yet even if there had been a smaller number of events in the past, such as heated assemblies and the misfortunes of aggressive ambition, by what other means could they have been handled than by adopting the principle of heredity?[103]

With characteristic, adroit cynicism, Mariana more than once advises his readers that human affairs are governed by what men believe is true rather than by the truth intrinsic to things themselves.[104] His epistemological pessimism is concomitant with

---

101 Ibid., p. 32, 'Deinde cum in omni populi parte improborum numerus sit multo maximus, si rerum potestas penes plures fuerit, in omni deliberatione pars sanior a peiori superabitur: neque enim suffragia ponderantur, sed numerantur, ac ne fieri quidem aliter potest.'

102 On Monarchomach and Leaguer political thought and use of the concept of the *maior* or *sanior pars* see J.H.M. Salmon (1973), 'Bodin and the Monarchomachs', in H. Denzer (ed.), *Verhandlungen der internationalen Bodin Tagung*, Beck, Munich, pp. 359-78 [now in: J.H.M. Salmon (1987), *Renaissance and Revolt, Essays in the intellectual and social history of early modern France* (Cambridge Studies in Early Modern History), Cambridge University Press, Cambridge, pp. 119-35]; and ibid. (1982), 'An Alternative Theory of Popular Resistance: Buchanan, Rossaeus and Locke', in B. Paradisi, *Diritto e potere nella storia europea*, Leo S. Olschki, Florence, pp. 823-49 [now in: as above, pp. 136-54].

103 *De rege*, p. 43, '(...) nolumus considerare in quae incommoda antiquis temporibus diversa ratione suscepta incurreretur. Quae videmus vitia aversamur, praeterita praesentibus potiora fuisse, foreque existimantes, unde malorum orbis recurrat. Quae tamen si minora antiquis temporibus extitissent, comitiorum aestus, ambitionis tetrae incommoda, qua alia ratione, nisi haereditate suscepta possint procurari.'

104 Ibid., p. 39, 'Et est natura datum ut res communes & imperia magis opinione hominum quam rebus ipsis gubernentur.'

his view of human nature. The generations following the 'first race' can no longer comprehend the 'true nature of things'. As a result, they cannot claim that any such knowledge could inspire their thinking and conduct. His comprehensive pessimism makes him wary of attempts to field the past against the present. His credo is that of a historian pained by disillusionment and a sense of permanent loss:

> The conduct of human affairs would be admirable, if what is undertaken sensibly to begin with were carried through accordingly, and if the outcome were related to and consonant with the beginning. But time and the worthlessness and depravity of man pervert everything. This is the human condition.[105]

However lamentable the destruction of the *civitas libera*, however despicable the institution of hereditary rule, however insufficient the majority of those who exercise it, there is no mytho-historical ideal which can be called up to challenge monarchical authority. The inevitable conclusion is that in constantly changing circumstances, in an unsafe world, hereditary monarchy still affords the best protection.[106]

The comparison between hereditary and elected princes in *De rege* is permeated by an awareness that primeval innocence and freedom are irretrievably lost to mankind. The mythical and ideal past may be preserved in collective memory. Mariana is prepared to concede that peoples will try to allocate the primordial *rector* a place in their national histories, usually in terms of a dimly sketched variation of the ideal philosopher-king of classical literature. The ideal, however, is to be banished to the realm of the unattainable ideal. 'Time and the wickedness of man' have created an impassable chasm between the pre-lapsarian and primordial ideal and the historic reality of kingship. This is why, despite the inevitable demise of dynasties, hereditary monarchy is to be strongly preferred to elected rulers. Monarchical government is best suited to deal with human corruption, and it is in this if in no other respect superior to both electoral monarchy and republican government. The introduction of hereditary succession is both a symptom of and a response to human moral degeneration.

Conclusion

Immediately after the Fall, *rector* and *unius principatus* represent the original, untainted and, indeed, ideal form of monarchical government. The leadership practised and experienced by the post-lapsarian 'race of men' is utterly distinct from subsequent historical actualizations of the principle of single rule. Mariana refers to both *regia*

---

105 Ibid., pp. 42-43, 'Praeclare cum rebus humanis ageretur, si quae a sano initio suscipiuntur eadem perseverarent, postremaque cum primis conea aptaque essent. Verum ignavia maliciaque hominum, tempusque cuncta depravat. Ea est humanae vitae conditio.'

106 Ibid., p. 32, 'Ut sunt res humanae fluxae inconstantesque, prudentis viri partes sunt, non omnia incommoda, sed maiora vitare, persequi quae maiores opportunitates affere videantur. Ac praesertim concordia inter cives retinenda (sine qua quid esset respublica?) aptissimus esse unius principatum nemo dubitabit.'

potestas and tyranny as manifestations of a corrupted and irredeemably lost ideal. He thus padlocks his perception of kingship with his profoundly pessimistic, Catholic-Augustinian view of human nature. Society and political authority are institutions established to regulate the wanton acts of invariably egotistical human beings. They are undeniably flawed products of the will and intellect of men damaged by original sin. Mariana continues to challenge the Thomist-Aristotelian view of civil society as the product of a natural order basically unharmed by the Fall. He widens the scope of his investigation into irreparably corrupted civil society, shifting his focus to the laws with which the 'first race' hoped to guide and restrain their leaders. If civil society and the principle of single rule are prone to deteriorate, so are the laws with which men sought to protect themselves. The following chapter investigates the momentous implications this has for the theory and ethics of early modern government.

CHAPTER TWO

Power and the Law

The first chapters of *De rege* confront the reader with a rather inauspicious account of the origins and development of civil society and monarchical authority. Mariana applies a consistently pessimistic view of human nature to his analysis of the secular body politic. He rejects the Thomist-Aristotelian axiom that civil society and political authority evolved from an order of nature essentially unharmed by the corruption of man after the Fall. Instead, humanist topoi describe a transition from a state of innocence to one of intrinsically corrupted civic life. How, then, is post-lapsarian society to establish and maintain political order? What kind of government is to arise from the need to negotiate life in the *civitas terrena*? The most pressing question that Mariana will now have to address, surely, is how law can bind and protect people left with no more than the memories and remnants of pristine order.

Custom and Corruption

De rege abounds in references to civil and canon law as well as laws of the Iberian realms. Yet Mariana does not discuss natural and positive law in the detailed and comprehensive manner of the scholastic theologian. This is not so much because of the constraints of his chosen genre. Mariana's approach is phenomenological. It is rooted in a distinctive perception of the relationship between human nature, law and power as manifest in secular history. The order of law is but another illustration of human corruption as manifest in history. 'Time and the great wickedness of men', Mariana explains, 'brought on the great multitude of laws, so that now we suffer no less from laws than from vices'.[1] The small number of plain laws with which people initially sought to hold down their princes' aspirations have multiplied inordinately, now resembling an impenetrable undergrowth. Each group of men organizing themselves into some kind of society will be affected in the same way. Starting out with few and clear laws, they will soon find themselves overwhelmed by their own creation. The excessive multiplication and concomitant degradation of laws is a recurrent theme of *De rege*, and it recurs in Mariana's acerbic critique of the political constitution of the Society of Jesus, the *Discurso de las enfermedades de la Compañia* [de Jesús].[2] Mariana's remarks amount to more than mere topical

---

1   *De rege*, p. 23.

2   Especially chapters one, seventeen and nineteen. The *Discurso* was first printed in a French translation in 1625, *Discours du Père Jean Mariana Iesuite Espagnol, Des grands defauts qui sont en la forme du governement des Iesuites*, transl. J. de Cordes, n.p. First Spanish edition (1768), *Discurso de las enfermedades de la Compañia. Con una disertación sobre el Autoró y la legitimidad de la*

criticism of legal bureaucracy and litigiousness in contemporary Castile.[3] He has resolved that laws and systems of law do not suffice as frame of reference for the construction of political order.

In Mariana's etiology of civil society and monarchy, positive laws spring from a defensive reflex on the part of the *populus*. The first laws emerge as a purported bulwark against princely power always likely to encroach upon the rights and liberties of *cives* or *subditi* (Mariana uses the terms synonymously). The *lex naturae* provided the point of reference for the 'fair system of law' with which men 'hedged about' their monarchs once they became aware of their ambition, greed and thirst for power.[4] *Lex naturae* is natural in that it facilitates self-preservation. It is identical with the force steering man and animal alike towards communal life, thus increasing their chances of survival and procreation. Natural law *after* the Fall is akin to instinct.[5] This is not the understanding of *lex naturae* or *lex naturalis* preferred by Saint Thomas Aquinas and his many followers. Francisco Suárez, for instance, refers to natural law 'in the proper sense of the term' as the law 'which pertains to moral doctrine and to theology'.[6] Unlike 'the execution of the natural inclinations of the brutes' it is not a result of necessity. Suárez disagrees with the *iurisprudenti* (effectively the civilian tradition) who suggest that 'brute animals' share in the law of nature in more than a metaphorical sense.[7] Again, Mariana clearly opposes the Thomist-Aristotelian outlook on civic society. He diminishes the rational force of natural law, and thus its redeeming influence on the making of positive law. Positive law in turn is even more prone to suffer from corrupting manipulation.

Like the institution of monarchy itself, Mariana says, positive laws were initially conceived by the people as a corporate body. The original mandate of princes, accordingly, was to preserve and administer primeval, positive law rather than make new laws. Over the course of time, however, the relationship between the prince and positive law disintegrated. Mariana perceives history to be dominated by princes successfully hollowing out or burying laws not to their liking.[8] Invariably, the student of history will have to admit that 'arms silence the laws' and that 'might is right'. Mariana concludes that positive laws will always be easy prey to princes who are subtle and ruthless in their pursuit of power. Though there are exceptions to the

---

obra y un apendice de varios testimonios de Jesuitas Españolas que concuerdan con Mariana, D. Gabriel Ramirez, Madrid.

3   On the widespread criticism of the proliferation of laws, lawsuits and lawyers in early modern Castile see R.L. Kagan (1981), *Lawsuits and Litigants in Castile, 1500-1700*, University of North Carolina Press, Chapel Hill.

4   *De rege*, p. 21.

5   Mariana echoes the civilian definition of natural law as the 'law shared by man and beast', especially *Inst.* 1.2.1. and *Dig.* 1.1.1.; also Cicero, *De re publica*, 3.11.19.

6   Francisco Suárez (1612), *De legibus, ac Deo legislatore*, D. Gomez de Loureyo, Coimbra, 1.3.9.

7   Ibid., 1.3.7-8.

8   See, for instance, *De rege*, p. 37 on the *viri prudentes* the Visigothic kings employed to subvert the customs of the realm.

rule, peoples are generally incapable of protecting themselves and their laws from the ambition of princes. This is one of the most lamentable aspects of the human condition. It is also one for which Mariana believes there is no real remedy.

Mariana's frequent use of the subjunctive mood and of modal verbs is conspicuous. Mariana talks about what princes *should* or *ought* to do. He is adamant that princes ought to see themselves as simple helmsmen or *gubernatores*. They receive 'rewards' for their efforts on behalf of the *populus*, of course. Yet they must look at these as gifts or grants (*mercedes*), and seek to ensure that the people can act of their own free will in making these rewards.[9] This is hardly meant as a description of the constitutional and political reality of government in early modern Spain. The language of *De rege* indicates that its normative frame of reference is noticeably different from that found in the legal and theological writings of Diego Covarruvias or Francisco Suárez. The latter, for instance, posits that the people had transferred irrevocable and 'absolute' power to the prince.[10] He arrives at definite and axiomatic conclusions by means of scholastic dissection and reconciliation of legal concepts. Mariana clearly disagrees with Suárez's contention, yet he does not offer an alternative interpretation of this vexed issue of transfer of power. Nor is he prepared to meet Suárez on his own terrain and engage with scholastic legal discourse. Throughout his treatise, Mariana determines to restrain the prince by means of indoctrination, and with recourse to virtue, prudence and necessity rather than the law.

Mariana is sceptical about positive law as the guardian of primeval rights and liberties not only because of the machinations of unscrupulous and ambitious rulers. He subjects the laws and the people who make them to severe criticism, too. For instance, he asserts that laws constituting the body politic are the product of *fortuna* rather than sound natural reason.[11] In making laws supposed to 'hedge about' the ruler, Mariana says, peoples are generally inspired by sudden whims and foolhardiness instead of wisdom (*sapientia*). The most likely outcome are laws that are deeply flawed. Even the laws established by the 'first race', Mariana suggests, would not have necessarily been worth upholding.

The worst outcome of the law-making process imaginable, according to Mariana, are laws that either *decrease* or *increase* the power of the monarch disproportionately. Injudicious laws seriously jeopardize the safety and stability of the realm as well as

---

9   *De rege*, p. 59, 'Neque enim se Princeps reipublicae & singulorum dominum arbitrabitur, quamvis assentatoribus id in aurem insusurrantibus, sed rectore mercede a civibus designata: qua augere nisi ipsis volentibus nefas existimabit.'

10   Suárez, *De legibus*, 3.4.

11   In the context of investigating the crucial question 'whether the authority of the commonwealth or that of the king is greater'. See ibid., pp. 87-88, 'Maximam quidem partem constituenda republica, legibus promulgandis quasi suo iure fortuna sibi vendicat: populus saepe non delectu alique & sapientia ducitur, sed impetu animorum & quadam temeritate. quo circa sapientes ea quae populus fecisset ferenda, non saepe laudanda iudicarunt.' On the varying conceptualizations of *fortuna* in humanist political thought, see J.G.A. Pocock (1975), *The Machiavellian Moment, Florentine Political Thought and the Atlantic Republican Tradition*, Princeton University Press, Princeton, pp. 31-48.

the liberties of the people. Laws that bestow 'excessive power very nearly verging on tyranny' on a single ruler are particularly common among 'barbaric peoples'.[12] These laws are to be deplored, and the people voluntarily subjecting themselves to the whim of their rulers are to be pitied. Yet these laws constitute legitimate governments. Each nation makes its own bed, and it will rest the better or the worse for it. The fact that the majority of human law testifies to the craftiness of rulers and the indifference or plain idiocy of their peoples is a staple theme of *De rege*. Readers are repeatedly reminded that laws are likely to prevent rather than encourage a balance of power from establishing itself. In fact, they are told to abandon all hope that monarchical government can be operated in terms of law.

The ambition of princes and the ineptitude of subjects are complemented by a third element equally important in the unmaking of political order already mentioned: the element of time. In the first instance, 'time and the wickedness of men' affect and corrupt all areas of human activity. However, time also appears to rank as one of the few remaining safeguards of the original compact. More often than not, time encases in custom the imprudent *leges* of 'barbarian tribes' knowing no better than to sacrifice their liberties at the altar of tyranny. Occasionally, however, time happens to preserve the *iura libertatis* with which more discerning nations sought to perpetuate the primordial consensus that led to the introduction of the *unius principatus* in the first instance. Does custom have the potential to obstruct the expansion of princely power, though?

Mariana's remarks in this respect paraphrase several *loci classici*. He echoes the civilian idea that custom supersedes statutory law.[13] He agrees with the prevalent opinion of the leading fourteenth-century lawyer Bartolus of Sassoferato (1314-57) that custom retains its authority against statutory law even if a people transfers law-making powers to its prince.[14] The 'Bartolist' concept of custom holds that the

---

12   *De rege*, p. 91, 'Est autem perspicuum, id institutum in quibusdam gentibus vigere, ubi nullus est publicus consensus, numquam populus aut proceres de republica deliberaturi conveniunt: obtemperandi tantum necessitas urget, sive aequum sive iniquum Regis imperium sit. Potestas nimia proculdubio, proximeque, ad tyrannidem vergens, qualem inter gentes barbaras vigere Aristoteles affirmatum reliquit. Nec mirum cum robore corporis, sine consilio, sine prudentia ad servitutem nati sint quidam; (...).' The reference is to Aristotle, *Politics*, 1285a16, who contends that non-Greek and especially Asiatic peoples are by nature more inclined to suffer oppressive rule.

13   Notably *Dig.* 1.3.32 [Iulian], 'De quibus causis scriptis legibus non utimur, id custodiri oportet, quod moribus et consuetudine inductum est. (...) Inveterata consuetudo pro lege non immerito custoditur, et hoc est ius quod dicitur moribus constitutum'; and *Dig.* 1.3.33 [Ulpian], 'Diuturna consuetudo pro iure et lege in his qui non ex scripto descendunt observari solet.' The authoritative statement for the opinion of the majority of jurists is the widely quoted gloss of Accursius on *Dig.* 1.3.32, 'Consuetudo vincit legem, sicut una lex vincit aliam'.

14   See e.g. Bartolus of Sassoferrato (1471), *Super prima parte Codicis*, Sixtus Riesinger, Naples, Vol. 1, p. 161r, col.2-161v, col. 1 [no page nos. in volume], ad *Cod.* 8, '(...) Guilelmus de Cuneo in dicta l. de quibus [*Dig.* 1.3.32] (...) fatetur quod in principem translata est potestas condendi legem expressam et scriptam, non autem consuetudinariam, quae

populus acting through their representatives or over long periods of time has the power to make laws redundant as well as to refuse to accept statutory laws. Laws are not simply valid because they are old. Laws are valid because their age manifests the continuous consent of the people. Law is made by popular consent. Desuetude, in turn, manifests the withdrawal of such consent. It may or may not be confirmed by representatives of the people. This is the notion of custom as 'second nature'. [15]

Mariana argues along the same lines, although only up to a point. He agrees that promulgation, whichever form it takes, does not imbue statutory laws with anything more than a mere nominal force. Promulgated laws still need to be confirmed by the consent of those for whom they are passed. [16] This is where he draws the line between statutory law and customary law. Customary law is law that has been corroborated by practice over a long period of time. Mariana suggests that the *consensus populi* is likely to be tacit rather than explicit (by means of assembly). It is enacted over potentially long periods of time during which a people come to accept laws into their lives. The 'fundamental laws' or 'laws of the land' represent the core of customary law, flagged up as cornerstones of a nation's identity. Laws, Mariana says, are finally approved only once persistent practice has established them as part of the customs (*mores*) of a people.

---

in eum non potuit transferri, quum procedat ex tacito consensu (…) et sic dicit hodie populum Romanum posse facere consuetudinem generalem, quum potestas ipsius legis consuetudinariae inducendae non sit translata in principem et (…) remanet in suo statu. (…) bene sequi debemus illud quod populus Romanus ex certa scientia fecit consuetudinem inducendo.' Bartolus in fact confirms the opinion of a contemporary civilian, Guilelmus de Cuneo [Guillaume de Cunh]. On Bartolus see D. Quaglioni (1983), *Politica e diritto nel Trecento italiano. Il 'De tyranno' di Bartolo di Sassoferrato (1314-57). Con l'edizione critica dei trattati 'De Guelphis et Gebellinis', 'De regimine civitatis' e 'De tyranno'* (Il pensiero politica biblioteca; 11), Olschki, Florence; and the contributions in D. Segoloni (ed.) (1962), *Bartolo da Sassoferrato. Studi e documenti per il VI centenario*, Giuffrè, Milan. On medieval juridical conceptualizations of the relationship between law and political authority see B. Paradisi (1983), 'Il pensiero politico dei giuristi medievali', in L. Firpo (ed.), *Storia delle idee politiche, economiche e sociali*, Vol. 2, Unione Tipografico, Turin, pp. 211-366; C. Fasolt (1995), 'Visions of Order in the Canonists and Civilians', in T.A. Brady, H.A. Oberman and J.D. Tracy (eds), *Handbook of European History, 1400-1600*, Vol. 2, Brill, Leiden, pp. 31-60, especially pp. 45-49; and the useful essays in M. Ascheri, I. Baumgärtner and Julius Kirshner (eds) (1999), *Legal Consulting in the Civil Law Tradition*, Robbins Collection Publication, Berkeley.

15 On the notion of customary law as 'second nature', see D.R. Kelley (1990), 'Second Nature: The Idea of Custom in European Law, Society, and Culture', in A. Grafton and A. Blair (eds), *The Transmission of Culture in Early Modern Europe*, University of Pennsylvania, Philadelphia, pp. 131-72, especially pp. 133-37.

16 *De rege*, p. 89, 'Idem de legum sanctione iudicium esto (…) tunc instituuntur cum promulgantur, firmantur, cum moribus utentium approbantur.' This formula, recurrent in *De rege*, echoes civilian vocabulary. See *Inst.* 1.2.9, 'Ex non scripto ius venit, quod usus comprobavit, nam diuturni mores consensu utentium comprobati, legem imitantur'; also *Dig.* 1.3.32 and 35.

Human nature, and its limits, provide perhaps the best protection of custom. Mariana warns that it is extremely dangerous to change the *patriae instituta* or customs of a country because it is likely to offend a major trait of human nature. Peoples and individuals, 'unless experience clearly instructs them to do differently', are 'by nature' inclined 'to stick to what they know'.[17] Mariana's unwholesome lessons from history clearly extend to the conviction that, generally, 'empires and commonwealths are changed only for the worse.'[18] Human deficiency, then, recommends the preservation of custom and tradition as one of the best means to preserve peace. Mariana adds another common adage, namely that change can be desired in prayers, but must never be actively pursued in politics.

True to his pessimistic credo, Mariana then goes on to point out that tacit consent is subject to manipulation and corruption no less than explicit consent. His remarks echo Saint Augustine, who posited a strict opposition between pre- and post-lapsarian nature. Custom was clearly allocated to the latter. The Father of the Church took the idea of custom as second nature to be irreconcilable with the idea of the corruption of both human nature and human law by original sin. In his eyes, as well as those of Mariana, custom reflected the corruption of the post-lapsarian *civitas terrena* just as much as any law positive or natural. Mariana duly points out that jurisconsults have always been eager to oblige princes by faking the evidence necessary to persuade the *populus* that new laws agree or are identical with established custom. He is not even too damning about these *letrados* or 'prudent men'. Some of them, he says, truly believe that they act in the best interest of the commonwealth. What is more, custom itself gives manifold expression to corrupted human nature. In the first instance, it is just as likely to be bent and twisted according to the will and whim of princes as statutory law. It is a matter of how princes go about changing custom rather than what they change. The salient point is that the bending and twisting ought to happen with the connivance of the *populus*. Whatever the objectives of a prince meddling with custom, Mariana says, failure to involve his subjects is tantamount to conjuring up the evil of civil war. Hence *De rege* abounds with entreaties and warnings that Philip III must not change fundamental laws, especially the laws of religion, taxation and succession without consulting the 'will of the people'. Again, however, Mariana is ambiguous about who 'the people' are, in what ways they ought to be consulted and how fundamental laws are likely to be affected during that process. He expounds his views when discussing the fundamental laws supposedly regulating royal succession in Castile.[19] In one of those sardonic turns of argument readers soon learn to expect from the author of *De rege*, Mariana explains that customary laws are more likely to stand the test of time if they reflect the human state of corruption.

---

17   Ibid., pp. 29-30.
18   Ibid., p. 36.
19   This discussion takes place in chapter four of Book one, pp. 48-55.

Laws of Succession: Breaking the Law, Preserving the Commonwealth

The Castilian laws of succession are Mariana's prime example. He denounces the introduction of hereditary succession straightaway as a corollary to the 'excessive power of kings', and a direct result of peoples' readiness to 'toady to the will of princes'.[20] However, the laws of hereditary succession not only mirror and accommodate, they also cleverly exploit principal traits of corrupted human nature. Peoples will always allow 'public affairs and governments' to be ruled 'more by opinion (...) than by the intrinsic merits of the question'.[21] Accordingly, the prime advantage of hereditary titles lies in the fact that they so easily deceive, overwhelm and intimidate men. A dynastic title is 'like the light striking in the eyes of the multitude as well as those of the chief men'.[22] Blinded by the appearance of dynastic tradition, both *populus* and *proceres* will stand 'restrained in their selfishness'. Their weakness of mind makes men tolerate 'with more equanimity an unfortunately sired hereditary prince than one who has been honestly elected'. Hereditary rule is an institution altogether wicked in origin and deeply rooted in both the 'recklessness of princes' and the 'ineptitude of the multitude'. It is vindicated primarily by its restraining influence on subjects. Rebellion is much less likely to occur during a dynastic transfer of power from father to son than under electoral rule. Mariana is by no means the only early modern author to make these and related points. He is still remarkable, however, for the rigour and consistency with which he draws on the notion of egotistical human nature in order to put *realpolitik* before laws.

Mariana's examination of the agnatic principle of succession prevalent in Iberian law and politics amounts to a case-study of the post-lapsarian relationship between law and power. Law is in effect replaced by historical experience as the primary frame of reference for establishing political and social order. He proceeds by contrasting legal principles enshrined in civil law and Iberian customary laws with lessons drawn from historical incidents. It quickly strikes the reader that what Iberian customary laws prescribe is difficult to reconcile with what historical evidence suggests actually happened. More often than not, political circumstances and the character of the individuals involved demand clear breaches of the spirit and the letter of the law. Mariana, again, is quick to make the point that human depravity is reflected in the corruption of laws. His way of resolving this dilemma is to let historical experience decide whether specific laws are likely to preserve the peace and improve the fortunes of the monarchy. History (and thus, at one remove, historiography) is called upon to assess the value of customary law.

Introducing his case study, Mariana reflects on laws of succession in general, and states that it would be most beneficial to public peace if the Iberian peoples had

---

20   Ibid., pp. 36-47, p. 37.
21   Ibid., p. 40.
22   Ibid., p. 41.

managed to fix the mode of succession once and for all.[23] Ideally, kings ought not to change the order of succession, not even among their own sons. Mariana immediately acknowledges that this is no more than wishful thinking. Neither succession nor any other similarly fundamental issue (religion and taxation in the first instance) will ever be 'settled for all time by law'.[24] The principal reason is that *consuetudines*, too, transform and develop according to changing political circumstances. It is often difficult to trace and explain these changes. As a consequence, Mariana says, codifications of the same body of customary law vary widely, and bitter wars of interpretation are fought over the value of conflicting traditions.[25] There is no easy way out. Custom invariably changes with the passage of time, and there will always be legitimate doubts concerning the right interpretation of written laws.

Mariana goes on to investigate whether the multitude of Iberian 'provincial laws' on hereditary succession can nonetheless be subsumed under easily identifiable juridical principles drawn from Roman law. The only unifying principle he is able to discern, however, is that of the agnatic principle of succession as handed down from the earliest Roman law of the Twelve Tables.[26] He warrants that limiting succession to male and female agnates is in general accordance with what the various customs of the peninsular realms as well as prudence and equity advise if a king has not left a male heir. There is a hitch, though. What is the order of succession among the brothers and sisters of an intestate ruler?[27] Does Roman law offer a way of preventing such a situation from exploding into civil war? Pursuing this question and working his way into the mind of a jurisprudent, Mariana stumbles upon another legal fiction from Roman law, the principle of *repraesentatio*.

This doctrine was particularly contested among French jurists of the period. Its application supported Henry of Navarre's (Henry IV) claim to the throne of France.[28] If applied to dynastic succession, *repraesentatio* demanded that a prince who died without male issue is succeeded either by his eldest sibling or that sibling's children according to order of birth. Mariana is not yet satisfied, however. What if brothers, sisters as well as all their children and grandchildren were already deceased,

---

23   Ibid., p. 48, 'Graves de successione rixae, exitiales contentiones vitantur successore in omne tempus per legem designato, neque relicto in cuiusquam arbitrio, defuncto aliquo Rege quis in eius locum substituatur: ne patri quidem Regi potestate permissa ex filiorum numero haeredem principatus, quem maxime voluerit designandi. In quo publicae tranquilitati consulitur, (…). Leges, quibus constricta est successio, mutare nemini licet sine populi voluntate, a quo pendent iura regnandi.'

24   Ibid., p. 48.

25   Ibid., p. 48, 'Sed de scriptis legibus, quomodo intelligendae sint, dubitari: consuetudines saepe pro rerum conditione mutantur. Inde totius controversiae difficultas existit: quam scribentium diversitas & altercatio magis etiam obscuravit.'

26   Ibid., p. 48, p. 52. On Roman law of intestate succession see Buckland, *Textbook of Roman Law*, pp. 367-72, especially pp. 368-69.

27   Ibid., pp. 50-52.

28   See R.E. Giesey (1961), 'The Juristic Basis of Dynastic Rights to the French Throne', *Transactions of the American Philosophical Society*, Vol. 51, pp. 3-47, especially pp. 24-25.

too? What is the precise order of succession among the cognates who would then come into play? Examining the opinions of 'the lawyers', Mariana finds himself perplexed and disconcerted by the great number of completely discordant views (he never tells us which jurisprudents he actually consulted). He considers such variety of opinion dangerous as it opens the doors to disagreement, discontent and civil war. He thus casts aside ideas of *repraesentatio* as 'fabrications and fictions', not least because they do not help to protect the *respublica* from the accession of women and minors.[29]

Still, Mariana believes that the 'more numerous and more erudite' among the *letrados* draw an analogy between monarchical succession and Roman private law of inheritance. They prefer 'blood' (*ius sanguinis*) to 'lineage' (*ius stirpis*). Rejecting the principle of *repraesentatio*, the jurisprudents propose to apply another civil law principle. This is the principle of even distribution of the possessions of an intestate, the so-called distribution *per capita*.[30] There is yet another crux, however. The immediate application of distribution *per capita* could entail division of the realm among the various dynastic cognates. To follow Roman law, in other words, would encourage cognate heirs to divide and thus weaken and eventually destroy the kingdom. The profession and tradition of law fail the all important test. They do not seem able to help preserve peace within the commonwealth. In response to this failure Mariana submits his own, utterly non-juridical interpretation of the civil law principle of division of cognatic inheritance *per rationem capitum*.

In fact, Mariana ceases to interpret analogies from Roman private law of intestacy in strictly juridical terms. Rather he explains civil law in summary terms of historical experience and reason of state. Roman law is exposed as a confused and confusing kind of political thinking which is largely detached from political reality. Mariana transforms the principle *per rationem capitum* into a qualitative rather than a quantitative category, advising that the male cognate 'distinguished in age, gender and virtues among those of equal relationship' ought to inherit the throne. This rationale, he contends in spite of what he said before, agrees with the 'very principles of nature', 'the customs of the Spaniards' and even the *ius commune*.[31]

---

29   *De rege*, pp. 50-51 Mariana repeatedly expresses his dissatisfaction with the fact that Roman law of intestate succession does not make any provision for excluding women from inheritance.

30   Ibid., p. 50, 'Numero tamen & eruditione potiores capitum rationem haberi iubent, negant stirpis: quod iure sanguinis regnum obveniat.' The relevant Roman law text is *Dig.* 38.8.1 [Ulpian]; especially *Dig.* 38.8.1, 10-11, 'Gradatim autem admittuntur cognati ad bonorum possessionem: ut qui sunt primu gradu, omnes simul admittuntur.'

31   Ibid., pp. 52-55, p. 52, 'Nostra disputatio ex ipsis naturae principis procedebat et iure commune: quae ratio Hispanorum moribus consentanea est. Constat enim iura regnandi in armis plerumque homines ponere malis artibus ambitiosos atque vaecordes: & qui minus iure, plus viribus saepe potest: silent enim inter arma leges. Nemoque est qui oblatam facultatem regnandi, legum arbitrio permittat. Neque negamus iure successionis controverso eam sequi partem rempublicam posse, modo voluntate certoque iudicio, quae rebus & tempori maxime

Mariana's confident, albeit confusing statement leads straight into his thinking about the nature and the uses of law.

Neither the *ius commune* nor many of the *leges provinciales* contain qualitative provisions of the kind he suggests. His assurance that his rationale agrees with the law of nature, Roman law and provincial custom is entirely misleading. Mariana is quite aware that this is the case. He says as much when conceding that his rationale ought to be applied *unless* the customary laws of individual *provinciae* make very different provisions.[32] Yet this does not appear to trouble him particularly. It is safe to assume that the 'very principles of nature' Mariana refers to are those of post-lapsarian corrupted nature. Even the 'customs of the Spaniards', as he has already pointed out, frequently do not in fact reflect the bare and brutal facts of the actual political process of dynastic inheritance. Custom is observed, generally, because it often turns out to be the best way to preserve peace among men ultimately abhorrent of change. Mariana's remarks to this effect echo civilian respect for local knowledge as well as the corresponding premise that laws and customs have to be in agreement with the character and environment of the people. Yet he is more than ready to give legal concepts a distinct makeover in terms of reason of state.

In fact, historical evidence tells Mariana that succession is determined by brute force and conspiracy rather than 'principles of nature' and *ius commune* enshrined in the 'customs of the Spaniards'. The history of succession to the throne of Castile is a chequered and bewildering one, with political circumstances of individual successions varying considerably over time. It does nonetheless permit the historian to draw clearly defined lessons. Mariana insists that an heir to the throne should be distinguished by 'age, gender and virtues', and that this is a principle supported by the 'customs of the Spaniards'.[33] This is the case because history proves that princes and nobles will always break laws according to the demands of expediency. Powerful and ambitious nobles will never forgo an opportunity to seize power, irrespective of the standards and procedures of legitimacy laid down in customary law.

Mariana, however, does not seem altogether too disturbed by the fact that force tends to prevail over custom. He goes on to demonstrate that the *salus publicis* can benefit from even the most blatant violation of customary law. In his *Historiae* (first published in 1592), he had already explained that after the death of Alfonso VIII of Castile in 1217, the crown of Castile *de iure* ought to have passed not to his younger daughter Berenguela, but to her elder sister Blanca, wife of Louis VIII of France.

---

accommodata videatur : unde varia in utramque partem atque illustria exempla manarunt, tum in aliis Christiani orbis partibus, tum praesertim in Hispania.'

32   Ibid., p. 50, 'Eoque, in pari propinquitate iubent, nisi lege provinciali secus sancitum sit, praestantissimum sexu, aetate, prudentia ex ea familia cognatorum que numero ad regni successionem vocandum'; see also ibid, p. 52. This notion is concisely expressed in the *Summa* of the thirteenth-century jurist Azo. His work was much consulted and quoted during the sixteenth and seventeenth centuries. The edition published in Venice in 1561, col. 123, states that 'the customs of a region must be followed' (*consuetudines regionis servandae sunt*).

33   Ibid., p. 52.

His contention that the Valois had a rightful claim to the throne of Castile caused some consternation.[34] He would retract it in the 1608 edition of the *Historiae*. In 1599, Mariana is content to add a rationale for the unlawful accession of Berenguela's son as Ferdinand III of Castile. A pithy commentator on human ambition and political expediency, he suggests the only reason that Ferdinand acquired the crown was that the nobility disliked the idea of a foreigner ruling Castile.[35] Whatever the motives and objectives of the nobles, though, Mariana makes clear that he cannot find any fault with their eventual decision. It was justified in retrospect by the 'uninterrupted success, blameless life and purity of habits' of King Ferdinand. Despite his dubious claim to the throne, Ferdinand III takes pride of place in Mariana's pantheon of rulers.[36] He is the revered 'champion of the Christian faith', and an example of good kingship to all who succeeded him as kings of Castile. Other, less laudable examples of accession in breach of custom include Sancho IV. He was preferred over the children of his elder brother because he had the military muscle and allies to conquer the throne. John I of Portugal is another example. He fought off lawful Castilian claims at the battle of Albujarrota, and went on to set up a dynasty 'conspicuous for all its prosperity and success'. Finally, there is the case of Henry I of Castile, who killed his brother and rightful King Peter because of his alleged descent into tyranny.[37] The examples of Ferdinand's and Henry's succession and subsequent reign demonstrate particularly well that 'it is almost unavoidable that every great example should have some evil in it'.[38] Breaking or misinterpreting the law is justified if the lawbreaker turns out to preserve peace by avoiding civil war or protecting the commonwealth from tyranny. In the view of this Jesuit theologian and resigned historian, the end, ultimately, justifies the means.

Mariana admits that studying history leads to the disconcerting conclusion that in most instances 'the right to rule is changed according to the will of the prince'.[39] He then adds a number of rhetorical questions, each of which further undermines the idea that corrupted man is able to contain political reality within the bounds

---

34   Mariana, *Historiae*, ix, 5, accuses the thirteenth-century historian and archbishop of Toledo, Rodrigo Jiménez de Rada of wittingly misrepresenting Berenguela as the eldest daughter and rightful heir to Alfonso VIII. See P. Linehan, *History and the Historians*, p. 457.

35   *De rege*, pp. 52-53, 'Henrico eo nomine primo Castellae Rege in tenera aetate sine prole defuncto e duabus sororibus Berengaria praelata est Ferdinandi Regis mater, eius cui vitae probitas Sancti cognomen adiunxit. Blanca Galliae Regina praetermissa est Ludovici itidem Sancti Galliae Regis mater, quae maior natu erat. Tametsi in eo proceres secuti videntur, ne externi in Hispania imperarent.'

36   See P. Linehan (1971), *The Spanish Church and the Papacy in the Thirteenth Century* (Cambridge Studies in Medieval Life and Thought, Third Series; Vol. 4), Cambridge University Press, Cambridge, p. 186.

37   *De rege*, pp. 43-45. See also ibid., pp. 53-54.

38   Ibid., p. 44.

39   Ibid., p. 54, 'Sic iura regnandi ex Principum voluntate mutantur (…).'

of an abstract and principled system of law.[40] Most laws of hereditary succession, Mariana says, were introduced by princes who were able to silence opposition. The ways in which the numerous succession crises in Spanish history were resolved shows the ability of nobles as well as princes to manipulate or simply disregard custom according to the dictate of what they perceived as expedient. Not every alteration or distortion of fundamental laws is necessarily detrimental to the *salus publicus*, not even those manipulations which clearly spring solely from the egotism and ignorance of the prince or *populus*. There is no reason either to object to changing laws 'by the will of the multitude when circumstances demand it'. Prince and people may break the law if necessary. They will be justified in their actions *as long as* they succeed in avoiding protracted civil war. Mariana exposes the 'definite decision and free agreement of all orders' he appeared to require for changes of customary law as one that is reached through conniving between noble factions and powerful individuals.[41] The way in which he treats legal principles testifies to Mariana's deeply pessimistic and cynical assessment of the relationship between power and the law. It is futile to assess the legitimacy of the actions of either kings or peoples in juridical terms. Recorded history reflects the demands of ad-hoc acts of expediency.

Cortes and Fueros: Preserving the Law, Preserving the Commonwealth?

Mariana repeatedly makes that point that princes are able to weaken customary law not least because of the subservience of many peoples, including the people of Castile. At the same time, he acknowledges that there are exceptions to the rule. Different nations have different ways of interacting with their rulers and looking after their bodies of customary law. Indeed, peoples can be told apart by the degree to which they buck the trend, and continually repel efforts to tamper with their rights and liberties. Mariana presses this point comparing the divergent fortunes of customary law and constitutional institutions in the Iberian peninsula. As far as the preservation of *iura libertatis* and *leges fundamentales* is concerned, the people of Aragon have been much luckier, and certainly pluckier than those of Castile.

The Castilian and Aragonese cortes retain very different degrees of actual political power. Both in Castile and Aragon, 'prudent and far-sighted ancestors' determined that kings must meet the representatives of nobility, clergy and towns in their respective cortes or corts.[42] Only the Aragonese cortes, however, to this

---

40   Ibid., pp. 54-55, 'Nimirum quod publicae salutis causa, & communi consensu statutum est, eadem multitudinis voluntate rebus exigentibus immutari quid obstet? Certe iure inter multos controverso, quis amplecti vetet consilium salutarius? An iniqui iudices in causa omnium gravissima esse velimus? Praesertim cum iura regnandi haereditaria fere sint facta magis dissimulante populo, & priorum Principum voluntati repugnare non auso, quam certa voluntate, liberoque omnium ordinum consensu: uti fore opus videbatur.'

41   Ibid., p. 48.

42   Ibid., p. 96, '(…) maiores nostri, providentes viri prudentes periculum, ut Reges continerent intra modestiae et mediocritatis fines, ne se nimia potestate efferent, unde publica pernicies existeret, multa sapienter sanxerunt atque praeclare. In his quam prudenter, quod

day unite representatives of the three estates.[43] Realizing early on 'that the rights of liberty are much weakened by small initial encroachments', the Aragonese installed one of the most peculiar institutions of Iberian constitutional history, the office of *justicia* of Aragon.[44] Determined to prevent a gradual debasing of their customs and liberties, *proceres* and *populus* endowed this 'middle sort of magistrate' (*medius magistratus*) with 'a tribune's powers', in particular with the right to overrule royal jurisdiction contravening the *fueros* or ancient laws of Aragon. Mariana clearly identifies the *justicia* as part of a tradition that stretches back to the Spartan ephor and the tribunes of the Roman plebs.[45] Admiringly, he reports that successive generations of *justicias* succeeded in keeping the power of the kings of Aragon within the boundaries envisaged in the original compact.[46] The *fueros* of Aragon even include the right of the Aragonese nobility to convene without informing their king if the protection of their ancient rights demanded the clandestine organization of resistance against royal intrusion. Mariana is in no doubt that the Aragonese prevailed because of the 'unswerving zeal' with which they defended their ancient rights against royal incursions.

From Mariana's point of view, the contrast with Castile could not be more striking. The people of Castile never created an office with powers similar to those of the *justicia*. It was up to the cortes to defend the Castilian *iura libertatis*. They completely failed to do so. *De rege* presents the cortes of Castile as a prime example of the damage and distortion suffered by original compacts. The cortes of his time, Mariana says, no longer represent Castilian society. The kings of Castile have succeeded in their persistent attempts to shed the constitutional restraints

---

nihil maioris rei sine voluntate procerum et populi sanctum esse voluerunt; eoque consilio, delectos ex omnibus ordinibus ad conventus regni, Ponitifices tota ditione, proceres, et procuratores civitatum evocare moris erat. Quod hoc tempore in Aragonia aliisque provinciis retentum, vellem nostri Principes reponerent.'

43   Mariana appears to mistake the cortes of the crown of Aragon (comprising the kingdom of Aragon and principalities of Catalonia and Valencia) for those of the kingdom of Aragon. The cortes generales of the crown of Aragon, the joint session of the cortes of the kingdom of Aragon and the corts of Catalonia and Valencia under the presidency of the king had three chambers. The cortes of the kingdom of Aragon, on the other hand, were divided into four rather than the usual three chambers, the noble estate being divided into two, the *ricos hombres* and the *caballeros*. Correspondingly, he may have come to regard the office of the *justicia* of Aragon as an institution specific to the crown rather than the kingdom of Aragon. On the constitutional structure of the crown of Aragon see J.H. Elliott (2002), *Imperial Spain*, 1469-1716, Penguin, London, especially pp. 26-31..

44   *De rege*, p. 88, '(…) Idem recentiori memoria in Hispania Aragonii praestiterunt, studio tuendae libertates acres & incitati, neque ignari a parvis initiis multum imminui iura libertatis. Medium itaque magistratum crearunt, tribunitiae potestatis adinstar (vulgo hoc tempore Aragoniae Iustitia dicitur) qui legibus, auctoritate & populi studiis armatus regiam potestatem certis hactenus finibus inclusam tentuit.' See also *Historiae*, I, 4.

45   Classical sources for the concept of *medius magistratus* are Plutarch, *Lycurgus*, 7; Aristotle, *Politics*, 1313a27; and Cicero, *De legibus*, 3.16.

46   *De rege*, p. 88.

that ancestral prudence had imposed upon them. The nobility and clergy are no longer summoned, and the cortes are no more than a shell of their former self.[47] The eighteen Castilian towns whose oligarchies still send delegates are anything but staunch defenders of the rights and liberties of the people of Castile. Some of the harshest criticism meted out in *De rege* is reserved for the *procuradores* of the eighteen towns.[48] Often selected by lot, rarely, if ever, chosen according to their intellectual and moral stamina, they are prone to be bribed or browbeaten into rubberstamping the king's wishes. Public affairs in late sixteenth-century Castile, if we believe this stern critic, are run by the 'capricious will of the king and the desires of the few'.[49]

The lavish praise heaped upon the laws and people of Aragon contrasts starkly with the scorn poured on kings and cortes of Castile. Not without reason, historians have therefore tended to take Mariana's remarks as evidence for the dogged survival of medieval constitutional thinking in Habsburg Spain. Yet Mariana differs from those humanist historians, lawyers and theologians who dwell upon the office and duty of magistrates when they come to extract rights of resistance from scripture or ancient customs.[50] It is conspicuous that he chastises court, *proceres* and *populus* of Castile alike for the state of disrepair into which the primeval body politic has fallen. The question is whether he does indeed go further, and wishes to intimate that Aragon provides the model for a constitutional overhaul of Castile. His brief comments seem to suggest that the constant hollowing out of primeval laws and institutions can be prevented or at least delayed. So, if the Aragonese have stemmed the deterioration and denigration of their primeval laws, does the Aragonese model provide a viable alternative to that of Spanish Habsburg rule in Castile?

De rege does not yield evidence that Mariana meant to suggest as much. To begin with, Mariana's comparison between Spartan ephors and Roman tribunes is incomplete and highly problematic, if not downright misleading. The tribunes were annually elected officials. The *justicia* of Aragon was appointed by the king until the office became hereditary in the Lanuza family from the mid-fifteenth century onwards. Neither ordained by God, nor elected by the people, nor both elected and ordained like the popular magistrates of radical Calvinist ilk, the *justicia* was a hereditary official of the crown of Aragon. It is doubtful that either Mariana or his readers would have been oblivious to the historical facts.

---

47   Charles V excluded them after the cortes of Toledo (1538) refused to grant him urgently required monies in the form of a new sales tax. Philip II continued his father's practice.

48   *De rege*, p. 96, 'Homines privatos, quales procuratores urbium sunt, qui soli hac tempestate supersunt, donis speque corrumpere conqueritur populus passim: praesertim non iudicio delectos, sed fortis temeritate designatos, quae nova corruptela est, argumentum reipublicae perturbatae. Quod prudentiores dolent, mutire nemo audet.'

49   Ibid., p. 96, 'Cur enim maiori ex parte antiquatum in nostra gente est, exclusis proceribus et Episcopis, nisi ut sublato communi consensu, quo salus publica continetur, Regis ad arbitrium, et ad pancorum libidinem res publicae et privatae vertantur.'

50   Most famously Jean Calvin in his *Institutio Christianae religionis*, IV, 20, 9-11 [references to the edition of 1568, Franciscus Perrinus, Geneva].

What is more, Mariana's altogether vague appraisal of the people and political institutions of Aragon does not include a single reference to the recent and very serious conflagration in Iberian politics. *De rege* makes no mention of the so-called Revolt of the Aragonese (1591-93). This short-lived upheaval followed in the wake of the 'Pérez affair'.[51] Antonio Pérez, Philip's former secretary, had escaped from his Madrid prison in 1591, fled to Zaragoza, and put himself under the protection of the *justicia*. Many Aragonese had long suspected Philip II of harbouring a desire to abolish their ancient rights and liberties, and saw this as an opportunity to take a stand. A naive *justicia*, Diego de Lanuza, offered Pérez asylum. Unwilling to offend the Aragonese, yet determined to lay his hands on Pérez, Philip II ordered that the latter be handed over to the Inquisition. When a mob freed Pérez on his way to the prison of the Inquisition, a short-lived revolt ensued. Supported by an army of 12,000 men, the king's envoys quickly negotiated the surrender of the rebels and the pacification of Aragon.[52] Philip II curbed the powers of the *justicia*.[53] Eager not to put even more stress on an already fraught relationship, however, the *rey prudente* left the ancient *fueros* largely intact. The punishment meted out to the ringleaders was followed by customary signs of royal favour.

It is possible that Mariana recognized that the political constitution of the crown of Aragon suffered only limited changes in the aftermath of the revolt. He might have decided that recent disturbances did not impair the image of Aragon as an example of a polity preserving its ancient rights and liberties. A staunch patriot who looked at the *monarquía española* as the epitome of Castilian achievement, he would hardly have wanted to associate himself with the traitor Antonio Pérez in any case. A man as outspoken as Mariana, a seasoned and daring critic of the ills of Castile as he saw them, should not lightly be accused of self-censorship. *De rege* is written in Latin rather than the vernacular, which increased his freedom to vent his anger at the dead king. He never hesitated to slate Philip II as a worthy successor to Nimrod, Alexander and Julius Caesar. *De rege* would not have stood out from among the many treatises and pamphlets published soon after Philip II's death, had Mariana chosen to condemn Philip II's handling of the affairs of Spain, including the revolt of the Aragonese. Readers of *De rege* are certainly left with a vision of the Aragonese constitution surviving the sixteenth century unscathed by royal incursions.

---

51   For the history of this scandal perturbing the inner core of Philip II's political machine for quite some time see Elliott, *Imperial Spain*, pp. 264-68, pp. 277-84; and G. Marañon (1954), *Antonio Pérez*, Espasa-Calpe, Madrid.

52   Pérez escaped to France. A fugitive for the rest of his life, he served the enemies of Spain and enriched European political mythology and nurtured the *leyenda negra* with a robust version of the history of the *fueros* of Aragon.

53   On changes of the Aragonese political constitution in the wake of the revolt see G. Colás Latorre and J.A. Salas Ausens (1982), *Aragón en el siglo XVI, Alteraciones sociales y conflictos políticos*, Departamento de Historia Moderna, Universidad de Zaragoza, Zaragoza.

Mariana does not indulge in the kind of 'constitutional antiquarianism' familiar from François Hotman or George Buchanan.[54] This is the case not least because Mariana the historian is not necessarily partial to Aragonese pride in their hallowed *fueros*. He is well aware that Aragonese patriotism was more likely to be rooted on fables than historical truth. The *Historiae* briefly touch upon the integral element of Aragonese constitutional mythology and ideology, the so-called *fueros* of Sobrarbe.[55] The legend of Sobrarbe relates the story of a small number of Aragonese knights who initiated the *reconquista* from their boltholes in the Pyrenees. Choosing a ruler from among their number, they required him to ratify their customs and traditions. They went on to take an oath asserting that they had the right to withdraw their allegiance should the ruler dare violate their customary rights and privileges. In other words, the legend of Sobrarbe is a prime example of the kind of original compact Mariana himself imagines. Discussing the authenticity of this tradition, however, he refuses to pass judgement.[56] The available sources do not make it possible to decide for or against its authenticity.

At the same time, Mariana is clearly aware that the legend of Sobrarbe matters to Aragonese politics irrespective of historical truth, determining the way in which they view and interact with their rulers. The historical tradition of Castile, however, provides no constitutional myth similar to that of the *fueros* of Sobrarbe. *De rege* does not refer to them even once. In this instance, Mariana is a far more scrupulous historian than George Buchanan or the polemicists of the French wars of religion. He is simply not prepared to rewrite the constitutional history of Castile, and no ancient customs are recovered for future restitution on the pages of his treatise. Instead, the example of Aragon serves to confirm the conviction that the binding force of law is fully dependent on a variety of local conditions and subject to the mutability of time. The 'rationale of different times' is 'varied and changeable'.[57] More often than

---

54   François Hotman's *Francogallia* is but one example of such blatant attempts at re-inventing history in the context of early modern confessional conflict. See the introduction to the edition of *Francogallia* by R.E. Giesey and J.H.M. Salmon (1972), Cambridge University Press, Cambridge. On Buchanan's deliberate distortions of history see J.H. Burns (1996), *The True Law of Kingship, Concepts of Monarchy in Early Modern Scotland*, Oxford University Press, Oxford, pp. 217-21.

55   There is no space here to recount the fascinating, yet labyrinthine and tortuously intertwined development of the legend of the kingdom, the *fueros* and the oath of Sobrarbe. R. Giesey (1968), *If not, not: The Oath of the Aragonese and the Legendary Laws of Sobrarbe*, Princeton University Press, Princeton, reconstructs the historiographical process which gave birth to the myth of the oath of Sobrarbe during the mid-sixteenth century. J.M. Ramos y Loscertales (1961), *Reino de Aragon bajo la dinastía pamplonesa*, ed. J.M. Lacarra de Miguel (Acta Salmanticensia; Serie de filosofía y letras; Vol. 15/2), Universidad de Salamanca, Salamanca, traces the legend of Sobrarbe and its place in Aragonese Renaissance historiography.

56   *Historiae*, especially VIII.1.

57   *De rege*, p. 429, 'Nos quidem certe non quid fuerit factum quaerimus, quia sciamus multa perturbata olim temporum aut hominum culpa fuisse (…). (…) Varia & commutabilis temporum ratio est. Multaque aliquando tolerata in perniciem vertant, si nostro tempore concedantur'. For further examples see p. 31, p. 209.

not, institutions and practices of the past have been 'confused through the fault of time and men'. Different peoples have different collective experiences that prescribe the form of government best for them.[58] Like Machiavelli, Mariana argues that the political system of a people has to be in conformity with its own time.[59] Political stability has preference over the actual form of government. The clock cannot be turned back. Aragon is not to be imitated, and Castile is just another confirmation of the decline of human institutions from pristine ideal to disappointing present.

For a brief moment, then, the Aragonese appear to have assumed the literary function of Tacitus's ancient Teutons. Making reference to Aragon is Mariana's way of reminding the Castilians of what is irretrievably lost to them as a result of 'time and the wickedness of man'. The *justicia* of Aragon serves as a mere foil with which to chastise the Castilian body politic. Sound scholarship and the human condition do not permit the invocation of past ideals or the transfer of constitutional models. *De rege* is a narrative of loss, not one of retrieval of constitutional tradition.

Conclusion

Mariana completely abandons the Thomist-Aristotelian perception of political order as comprehensible in terms of a rational system of interlocking natural and positive law. Natural law is reduced to a simple, even simplistic doctrine of sheer self-preservation. Human reason, in turn, cannot create systems of positive law closely reflecting the rationality and morality of divine law. Mariana's ideas on law correspond to his pessimistic assessment of the human ability to overcome original sin. *De rege* is the work of an author for whom post-lapsarian law is invariably tainted as much as the human beings who create it.[60] This is a far cry from the Aristotelian notion of positive law as the expression of *mens sine affectu*.[61]

The chances of a people preserving their customs against the onslaught 'of time and the wickedness of men' are slim. The focus is on the historical and changeable nature of custom. Continually being created, custom is continually becoming obsolete. Custom can be bent and undermined by a succession of strong-willed rulers helped by an acquiescing populace. Such manipulation may turn out to profit the *salus populi*, but in any case custom is hardly the weapon to defend the original compact. Mariana thus makes the Bartolist concept of tacit consent sound hollow. Though the people appear to remain the ultimate lawgiver, the prince can always find ways of manipulating popular consent, perverting custom or introducing 'new' custom. Desuetude affecting customary law is first and foremost a matter of *de facto* power.

Mariana's examples of *respublicae* with constitutional arrangements that closely resemble the original compact provide no real respite. Spartan kings, it is true, had

---

58 Ibid., p. 29.

59 See, for instance, *Discorsi*, III, 9.

60 Echoing Saint Augustine, for example in his *Contra Julianum Pelagium*.

61 See Aristotle, *Politics*, 3:5.

authority only in matters of war and religious doctrine.[62] The Aragonese established the office of *justicia*, so popular with the Monarchomachs. These examples represent good practice, yet they are historically contingent. Mariana immediately concedes that 'other provinces where the authority of the people is less and that of the kings is greater' may well have organized themselves in the manner that suits them best.[63] Mariana does not just make allowance for the heterogeneity and diversity of historical experience. He refuses to translate historical experience of good government into metahistorical (juridical or philosophical) norms. If good custom dwindles away, as in the case of Castile, it cannot be restored by the people. Prudence nurtured on history ordains the well-meaning and well-informed prince as the only legitimate agent of change. Mariana is not shy to draw drastic conclusions. Chapter three examines the way in which he recasts the language of law into a language of prudence or reason of state.

---

62   *De rege*, p. 88, 'Quod inter Graecos olim Lacedaeones fecerunt Regi tantummodo dantes belli curam, atque sacrorum procuratione.' See Aristotle, *Politics*, 3:14.

63   Ibid., p. 88, 'In aliis provinciis, ubi minor populi auctoritas est, Regum maior: an idem iudicium sit, & an rebus communibus id expediat, considerandum est.' Salmon, 'Catholic Resistance Theory', p. 241, observes that 'Mariana said clearly what royalists read into all Jesuit writers, namely that no people would establish a governor under terms that would permit him to oppress them.' Salmon does not, however, take Mariana's historicist conception of law and custom into account.

CHAPTER THREE

'True Power': Abandoning the Discourse on Sovereignty

The first chapters of Book one of *De rege* disparage the legal fetters and constitutional agents conventionally thought to restrain wayward rulers. His pessimistic view of human nature and history induces Mariana to dismiss customary laws, cortes and magistrates of Castile as ultimately incapable of checking the power of her kings. He nonetheless acknowledges mixed or limited monarchy as the best form of government. All said, it is the one most likely to mitigate the impact of human depravity on society. Mariana has thus set himself a twofold task. Firstly, he has to devise a political doctrine which reconciles the notion of limited monarchy with his disillusioned view of princes, nobles and subjects. Chapters three and four of this study deal with Mariana's attempt to do so by subsuming different modes of political thinking into a refined code of political prudence or reason of state. Secondly, he has to identify an institutional framework within which princely administration of reason of state can be monitored, and, if necessary, contained. Chapter five investigates Mariana's proposals for apposite and comprehensive reform of Castilian government.

Power that is both Limited and Absolute

Initially, the many snippets of canon and Roman law which permeate Book one of *De rege* compel readers to assume that Mariana sees limited monarchy in terms of familiar juridical norms. Many of the themes, terms and notions advanced are of the kind scholars in the history of political thought commonly associate with later scholastic conceptualizations of limited monarchy, popular sovereignty and their radical development during the later sixteenth century. As a result, Mariana has been credited with being one of the few sixteenth-century political theorists perceptive and bold enough to weave those strands into

> a theory of popular sovereignty which, while scholastic in its origins and Calvinist in its later developments, was in essence independent of either religious creed, and was thus available to all parties in the coming constitutional struggles of the seventeenth century.[1]

---

1   Skinner, *Foundations*, Vol. 2, p. 347. Salmon (1991), 'Catholic Resistance Theory', p. 241, notes that Mariana gives less emphasis to the deposition of a king by the representatives of the community than he did to the right of private men to kill a tyrant who prevented the assembly of the estates or *cortes*.

Professor Skinner's appraisal of Mariana's legacy to European political thought is characteristic for the kind of appreciation he enjoys. The author of *De rege* is said to have joined an almost pan-European debate. Its participants are understood to have thought invariably in terms of a strict dichotomy between unlimited or absolute (irresistible, that is arbitrary, despotic or tyrannical rule) and limited (resistible) monarchy. Glenn Burgess sums up the underlying assumptions of this ultimately legalistic approach to early modern political thinking. They are

> [f]irstly, (…) that a monarch is not *limited* if those limitations cannot be enforced by human agency. And, secondly, (…) that, (…) in the last resort, forcible resistance constituted the only viable means of limitation in early modern politics. Taken together, these assumptions conflate the separate issues of *limitation* and *resistance*.[2]

The assumption is that early modern rulers were considered limited only if their subjects possessed constitutional rights of active resistance including the right to depose or even kill a tyrant. There is a strong tendency to scour texts for articulations of a theory of sovereignty that lodges ultimate sovereignty in either the king or the people. The value of a text scrutinized in this manner is frequently measured in terms of the degree to which it anticipates an ideal type of modern parliamentary constitutionalism.[3] This is a practice often favoured by historians examining *De rege* from the vantage point of the parliamentarian hermeneutics of the English civil wars of the seventeenth and the polemics of the French Wars of Religion of the sixteenth century. It is also present in Spanish historians concerned to identify a strong liberal tradition in Spanish political thinking.[4] Deeply rooted in Anglo-Saxon history and historiographical perceptions, it is deemed applicable nonetheless to early modern Castile.

De rege highlights the limits of an interpretative paradigm applied to thinkers writing within intellectual climates and political contexts as diverse as those of early modern England, France or Spain. Habsburg Spain appears to have provided a more favourable environment for 'institutions of moral restraint' than, for instance,

---

2   G. Burgess (1996), *Absolute Monarchy and the Stuart Constitution*, Yale University Press, New Haven and London, p. 19. Burgess shows how the simple dichotomous theory distinguishing between unlimited and limited monarchy, developed as part of the parliamentarian hermeneutic and propaganda of the English civil wars from the 1640s onwards, continues to flourish in the study of English intellectual history. For a succinct criticism of legalistic conceptualizations of early modern monarchy see also J.H. Burns (1986), *Absolutism: The History of an Idea* (The Creighton Trust Lecture), University of London, London.

3   See the useful discussion in Höpfl and Thompson, 'The History of Contract'; and Oakley, 'Anxieties of Influence'.

4   Frequently, these approaches rely on the explanatory concept of 'absolutism'. The latter, however, has lost much of its interpretative potency. See, for instance, N. Henshall (1992), *The Myth of Absolutism: Change and Continuity in Early Modern European Monarchy*, Longman, London.

its war-torn neighbour France.[5] Revolt was much less endemic in sixteenth-century Spain than it was in other European monarchies.[6] Juan de Mariana had no compelling reason to join a European discourse on sovereignty on the same terms as French Huguenot or Leaguer authors. Unlike the Monarchomachs or the polemicists of the English civil wars who subsequently exploited their writings, he did not live in a situation of actual religious civil war.[7] The treatises of Jean Boucher and François Hotman were completed under immediate pressure to justify resistance *in extremis*. Mariana simply had no need to develop existing legal idiom into a political theory bestowing ultimate sovereignty on one or other party in a situation of civil war. Who had the right to depose or even kill a king would have been more of a 'theoretical' issue for him. His focus is on Castile and the Iberian peninsula.

Mariana was, of course, acutely aware of the general European situation. *De rege* testifies to his concern that the Spanish monarchy could fall prey to confessional conflict fomented by a disaffected and self-serving aristocracy. Reminding his readers of what he perceives as the failure of the late Valois kings to preserve France from internecine conflict, he asks them to

> imagine, that a prince is left by his father at an early and weak age, (...) imagine that he has low morals and is contaminated with new ideas about religion, with the result that he changes the established ancestral religious practices. (...) Imagine that a conspiracy is formed and civil war is stirred up by the nobles. (...) It has been my view all along that the present bad conditions are mere trifles in comparison with what I have in mind as possible (...).[8]

Preserving Spain from the horrible fate that had befallen her neighbour and rival France is one of the principal objectives of the treatise. That Philip III will repeat the sorry mistake of John II of Castile, and deliver his person and kingdom into the hands of a favourite is the stuff of his nightmares. Mariana's gaze is fixed on the flaws of princes and the manifold machinations of a restless nobility. Unwilling to entrust either nobles or burghers with putting in force existing normative constraints of monarchical rule, he turns, in the first instance, to pleading with the prince himself.

---

5   On institutions of moral restraint in early modern Castile see I.A.A. Thompson (1990), 'Castile', in J. Miller (ed.), *Absolutism in Seventeenth-Century Europe*, Macmillan Education, Basingstoke, pp. 69-98, especially pp. 76-84; and ibid. (1994), 'Castile: Absolutism, Constitutionalism and Liberty', in P.T. Hoffmann and K. Norberg (eds), *Fiscal Crises, Liberty, and representative Government, 1450-1789*, Stanford University Press, Stanford, pp. 181-225.

6   See J.H. Elliott (1969), 'Revolution and Continuity in Early Modern Europe', in *Past and Present*, Vol. 42, pp. 35-56 [reprint: ibid. (1989), *Spain and its World, 1500-1700. Selected Essays*, Yale University Press, New Haven and London, pp. 92-113].

7   On the adaptation of monarchomach political thought during the English civil wars see J.H.H. Salmon (1959), *The French Religious Wars in English Political Thought*, Clarendon Press, Oxford.

8   *De rege*, pp. 112-13.

Mariana requires the prince to accept that even if his power is *de facto* 'absolute', it will be limited in many practical ways nonetheless. Prudence therefore requires voluntary restraint on his part, not least because a prince abusing his legitimate power can expect to be challenged outside rather than within existing constitutional frameworks. Mariana thus keeps apart the issues of *limitation* and *resistance*. The need for resistance of whatever kind arises only if the prince has exhausted his capacity to restrain himself. If resistance to legitimate authority occurs, the relationship between prince and people has already collapsed. What follows on after such a breakdown has to be discussed in terms of what is likely to happen *de facto* rather than what ought to happen by law. Mariana's understanding of monarchical authority is comprehensible neither in familiar terms of scholastic political theology, nor in those of modern perceptions of constitutional procedure concerning the exercise and control of power.

Humanist Rhetoric and the Conversion of Law into Prudence

Mariana's appeal for self-restraint in a prince takes the form of a humanist moral and rhetorical discourse. The preface of his treatise employs conventional topoi of epideictic oratory.[9] Allegedly, the decision to write up his thoughts was made during a lively dialogue concerning the education of princes between learned friends ambling through beautiful landscape near Talavera de la Reina. Towards the end of the conversation, Mariana resolves to provide his friend García de Loaysa with a manual for the education of prince Philip. The text will discuss *regulae artis gubernandi*, but not as part of a systematic exposition of first principles of natural and divine law in the form of the scholastic *lectura*, *quaestio* or *quodlibet*. Rather it will take the form of a learned yet entertaining dialogue discussing and illuminating the rules of statecraft by means of historical examples. From the outset, then, Mariana makes plain that he subscribes to the central assumption of the humanist rhetorical tradition, namely

> that reading is a form of prudence or of deliberative rhetoric and that a text is valuable insofar as it engages the reader in an activity of discrimination and thereby educates the faculty of practical reason or prudential judgement which is essential to the active life.[10]

Mariana aspires to engage readers in the discursive pursuit of prudence and practical thinking. This is the mode of discussion most likely to engage a disparate audience of lay and clerical readers of varying levels of education. It is also a form of discourse that gives authors generous leave to manipulate and control their audience. Mariana is able, for instance, to shirk the detailed discussion of potentially controversial

---

9   *De rege*, pp. 1-5. On early Renaissance epideictic oratory see E. Rummel (1995), *The Humanist-Scholastic Debate in the Renaissance and Reformation* (Harvard Historical Studies; 120), Harvard University Press, Cambridge, Mass. and London, especially pp. 2-7.

10   V. Kahn (1985), *Rhetoric, Prudence and Skepticism in the Renaissance*, Cornell University Press, Ithaca and London, p. 11.

statements whenever it suits him.[11] Frequently, he puts forward his points implicitly rather than explicitly. Examples from history tend to differentiate, even undermine the statements they are supposed to back up. Readers are in effect free to pursue avenues of thought merely hinted at in the text. *De rege* is one of those early modern texts which empower their readers, often wittingly, at other times unwittingly.

Food for thought and debate is filtered from a wide range of sources ranging from medieval theology to classical and humanist literature and history.[12] The way in which Mariana organizes his material is one well suited to subsume historical *exempla*, literary quotations and legal formulae into a coherent argument. *De rege* presents practical knowledge in the form of the *locus communis* or commonplace.[13] The term *locus communis* carries a great array of frequently intersecting meanings. In the first instance, it refers to 'places of wisdom' or headings under which to collect and arrange pertinent precepts of moral conduct, mostly in the form of quotations appropriated from a great variety of literatures. *Locus communis* also denotes theses tenets of morality and sagacity themselves. Commonplaces fulfil the rhetorical convention that an author ought to accommodate an argument as far as possible to the received opinions and beliefs of the audience admirably. The speaker or writer invokes popular maxims and familiar arguments so as to persuade listeners that the particular course of action advised is acceptable to anyone already endorsing these general principles. Contemporary readers familiar with but not necessarily well-versed in a great variety of terminologies find them configured in an easily accessible, yet often also manipulative way. Certainly, Mariana's adroit use of commonplaces allows him to dislocate, adapt and merge a host of tenets from law, theology and classical and humanist literatures into a pragmatic ethic and political doctrine of his own.[14] Each of these strands gain value and meaning

---

11   A good example is (Desk.ed. example singular??) Mariana's brief and ambiguous observations concerning conciliar versus papal authority. See *De rege*, pp. 93-95, pp. 101-103.

12   Mariana rarely identifies his sources. He is intent on transmuting knowledge gathered into something that is both 'his own' and corroborated by 'authorities'. He follows humanist practice as inspired by Seneca, *Epistulae morales*, lxxxiv, 3-9, 9, 'I do believe that it is possible for them [arguments and ideas taken from various writers] not to be detected if the writer has great talent and has put his own stamp on all the things he has taken from his various models, with the result that the end product is a coherent whole.' Quoted in A. Moss (1999), *Printed Commonplace-Books and the Structuring of Renaissance Thought*, Oxford University Press, Oxford, p. 13.

13   Early modern authors can be obsessed with creating commonplace-books or 'treasure chests of wisdom' (*Tresors de sapience*). They serve as quarries from which authors draw headings organizing their works as well as the actual notions to be developed into an argument of their own. I discuss the use of *loci communes* only in so far as it is immediately relevant to our understanding of Mariana's argument. On the commonplace as a core constituent of early modern textual thinking see Moss, *Commonplace-Books*, especially pp. 101-33.

14   Mariana's rhetoricization of legal doctrine reflects profound changes in the epistemology of rhetoric and the nature of evidence during the post-Reformation period. See the perceptive studies by J.D. Lyons (1989), *Exemplum, The Rhetoric of Example in Early*

only within the generic form adopted and the overarching educational and political objectives defined by the author.

The formal structure of *De rege* as an educational and rhetorical exercise thus determines its ideological content.[15] A point that has so far been overlooked. Mariana's resolve to put his mark on the matter under consideration is particularly evident with regard to the transformation of juridical language into a language of political prudence. Legal formulae appear as chapter headings or 'topics' as well as maxims of prudence in the form of *dicta*. These *dicta* or *preceptos, avisos y reglas de la vida Real*, again, are effectively subdivided into what Justus Lipsius differentiated into *monita* and *sententiae*.[16] A *monitum* states (possibly axiomatic) knowledge which *sententiae* develop further and make comprehensible in terms of desirable (moral) conduct. Though Book one occasionally explores the issue of the origin of royal power in the manner of the scholastic dialectician, Mariana does not persist in the conventional scholastic method of dissecting and realigning terminologies by comparing, contrasting and reconciling established *auctoritates*. His knowledge of political conduct past and present intervenes to provide guidance on what is best practice in princely government. History or historical experience is set up to judge whether legal doctrine can pass as practicable knowledge.

Throughout Chapters eight and nine of Book one, for instance, Mariana posits the question of 'whether the power of the prince originates in the people'.[17] The conclusion takes the form of a frequently repeated *monitum* ('The power of the prince has its source in the people'). Mariana does not, however, go on to assert the relevance of this principle as one that is to be understood in constitutional or strictly juridical terms. Rather he explains that 'the people' are always likely to retain the power originally delegated to the prince, irrespective of whether the laws actually say so. A number of interrelating *sententiae* elaborate in terms of reason of state why this is the case. A prince always ought to bear in mind that he is 'not free from the law' because of the extra-legal or extra-constitutional means to which a people feeling oppressed by their ruler will resort. This is where the spectre of tyrannicide comes into play. Tyrannical inclinations are curbed by moral restraint, a lucid sense of expediency and a well informed sense of self-preservation on the part of the prince.

Three *sententiae* in particular drive the transition from legal thinking to thinking in terms of reason of state. These are that 'the prince should always wish to rule

---

Modern France and Italy, Princeton University Press, Princeton; and B.J. Shapiro (1983), *Probability and Certainty in Seventeenth Century England*, Princeton University Press, Princeton.

15   On the rhetorical presentation of political doctrine and its epistemic implications see the literature quoted above and Q. Skinner (1996), *Reason and Rhetoric in the Philosophy of Hobbes*, Cambridge University Press, Cambridge, Part I, Classical Eloquence in Renaissance England, especially chapters one to three.

16   See Justus Lipsius (1605), *Monita et exempla politica libri duo*, Plantin-Moret, Antwerp, preface. Though Mariana himself does not explicitly differentiate commonplaces into *monita* and *sententiae*, Lipsius's distinction serves to illuminate the way in which he changes the methodological and semantic context of primarily juridical terminologies.

17   *De rege*, I:8, pp. 87-99; I:9, pp. 99-107.

over willing subjects' (CI), that 'force is not as easily applied to the mind as it is to the bodies of subjects' (CII), and that the *respublica* 'is held together by reward and punishment, fear and hope'(CIII). The prince is to seek the approval of his subjects (CI), and to use persuasion rather than force in acquiring that approval (CII). Both *sententiae* stress the material and effective power of the *populus* as the principal reason to rule consensually. The explanations embellishing the *locus* on 'fear and hope, reward and punishment' (CIII) are concerned with how a prince is to make sure that he rules over pliant subjects. Together, these *sententiae* convey Mariana's sense of what it means to be a truly powerful prince.

Putting forward his argument in terms of *loci* certainly makes it easier for Mariana to turn scholastic legal language into a discourse of reason of state. His Catholic-Augustinian view of human nature facilitates the transition in ways already shown above. The discussion of the origins and limits of royal power, scholastic in its roots and terminology, becomes part of a discourse on the treatment of powerful subjects and the relevance of religion for the survival of the commonwealth. Commonplaces cross-reference the themes and chapters of the book and provide the core of a flexible, encompassing, yet coherent argument. Readers quick to pick up on references to contemporary literature on reason of state would have read Mariana's interlocking maxims as an analysis and confirmation of Giovanni Botero's assertion that '[i]t should be taken for granted that in the deliberations of princes interest prevails over every other consideration.'[18]

The rhetoricization of scholastic idiom makes it absolutely plain that power is a matter of reason of state. Yet arranging tenets of scholastic jurisprudence in a different mode of speech changes their meaning profoundly. A sentence from canon law extracted from its germane environment and deployed as a *locus communis* changes its semantic together with its epistemic value.[19] A clever humanist rhetorician, Mariana would have been well aware of the epistemic changes he operates. This, then, is one of the most salient points about Mariana's rhetoricization of legal terminologies. *Loci communes* are part of a mode of argument that is by definition not supposed to provide 'certain knowledge' of how to deal with political affairs, but merely knowledge that is plausible and probable. There are two sides to each argument, and commonplaces can be found to give equally convincing support to either side. Each argument can be discussed as well as decided *in utramque partem*. One of the places for this common humanist view is in Cicero's *De oratore*, where interlocutors agree that oratory is *ars*, and that its subject matter does not consist 'in things thoroughly examined and clearly apprehended, (...) which are outside the control of mere opinion and within the grasp of exact knowledge.'[20] The claim of an argument to absolute or varying degrees of relative truth depends on the nature of the proof provided. Committed to the

---

18   Botero, *Della ragion di stato*, 2.6.

19   Aristotle's *Topica* lists commonplaces for the use of those who sought to support conclusions which they had already reached.

20   I quote the English translation by E.W. Sutton (1942), *De oratore*, Books I-II, Loeb classical library, Cambridge, Mass. and London, 1:22, p. 108.

intellectual and linguistic standards of the particular audience addressed, the speaker or writer wants to persuade rather than enlighten, deliberately excluding himself from participating in the pursuit of unshakeable truth.[21]

During the sixteenth and seventeenth centuries, commonplaces are transformed from arsenals of contingent arguments to prime categories used to organize moral philosophy and speculative theology. Reformed as well as Catholic post-Tridentine theologians increasingly adopted the humanist view that conventional scholastic discourse failed to express the reality it was supposed to make comprehensible. Scholastic dialectic based on allegedly pure logical categories and operations is frequently replaced by a rhetorical dialectic relying on the commonplace as the method of proof and argument. The time-honoured distinction between knowledge (logic) and opinion (*sensus communis*, encapsulated in *loci communes*) becomes increasingly blurred. As a result, opinion slyly sneaks into areas of investigation that were formerly the preserve of exact knowledge. This development in speculative and controversial theology allows Catholic theologians to respond more flexibly to the moral dilemmas of early modern governance.

Mariana's writing exemplifies this tendency. By transferring legal formulae from a jurisprudential into a rhetorical discourse, he makes a statement with regard both to the nature of knowledge and the epistemological validity of his argument.[22] While valid under changing circumstances, juridical formulae articulated in the form of commonplaces offer no more than ballpark guidance on what ought or ought not to be done. Deployed as maxims of prudence, juridical concepts lose a good deal of normative authority. What is more, Mariana frequently employs specific modal verbs (what a king 'ought to do', 'should do', or 'must do' in order to survive). He also makes ample use of the conditional mood. The modal verb, the subjunctive and the commonplace jointly effect the process of semantic transformation of legal language. Enhancing the persuasive force of Mariana's argument, they also testify to his predicament in providing practical political advice. The linguistic means employed demonstrate Mariana's difficulties and his reservations about extracting guidance from a world perceived as corrupt and characterized by morally confusing volatility is difficult. They relay a strong sense of the precarious and fluid relationship between desirable moral standards and the unsettling demands of political reality.

---

21   The interlocutors in *De oratore* defend the view that this is the only kind of knowledge available to those dealing with political affairs against Plato and Aristotle. See Plato, *Phaedrus*, 260C, 261A; Aristotle, *NE*, 1173ᵃ. See J.E. Seigel (1968), *Rhetoric and Philosophy in Renaissance Humanism. The Union of Eloquence and Wisdom, Petrarch to Valla*, Princeton University Press, Princeton, pp. 9-12; and Kahn, *Rhetoric*, pp. 30-36.

22   See I. Maclean (1993), *From Prudence to Policy: Some Notes on the Prehistory of Policy Sciences*, University of Nijmegen, Nijmegen, pp. 8-10; and Kahn, *Rhetoric*, pp. 19-28.

Rex maior singulis, minor universis

Mariana's discussion of the question 'whether the power of the commonwealth or the king is greater' is exemplary for his mode of argument.[23] The heading of Book one, Chapter eight invokes a well-known canon law principle that continued to be significant to the early modern debate on the origin and limits of royal power long after fifteenth-century conciliarists had revived it: the maxim *rex maior singulis minor universis*. The formula epitomizes the medieval notion of a corporation (*universitas*) as a *persona ficta* or single person by fiction of law. The *universitas* was made up of men in their corporate aspect (the *universi*), that is, men who could act only as a corporate whole or through their representatives. According to this legal maxim, the king is inferior to men acting as a corporate whole (*universi*), but superior to any private individual (*singulus*).

Already the first paragraph shows Mariana's intention to shift the conceptual parameters of a debate on popular sovereignty and resistance which in Spain as anywhere else in Europe evolved from medieval and early modern juridical theory. He starts out with a seemingly unambiguous answer to the question of whether the power of the people or the king is greater. The *respublica*, he says, ought to be seen as enjoying the greater power because, invariably, 'the power of the king, if it is legitimate, has its source in the citizens'.[24] The opposite idea that the king is greater than the commonwealth and therefore *maior* rather than *minor universis* amounts to 'mistaking the child for the parent' or 'the river for the spring'. Peoples devised laws in order to prevent princes from sliding into tyranny. The Aragonese, for instance, created and in fact still practise laws which place the *respublica universa* or 'men of the first rank selected of all the orders' on a par with the king.[25] Mariana thus turns against jurisprudents and theologians like Francisco Suárez who defended the view that the law of nature institutes the king of Castile as natural lord of the realm (*proprius dominus* or *señor natural*).[26]

Whatever the particular constitutional arrangements of a nation, princes always are most likely to find their match when it comes to raising taxes. Historical experience has taught the kings of Castile, for instance, that they cannot impose new taxes against the will of their people.[27] Defiance in the face of royal demands for more money can take various forms of collective and individual action. Drawing on his rich fund of medieval anecdotes, Mariana recounts an episode during the

---

23 *De rege*, 1.8, 'Reipublicae an Regis maior potestas sit', pp. 87-99, p. 87.

24 Ibid., p. 88, 'Me tamen auctore, quando regia potestas, si legitima est, a civibus ortum habet, iis concedentibus primi Reges in quaque republica in rerum fastigio collocati sunt: eam legibus & sanctionibus circumscribent ne sese nimia efferat, luxuriet in subditorum perniciem, degeneretque in tyrannidem'.

25 Ibid., pp. 95-96.

26 See Suárez, *De legibus*, III, 4, 9. See ibid., I, 7, 11, for the notion of the identity of the common good and the king understood as 'common and public person'.

27 *De rege*, p. 89, 'Quod experimento comprobatur in Hispania, vectigalia imperare Regem non posse populo dissentiente.'

siege of Cuenca (1177). Running out of funds, and hesitant to levy further taxes on an exhausted population, Alfonso VIII of Castile turned to his nobility. The king asked his nobles for what Mariana himself considers a rather modest voluntary contribution. The count of Lara, however, interpreted Alfonso's plea as a veiled attempt to undermine the nobility's exemption from paying taxes. He responded by conspiring with other nobles to prepare for civil war, and openly threatened the king with violence. Realizing that he was in danger of being perceived as a tyrant, Alfonso decided to withdraw his appeal. Mariana does not suggest that Alfonso VIII's appeal for a gift or *merced* was ever meant to erode the right of the nobility to be exempt from taxation. The king is shown as motivated solely by personal zeal to overcome the Muslim enemy. He is hampered in his efforts by nobles suspecting a hidden agenda, and who are determined to defend their privileges at all costs. In several chapters, Mariana severely chastises Castilian nobles for their luxurious lifestyle, insistence on being exempt from taxes, effeminate behaviour, continuous plotting against the king and the clergy and their haughty belief that they are above the law.

This, then, is a more than ambiguous tale about the successful defence of ancient rights and privileges. That it does not amount to a wholehearted endorsement of notions of 'medieval constitutionalism' is indicated already by the fact that Mariana denotes the people defending their rights indifferently as *respublica*, *populus* or *multitudo*. The two latter terms more often than not carry their usual pejorative connotations ('mob'; 'the headless monster'). The *populus* is not depicted as a rational political actor, and the picture of the relationship between princes and peoples is one of shades of grey rather than one of black and white. In fact, the question is not whether or not a political action is rooted in the fundamental laws of the realm, but whether it maintains or restores a healthy balance of power that will help preserve the peace of the realm. The count of Lara could rightly be accused of treason, and dealt with accordingly. If his actions are worthy of consideration, of praise even, that is because they demonstrate the dangers of violating custom and upsetting powerful subjects even in circumstances of real expediency. Princes can learn from bad examples. Alfonso VIII learnt his lesson, captured Cuenca after a lengthy siege, and continued a successful reign. Reading *De rege*, Philip III, too, has the opportunity to avoid dangerous mistakes.

Mariana appeals to historical experience rather than the law. He calls up historical incidents rather than legal precedents. It is equally characteristic for his perception of the ambiguity of historical experience that he adds a caveat to his illustrations of the power and authority of the people. The *respublica universa* or her representatives are likely to prevail over the designs of kings only if 'gathered in one place and united in one resolution'.[28] Any attempt to make the quarrelsome minds of powerful men agree is beset with difficulties in the first instance. The fact that the king 'will persuade by words, hopes and promises (...)' as well as threats makes it almost impossible for subjects to resist firm demands for an increase in

---

28   Ibid., p. 89, p. 92.

revenue.[29] In a typical aside, Mariana states that he does not wish to discuss whether or not kings of Castile are within their rights when putting various pressures upon the *procuradores* of the cortes of Castile, for instance.[30] Whatever the laws say, kings in urgent need of funds will always seek to manipulate cortes and individuals. The question is that of the potential effects of their actions on the long-term relationship with their subjects. The count of Lara's behaviour may well be the exception rather than the rule. It still exemplifies what can happen if subjects, rightly or wrongly, feel threatened with oppression.

Quod omnes tangit, ab omnibus approbari

Maior singulis, minor universis is just one of several legal formulae put forward to remind rulers of their very immediate dependence on their subjects. Other *dicta* drawn from the body of scholastic juridical norms continue to make this point. One is the canon law principle *Quod omnes tangit ab omnibus approbari* ('What concerns all, must be approved by all').[31] It is employed to warn that disregard for the 'laws of the land' amounts to dangerous ignorance of the *de facto* power of the people.[32] Princes are told to be particularly wary of changing legislation concerning taxation, royal succession and religion without 'the consent and definite knowledge of the whole people'. The people's trust in the ruler will be undermined, royal power will be weakened to the point of collapse and the horrors of civil war unleashed. Considerations of *realpolitik* give the 'laws of the land', previously portrayed as the pitiable victim of princely ambition, a new lease of life.

---

29   Ibid., p. 89, 'Utetur quidem ille arte, praemia civibus ostentabit, nonnumquam terrores pertrahendis caeteris in suam sententiam: solicitabit verbis, spe, promissis (quod an recte non disputamus) sed si restiterint tamen, eorum potius iudicio quam Regis voluntati stabitur.'

30   Ibid., p. 89.

31   Originally specific to the institution of joint guardianship in Roman private law, this legal principle was subsequently applied to describe the function of the head of the ecclesiastical and secular body politic. See, for instance, *Cod.* 5.59.5, 2-3, '(...) quod omnes similiter tangit ab omnibus comprobetur'; and *Liber sextus, regulae iuris,* 29 (Friedberg, II, 1122), 'Quod omnes tangit debet ab omnibus approbari'. The formula permeates medieval and early modern attempts to describe the boundaries of secular and spiritual power as well as subsequent scholarly debate. For focused examinations of its bearing on medieval political thinking, see G. Post (1946), 'The Romano-Canonical Maxim "quod omnes tangit" in Bracton', *Traditio,* Vol. 4, pp. 197-252; Y. Congar (1958), 'Quod omnes tangit ab omnibus tractari et approbari debet', *Revue historique de droit français et étranger,* Vol. 36, pp. 210-59; and the work of B. Tierney, namely his (1998), *Foundations of the Conciliar Theory: the Contribution of the Medieval Canonists from Gratian to the Great Schism,* new, enlarged edn (Studies in the History of Christian Thought, Vol. 81), Brill, Leiden. For later medieval and early modern developments, see the work of Oakley; and also K. Pennington (1993), *The Prince and the Law, 1200-1600: Sovereignty and Rights in the Western Legal Tradition,* University of California Press, Berkeley; and M.S. Kempshall (1999), *The Common Good in Late Medieval Political Thought: Moral Goodness and Material Benefit,* Clarendon Press, Oxford.

32   *De rege,* p. 102, p. 106.

Mariana provides his readers with a digest of the laws which 'are fixed in the customs of almost all peoples', and are therefore particularly worthy of respect.[33] Showing respect for deeply entrenched custom will help prevent a people 'from arbitrarily repealing what has already been decided by the king, or departing from decisions he has already reached'. At the same time, Mariana does not contend that those laws shared by most peoples enjoy anything like universal validity.[34] He is noticeably cautious, speaking of laws common to 'almost all peoples' rather than 'all peoples'. In a brief aside characteristic of his balanced way of looking at things, Mariana concedes that not every people will find that customs thoroughly approved by the majority of nations further its best interest and welfare. He merely wishes to consider what 'perhaps ought to be observed' (*fortassis sentiendum*). Like Bodin, he stresses the difference between the positive law of nations and law natural and divine. Much more forcefully than Bodin, however, Mariana emphasizes the historicity and particularity of human positive law. In *De rege*, custom never progresses to become 'second nature'. As a result, Philip III is asked to regard the 'custom, statute and undoubted law' of 'most nations' largely as useful instruction on how to ensure that the legitimacy of his rule will not be doubted.

Mariana now turns to the part of royal authority that can generally be exercised both fully *and* safely. Included are the authority to declare and end war, to appoint magistrates and to dispense justice.[35] The jurisdiction of the prince also ought to comprise the duty to 'improve old laws and make new laws when circumstances require him to do so'.[36] In this respect, Mariana is prepared to attribute *suprema et maxima auctoritas* or *suprema potestas* to the prince. The prince '(…) will have greater authority not only than the individuals but also than the whole body, so that no one resists him and he does not give an account of his actions to anyone.'[37] The reader is never told what kind of circumstances entitle a prince to make new or reform old laws. Nor does he raise the obvious question whether circumstances may demand the unmaking of the fundamental laws of the realm. The possibility at least is not excluded, and the issue never resolved. Instead, the prince is persistently cautioned to the effect that his power is simultaneously supreme *and* limited.

---

33   Ibid., p. 92, 'Quod moribus populorum ferme omnium fixum videmus, ne a Rege constituta retractare cuiquam liceat, aut de illis disceptare.' This is a reference to the 'law of nations' (*ius gentium*) commonly understood as the law common to all peoples. Bodin, *Six livres*, 1.8 refers to the *lex omnium gentium communis*.

34   Ibid., p. 89.

35   Ibid., p. 89, 'Plerique omnes [nationes; H.B.] Regem rectorem reipublicae & caput esse concedunt, rebus gerendis supremam & maximam auctoritatem habere, sive bellum hostibus indicendum sit, sive iura subditis in pace danda (…)'; also ibid., p. 92, '(…) regiam potestatem supremam in regno esse iis rebus omnibus, quae more gentis, instituto, ac certa lege Principis arbitrio sunt permissae: sive bellum gerendum sit, sive ius dicendum subditis, sive duces magistratusque creandi (…).'

36   Ibid., p. 92, p. 101.

37   Ibid., p. 92, '(…) maiorem non singulis modo, sed universis habebit potestatem, nullo qui resistat aut facti rationem exigat.'

Eager to accommodate the reality of governing the *monarquía española*, Mariana adds a new angle to the notion of a king who is *maior singulis*. The customs of most nations agree that 'the *potestas imperandi* of the one is greater than that of individuals, *be they citizens or peoples* [my emphasis; H.B].'[38] This is the case when a king rules over more than one *provincia*. The relationship between the king of Castile and the various nations united under his rule is one that is to be understood in terms of the relation between the head of a corporate body and the private individual. Insofar as they represent the *provinciae* making up the Habsburg monarchy, the peoples of Castile, Flanders, Milan or Aragon must be regarded as *singuli* or private individuals. Brutalizing the *rex maior singulis, minor universis* epithet in order to describe the complex structure of the Spanish monarchy, Mariana unwittingly highlights the fact that contemporary legal theory had yet to find ways of conceptualizing the federal structure of early modern composite monarchies.[39]

Mariana's statements to the effect that the power of the commonwealth 'as a whole' is greater or at least equal to that of the king are ambiguous, and not easily reconciled with his appreciation of royal *suprema potestas*. *Suprema potestas* cannot possibly rest in both the king and the people as a corporate whole at the same time. If the *respublica* does indeed need to retain 'power greater than that of kings', the relationship between these two powers cannot be comprehended in merely juridical terms.[40]

Lex regia

Towards the end of Chapter eight, Mariana finally lays bare his intention of abstaining from attributing ultimate and absolute jurisdiction to either the ruler or the people. The occasion is entirely appropriate. He discusses a juridical theme at the very heart of medieval and early modern discourses of sovereignty, the so-called *lex regia*.[41] The relevant passages in the *Corpus Iuris Civilis* allege that the Roman people fully and irrevocably transferred their *imperium* to Augustus at the beginning of his reign.[42] Describing the supposed law rather than reproducing its text, however, Justinian's jurists ascribed a transfer of power greatly in excess of the historically verifiable grant of *tribunicia potestas* which Augustus apparently requested

---

38   Ibid., p. 89, 'Neque dubitant [i.e. the majority of nations; H.B.] maiorem unius quam singulorum tum civium tum populorum imperandi potestas esse.'

39   For the ideologies and languages of empire emerging in the wake of the discovery and colonization of the Americas see A. Pagden (1995), *Lords of all the World, Ideologies of Empire in Spain, Britain and France c. 1500 – c. 1800*, Yale University Press, New Haven and London, especially pp. 11-62. For attempts at conceptualizing 'federalism', see ibid., especially pp. 178-200.

40   *De rege*, p. 89.

41   Ibid., p. 94.

42   *Dig.* 1.4.1 (Ulpian); *Cod.* 1.17.1.7; see also *Inst.* 1.2.6. In classical Rome, the terms *imperium, merum imperium* or *summum imperium* described supreme civil and military authority.

and received.[43] Early modern advocates of strong monarchy as diverse as Barclay, Bodin or Suárez seized upon this tradition in order to dissociate royal power from its source in the people, and elevate it well above human positive law.

Mariana, in turn, feels compelled to confront the opinions of nameless 'men outstanding in their reputation for erudition' who, despite evidence to the contrary, maintain that 'the king is greater not only than the individual citizens but also than the whole body (…)'.[44] Determined to lodge *suprema potestas* in the king, they will 'not permit royal authority to be circumscribed by any limits'.[45] He takes particular issue with two strands in their argument, one legal and one philosophical. Firstly, these *viri eruditi* refer to canon law. They draw an analogy between the king of Castile and 'bishops, who enjoy authority that is greater not only than that of the individuals of the cathedral chapter (*singuli in diocesi*), but also that of the chapter as a whole (*universi in diocesi*)'.[46] Secondly, they root themselves in Aristotle, equating the supreme power of the king over the people to that of a father over his household. Both comparisons are invalid. The rule of the *paterfamilias* is that of a despot, equal to that of a master over his slaves, and cannot therefore reasonably be compared to the *principatus liber* or *principatus civilis* exercised by a legitimate king over free men.[47] The rule exercised by *reguli* or lesser princes, too, must not be confused with proper kingly rule. Princes as well as bishops may actually be considered greater than their *subditi universi* or subjects as a corporate body. That is the case because kings and Popes are always at hand to restrain them on behalf of the *respublica*. Mariana does not elaborate on the kind of jurisdiction over princes or bishops respectively that kings and Popes enjoy. He simply states that Pope and king have well-established powers to correct, restrain or punish a tyrannical bishop or prince for their sins.

---

43   The only surviving evidence of a transfer of summary powers to an emperor is a *senatus consultum* from AD 69, the *lex quae dicitur de imperio Vespasiani*. Early modern authors tend to equate it with the *lex regia*. The text of the *lex de imperio* in *Fontes iuris romani antiqui* (1909), ed. C.G. Bruns, 7th edn, I.C.B. Mohr, Tübingen, p. 202. For a concise discussion see H.F. Jolowicz (1954), *Historical Introduction to the Study of Roman Law*, 2nd edn, Cambridge University Press, Cambridge, p. 324 and p. 365.

44   *De rege*, p. 90, '(…) non deesse viros eruditionis opinione praestantes, qui secus statuant: Regem non singulis modo civibus, sed etiam universis maiorem esse, (…).'

45   Ibid., p. 91, '(…) neque ullis finibus circumscribi permittunt.' Mariana briefly refers to Bodin's notion of the indivisibility of power, ibid., pp. 90-91, 'Quoniam alioqui regius principatus popularis potius esset: quando summa rerum penes multos atque adeo penes omnes cives manet. Quod ea sententia suscepta, liceret a Regis sententia ad rempublica provocare. Quae libertas si suscipitur, magna esset rerum omnium confusio, magna iudiciorum perturbatio'. This seems a likely paraphrase of Bodin, *République*, I, 8. There is no direct evidence that Mariana read Bodin's work in the original French or in translation.

46   Ibid., pp. 90-91.

47   Ibid., p. 93, 'De patrefamilias, regulis, Episcopis laborare non attinet. De primo, quoniam subditis ut servis principatu despotico praeest. (…) Duos alios subditis praeferre universis nihil impedit, cum maior potestas in republica, nempe Regis aut Pontificis Romani sit: qua, si quid illi peccaverint, meliori censura corrigatur.'

Papal jurisdiction as such is not discussed any further either here or elsewhere in *De rege*. Mariana is unwilling to associate himself too closely with conciliarist arguments. Somewhat cautiously, he points out that 'many wise and serious men' go as far as to suggest that as far as the limits of papal authority is concerned, the supreme pontiff is subject to the general council of the Church in matters of religious doctrine.[48] Though his authority is 'next to divine', the Pope, however, cannot claim to be the source of secular *auctoritas*.[49] Much more concerned with the limits of secular than spiritual power, Mariana quickly goes on to ponder how to ensure the survival of the free or civic principate.

Again, he insists on weighing contrasting positions equitably. He does not rule out that the *lex regia* can be enacted just like those 'men outstanding in their reputation for erudition' suggest. 'No one can deny', he concedes, 'that the commonwealth can confer upon the prince supreme and maximum authority, without exception'.[50] Peoples are free to confer irrevocably power without limits upon their prince. Whether or not an irreversible transfer of power is legal in the first instance, however, is beside the point. What matters is the impact such a grant of unlimited power is likely to have upon the relationship between *princeps* and *subditi*. Granted such power, a prince will find it ever more difficult to think of himself as a *rector* of his people. He will be even more liable to turn himself into a despot or tyrant unfit to rule over free men. Mariana feels entitled to chastise the *viri eruditi* for their lack of prudence.

These 'learned men', Mariana says, eagerly claim that the corruption of humankind demands that the ruler be granted *suprema potestas*. They contend that a prince enacting absolute power will find it so much easier to command the respect of the 'multitude'. Mariana accepts that these are considerations rooted in dire human experience, yet he insists that the argument from human nature must be applied not only to the unruly *populus*, but also to the ruler. The monarch is as fallible as any other human being, while at the same time his mind and character are much more likely to be affected by the allure and exercise of power. To think that a king cannot be corrected or deprived of his title or his life, even if he 'is vexing [his people] with his low morals and is degenerating into open tyranny (…)' means to ignore well-known lessons from history.[51] Why, in the first instance, would a people

---

48 Ibid., p. 94.

49 Ibid., p. 93.

50 Ibid., p. 90, 'Praeterea cum negare nemo possit, quin respublica supremam & maximam potestatem possit sine exceptione Principi deferre: quid prohibet id factum concedere, quo maior esset auctoritas imperandi, maior populis obsequii necessitas, minor rebellandi facultas: qua re salus omnium & tranquillitas publica continetur?'

51 Ibid., p. 90, 'Preaterea Regem pravis moribus rempublicam vexantem, atque in apertam tyrannidem degenerantem comprimere eadem respublica qui posset, principatu & vita, si opus sit, spoliare, nisi maiori potestate penes se retenta, cum Regi suas partes delegavit?'; see also ibid., p. 93, '(…) Principis malo coercendi potestatem in republica residere: si vitiis & improbitate infectus sit, ignoransque verum iter gloriae, metui a civibus quam amari malit: metuque paventibus & perculsis imperare, iniuriam facere pergat factus

conscious of the perils of monarchical rule not want to 'retain within itself the greater power when it delegated some of it to the king?' Does not prudent appraisal of history suggest that 'it is improbable that the *cives universi* would have wanted to deprive themselves entirely of their own authority and transfer it to another without exceptions, limitations and restrictions?'[52] In response to his rhetorical questions, Mariana states that it is simply not necessary for a people to arrange things in such a way that 'a prince possibly subject to insufferable corruption and depravity has a greater power than all the citizens'. It is a matter of common sense to assume that there is some kind of residual authority in the *respublica*. Again, complex legal argument is reduced to one of common sense based on historical experience.

While Mariana has made it plain that he prefers to think that 'the power of restraining the prince abides in the commonwealth', he has yet to be definite about the exact nature of that authority and power. Though fully aware that his readers by now expect him to reveal where ultimate authority is lodged, Mariana refuses to resolve the issue in definite juridical terms. This is one of the rare occasions where he directly addresses his interlocutor. It is worth quoting in full.

> If you persist in asking inquisitively whether it is not within the prerogative of the commonwealth to abdicate and give full and unlimited authority to the Prince (…). Indeed I would not argue the matter much, nor would it make much difference to me how it is decided, provided that it is granted that the commonwealth would act unwisely if it surrendered, that the Prince would be rash to accept that power which will make his subjects slaves instead of free men, and that the principate, constituted for the public good, would degenerate into tyranny.[53]

One can easily imagine Mariana being pressed by a fellow theologian or by a jurisprudent demanding to know by means of which juridical axiom he intends to decide the question of the ultimate *locus* of secular power. His cool, albeit somewhat veiled response is that lawyers' and theologians' strained efforts to resolve issues of political power in such definitive terms are ultimately futile. The relations shaping the fortunes of monarchical regimes cannot be comprehended in terms of juridical-theological designations of supreme power to either the king or the people.

---

tyrannus. (…) Quid vero populare imperium effici dicat republica praelata, cum rebus gerendis, singulisque reipublicae partibus administrandis nulla potestas populo relicta sit, nulla proceribus?'

52 Ibid., p. 90, 'Neque sit verisimile sua se cives universos penitus auctoritate spoliare voluisse, transferre in alium sine exceptione, sine consilio, rationeque: quod necesse non erat, effecisse, ut Principe corruptioni obnoxius & pravitati, maiorem universis haberet potestatem (…).'

53 Ibid., p. 94, 'Quod si pergas curiose rogare, sit ne in arbitrio reipubliae plenam sine exceptione potestatem, de qua disceptatio est, sibi auferre, Principi dare? Equidem non magnopere contendam, neque in magno ponam discrimine utrovis modo sentiatur: modo illud concedatur imprudenter facturam rempubliam si dederit: Principem temerarie accepturum, per quod subditi e liberis servi evadant, principatus ad salutem datus, degeneret in tyrannidem.'

Mariana has no confidence in extracting universal and ultimately binding juridical logic from the customs of nations. He does not search and manipulate texts so as to locate *suprema potestas*. The historicity and mutability of law and custom ensure that neither the authority of the king nor that of the people is immune to being revised by 'time and the wickedness of man'. Both the act of transfer of power and the act of circumscribing the authority of the ruler with laws are entirely human in origin. Kings are free to rule *more tyrannico* if they obtain the tacit or express consent of a subservient people. What the study of the laws of nations does strongly suggest, however, is that it is very unwise on the part of both ruler and people to seek or condone a situation where ultimate power is lodged in the one or the other. Politics is not so much what the law says, but what prudence suggests a prince or people ought or ought not do. Power has to be limited and absolute at the same time, and it is the responsibility of the prince to establish and maintain this precarious equilibrium. Comparing the laws and customs of nations will provide rulers and their advisers with clues as to how this balance of power may be construed and sustained – no less, no more.

Mariana epitomizes the virtue of prudent self-restraint in a ruler by calling up a figure prominent in early modern political debates on the limits of sovereignty: the Spartan king Theopompus.[54] After establishing the ephorate as a means to gather and steer public consent on matters essential to the survival of the *respublica*, Theopompus was accused by his wife of having needlessly diminished the inheritance of his sons. His alleged response was that though he left his sons with less power, he certainly left them with power much more secure and stable. The maxim of prudence corresponding to the fable of king Theopompus, and summing up Mariana's treatment of canon and Roman law dicta is that 'princes, by placing reins on their own fortune, rule themselves, that fortune and their subjects more easily.'[55] Rulers are all too easily 'deceived with an appearance of greater power, (…) not giving the matter sufficient consideration, and not realising that power is finally safe only when it places a limit on its own strength.'[56] Good government ultimately depends not on human positive law or the representatives of the people, but on whether or not the prince is brought up in a manner that enables him to recognize what is in his own best interest.

Princeps Legibus Solutus

In Chapter nine, Mariana elaborates on his theme of power that is both limited and absolute at the same time. Civilian formulae which define the prince as being above the law are qualified in a manner confirming the perils of arbitrary rule, the dispensability of legalist thinking and the value of prudence. Already the title of

---

54   Ibid., p. 95. For classical versions of the story, see Aristotle, *Politics*, 1313a27; Plutarch, *Lives*, VII, 1-2, 'Lycurgus'; Valerius Maximus, *Facta et dicta*, IV, i, 8. François Hotman, *Francogallia*, p. 312, refers to Theopompus. See also *Vindiciae contra Tyrannos*, pp. 88-90.

55   Ibid., p. 95.

56   Ibid.

Chapter nine snubs the suggestion that the prince can deem himself *legibus solutus* or 'free from the laws'.[57] The reference is to Digest 1.3.31 ('The prince is not bound by the law'), a brief passage from the *Corpus Iuris Civilis* that was to reverberate through western political thinking.[58] Medieval and early modern political theorists keen to establish the will of the prince as the only source of law adopted and developed this as well as a variety of similar formulae into theories of sovereignty.[59] Their efforts were met by those of writers who wished to develop legal maxims locating *suprema potestas* not in the prince but in the people as a corporate body or the people as a whole. Mariana's sympathies are with the latter. Yet his observations in previous chapters have also shown that he does not believe that placing supreme or absolute power in the one or the other is the way forward.

Neither prepared to accept that the prince is 'above' or 'free from the laws', nor willing to discuss this issue in strictly juridical terms, Mariana is helped by the fact that civil law in itself is ambivalent regarding the nature and limits of the power of the *princeps*.[60] While several passages in the *Corpus Iuris Civilis* do proclaim that the power of the prince is of divine origin, others assert that it comes from the people.[61] Medieval and early modern civilians intent on defining the nature and scope of princely *potestas* generally sought to resolve the issue by deciding on whether or not the prince was above human positive law. Though they agreed that the *princeps* was subject to divine and natural law, civilians were coy to identify any agent entitled to enforce it other than the prince himself. The majority tended to see the relationship between *princeps* and *leges* in strictly hierarchical terms. Their conclusion was that the prince was unrestrained by human positive law. Yet to maintain that the will of the prince served as its own justification opened up the possibility of rulers entertaining

---

57   Ibid., 1:9, 'Princeps non est solutus regibus', pp. 99-107. The postglossator Accursius saw the formula *princeps legibus solutus* as derived from the *lex regia*, the law which had supposedly conferred all the power and *imperium* possessed by the Roman people on Augustus. His gloss on *Cod.* 6.23.2 is quoted and discussed in B. Tierney (1963), 'The prince is not bound by the laws: Accursius and the origins of the modern state', *Comparative Studies in Society and History*, Vol. 5, pp. 379-400 [also in ibid. (1979), *Church Law and Constitutional Thought* (CSS; 90), Ashgate Publishers, Aldershot, III]. On the development of this Roman law maxim in medieval and early modern political thought see D. Wyduckel (1979), *Princeps legibus solutus, Eine Untersuchung zur frühmodernen Rechts- und Staatslehre* (Schriften zur Verfassungsgeschichte, Vol. 30), Duncker und Humblot, Berlin, especially pp. 163-67.

58   For a brief survey of the complex history of civilian influence on western political thinking, see Kelley, 'Law', in *CHPTh*, pp. 66-94.

59   *Dig.* 1.3.31 usually appears as a double bill with *Dig.* 1.4.1, *Quod principi placuit leges habet vigorem* ('What pleases the prince has the force of law'). Medieval jurisprudents quickly found a way of equating regal with imperial power: the formula *rex imperator in regno suo* ('the king is emperor in his realm').

60   Several aspects of this ambivalence have been worked out by E.H. Kantorowicz (1957), *The King's Two Bodies. A Study in Medieval Political Theology*, Yale University Press, New Haven and London, especially pp. 97-192.

61   On divine origin, for instance, *Dig.* Prologue (*Constitutio Deo auctore*) and *Nov.* 73.1; on popular origin *Inst.* 1.2.6, *Cod.* 1.17.1, *Dig.* 1.4.

a capricious disregard for the law. Civilians saw the *princeps* as a creation of those laws from which his office and power derive as well as a creator of laws through which he rules. A prince undermining the rule of law invariably undermines public confidence in his ability and legitimacy, and thus destroys the foundation of his power.

The majority of civilians agreed to resolve this dilemma by interpreting the categorical pronouncement of Digest 1.3.31 in the light of Codex 1.14.4 ('It is a statement worthy of the majesty of the ruler that the prince professes himself bound to the law'), the equally famous *lex digna vox*.[62] *Lex digna vox* suggested that although the prince is under no obligation to obey the laws, he will nonetheless want to act as if he was. Intent on preserving and enhancing the rule of law by which he distinguishes himself from arbitrary regimes, the *princeps* will not formally declare that he is bound by the laws, but be clear about his intention to act in accordance with them. One of the most original postglossators, Baldus de Ubaldis, sums up the civilian response to the problem of power that has got to be limited and absolute at the same time:

> The *princeps* should live according to the laws because his authority depends on the law. Understand that this word, 'should', is interpreted as applying to the obligation of honesty which the emperor should possess to the highest degree. (...) Note that the emperor says he is bound by the laws and this is so out of his good will and not out of necessity. The emperor is *legibus solutus*, yet at the same time does not act *supra legem*.[63]

Though Baldus strongly indicates that the authority of the prince is tied to that of the law, he posits the matter of whether or not the prince actually supports the rule of law as one that is entirely dependent on his will and moral integrity. Defining the obligation of the prince to uphold the law exclusively in terms of his personal *honestas*, the civilian tradition of interpreting Digest 1.3.31 in the light of *lex digna vox* lent itself to being read in terms of political prudence. Chapter nine of *De rege* takes its cue from the civilian tradition, exploring a polarity encapsulated in two contrasting and highly influential texts from the Justinian body of law: the polarity of power that has got to be absolute, yet at the same time limited by those who exercise it.

Unlike the glossators and postglossators, Mariana has a rather glum view of the *honestas* or moral aptitude to be expected in a prince, who is 'so continuously beset with the flatteries of the court (...) that he is hardly able to have control of himself.'[64] Nor, on the other hand, is he prepared to put any faith in the will and

---

62 *Cod.* 1.14.4 [*lex digna vox*], 'Digna vox maiestate regnantis legibus alligatum se principem profiteri: adeo de auctoritate iuris nostra pendet auctoritas. Et re vera maius imperio est submittere legibus principatum. Et oraculo praesentis edicti quod nobis licere non patimur iudicamus.' On the exposition of the *lex digna vox* in medieval political thought, see Tierney, 'The Prince is Not Bound by the Laws', pp. 391-93; see also *Vindiciae*, p. 101, fn. 223; and Canning, *Baldus*, pp. 74-75.

63 Quoted in Canning, *Baldus*, p. 75.

64 *De rege*, p. 97.

ability of the *populus* (cortes, nobility, or magistrates) to uphold the laws against cunning and powerful rulers. Too many kings have successfully challenged the authority and resilience of the *respublica*. Mariana acknowledges this fact. Readers familiar with the works of the historians, after all, will be well aware of it, too. Engaging in a heated conversation with his interlocutor, he sets out to explain why a prince should nonetheless want to put himself on a par with subjects 'whom he surpasses so far in terms of the means of power'.[65] The interlocutor proposes that 'laws are protected only by the fear of superior power'.[66] It would be ridiculous, therefore, to want to impose laws on a king who cannot effectively be coerced 'by fear of trial or judgement'. Mariana readily agrees that it would be folly to rely on laws and courts of law when it comes to restraining princes. There is a solution though. He now sets out to prove that princes obey the law not so much out of goodwill rather than sheer necessity, and, indeed, out of fear. Again, Mariana grabs an opportunity to translate a controversial constitutional issue into one of political wisdom.

Prudence, Fear and Tyrannicide

Mariana's vehicle for persuading princes of the necessity to respect the laws is fear. His contention is that a prince has to be aware and, indeed, afraid of the many, rarely 'constitutional' ways in which his people may punish him for sustained breaches of law. The prince has got to respect the laws of the land because the authority and power of the commonwealth are likely to surpass his, 'no matter how great the power on which he relies.'[67] Not even the most powerful monarch can afford to ignore the fact that his people, ultimately, command much larger resources in terms of money, manpower and sheer determination than he does. Fear encourages princes to acknowledge the responsibilities and personal qualities traditionally associated with good kingship.

The main effect of fear is that it raises the degree to which princes become aware of the expediency of law-abiding kingship. Mariana's *leitmotif* in this respect is one of the basic principles of Renaissance humanism from Petrarch onwards, namely that 'we are more effectively moved to right action by the examples of poetry and history than by the precepts of philosophy'.[68] He vigorously applies this humanist tenet throughout his treatise, not least to the relationship between prince, people and the law. One of his favourite maxims is that 'people give more credit to example than to laws'.[69] The prudent prince therefore willingly embraces the authority of laws 'lest he induce contempt for the laws in his subjects.' If he desires subjects 'well

---

65   Ibid., p. 105.

66   Ibid., p. 105.

67   Ibid., p. 90, 'Et quis sentiat reipublicae cui maiores vires sunt, maioresque copiae quam Principis quantavis potestate nitatur, (…), auctoritatem fore.'

68   See Kahn, *Rhetoric*, p. 10.

69   *De rege*, pp. 101-102, 'Iam quantum illud est, subditos velle obsequentes habere, probitate conspicuos: ipsum vitae licentia impudicitiam improbitatemque sancire: credunt

disciplined and outstanding in probity', the prince cannot afford his own example to 'sanction licentiousness and wickedness'.[70] Princes exhibiting vices rather than virtues will find their subjects faithfully imitating their conduct. Conspiracy and rebellion are the inevitable outcome. The prince who undermines the legitimacy of his rule by public displays of 'wicked deceit (*dolus malus*), violence, and adultery' is like the armed madman hell-bent on destroying himself as well as others.[71]

Mariana's discussion of lawful conduct as a dictate of prudence results in a number of rules of thumb for maintaining the authority of the prince. Firstly, princes ought to act as if they enjoyed power no greater than the *potestas universa* held by the people themselves prior to the point at which they transferred their power onto the single ruler. With regard to respect for the laws, princes, again, are admonished to consider themselves free from their own laws only to the degree that they would wish to exempt the most powerful nobles of his realm.[72] Such observations on government by example, and on fear as the pilot of prudence are not what could be described as principles of proto-constitutional government. Issues of legitimacy are discussed as a matter of personal wisdom and conduct.

Tyrannicide as a Constitutional Issue

Mariana's most potent, controversial and misconstrued explication of fear as a political factor is his discussion of tyrannicide. It was possibly the thorniest issue an early modern author could tackle. One man's tyrant was another man's just and firm ruler. What was an act of regicide to some, was tyrannicide to others. Mariana was clearly aware that he was dealing with a highly divisive issue. He makes an effort to present his discussion of tyrannicide as being about the psychology of fear and its healthy effect on powerful princes. Ultimately, though, and not without responsibility of his own, he failed to disperse suspicions that he set out to promote a radical theory of resistance.

Mentioning tyrannicide in a treatise was bound to be problematic. It had been impossible to define tyrannicide in unequivocal terms. Even leading lights of medieval theology felt driven to despair. Jean Gerson (1363-1429) despondently remarked that the charge was so vague that it could be levelled against anyone at any time.[73] Gerson witnessed events during the tumultuous period of the Great Schism

---

enim homines magis exemplis quam legibus, & genus obsequii putatur Principum studia imitari, sive prava illa sint sive salutaria.'

70   Ibid., p. 102.

71   Ibid., p. 107.

72   Ibid., p. 102, 'Quid vero quod Princeps non maiorem potestatem habet quam universus populus, si principatus popularis esset, aut quam viri primarii, si potestas universa ad eos esset devoluta (...) non ergo se magis liberum putet a suis legibus, quam singuli populares aut proceres ab iis essent exempti, quas pro iure arreptae potestatis isti sanxissent.'

73   Jean Gerson (1963), *Oportet haereses esse, Oeuvres complètes*, ed. Palémon Glorieux, Vol. 5, Desclée, Paris and New York, pp. 420-35, p. 423.

of the Western Church (1378-1415). Serious controversy among theologians concerning the murder of a legitimate ruler had been aroused in 1407, when the duke of Orleans was assassinated by orders of his powerful vassal, the duke of Burgundy. One of Burgundy's clients, the theologian Jean Petit caused a scandal by defending his patron's action on the ground that it was lawful to murder a tyrant. Under considerable pressure from secular princes to anathematize regicide, the Council of Constance (1414-18) resolved to meet Petit's mercenary teachings head-on. It condemned as heretical his proposition that:

> Any tyrant can and ought to be killed, licitly and meritoriously, by any of his vassals or subjects, even by means of plots and blandishments or flattery, notwithstanding any oath taken, or treaty made with the tyrant, and without waiting for a sentence or a command from any judge.[74]

Though the Council's condemnation was far too general to settle the issue, Catholic theologians, with the notable exception of Mariana, subsequently felt obliged to profess themselves in agreement with the Fathers of the council. Conveniently, the Council's anathema was open to interpretation. It could be understood to allow for the killing of *certain kinds* of tyrants. Yet even if *some* tyrants could be lawfully killed, the question remained by what judicial procedure a verdict could be reached. In a nutshell, the issue was that killing a tyrant invariably meant killing a natural superior, with potentially disastrous consequences for the accepted hierarchical order. Whoever had the right to decide whether or not a prince had lapsed into tyranny automatically enjoyed authority superior to that of the prince.

The first distinction commonly employed to tackle this problem was adopted from Bartolus of Sassoferrato's *Tractatus de Guelphis et Ghibellinis*.[75] Bartolus had provided a *locus classicus* by distinguishing a legitimate ruler who behaved tyrannically from an invader or usurper of the throne. The latter had no title to his office and could be removed by force or slain by any subject. The commonwealth or private person merely exercised the natural right of *vim vi repellere*. The only restriction was that such an action must not threaten to make the situation worse. This was the position adopted by the vast majority of Catholic theologians, including prominent Jesuits like Luis de Molina. The latter declared that unless such action was likely to cause greater evil, a tyrant who is a usurper or invader 'can be justly killed by any member of the commonwealth'.[76]

---

74   The sentence formally condemned by the Council during its fifteenth session, 11 July 1415, runs as follows, 'Quilibet tyrannus potest ed debet licite et meritorie occidi per quemcumque vassallum suum vel subditum, etiam per insidias, et blanditas vel adulationes, non obstante quocumque praestito iuramento, seu confoederatione facta cum eo, non expectata sententia vel mandato iudicis cuiuscumque', *Conciliorum Oecumenicorum Decreta* (1962), ed. Istituto per le scienze religiose die Bologna, cura di G. Alberigo, Herder, Basle, p. 408.

75   On Bartolo see the literature quoted above, chapter two, p. 43, footnote 14.

76   See for instance, Luis de Molina (1615), *De iustitia et iure*, Johannes Keerbergius, Antwerp, tract. III, disp. VI.2. I am obliged to the concise survey of Jesuit positions on

The much more common and much more difficult case, of course, was that of a ruler using his legitimate authority to govern tyrannically. The crux of the matter was to find a morally and legally convincing way of extending the principle of *vim vi repellere* to the tyrant 'with a title': (*tyrannus cum titulo* or *tyrannus ex parte exercitii*). For theologians largely concerned with maintaining the order of superiority and inferiority between prince and subject there was no easy way out. To judge a legitimate ruler behaving tyrannically meant to judge a superior. Who was to judge whether or not a prince had turned into a tyrant in the first instance, and then decide how to proceed against him? No Catholic or Jesuit theologian with the possible exception of Mariana, ever argued outright that it was justifiable for a private person simply to go forth and kill a lawful prince on his or her own authority. It was commonly agreed that a legitimate ruler using his authority tyrannically could not be killed by any private individual, but that it belonged to the commonwealth to establish and execute a valid judicial procedure. Jean Calvin and the French Huguenot writers, too, chose to exclude private individuals by empowering 'lesser' or 'popular magistrates'.[77] Yet even if it was up to the *respublica* or its lawful representatives to confront, depose or execute a tyrant, the question remained on what authority it would do so. The need to establish by what right the *respublica* was to judge a tyrant 'with a title' remained. In an age of confessional conflict, the doctrinal resolution of the issue of tyrannicide became an ever more remote possibility. Almost two hundred years after Gerson's comment, Francisco Suárez could still share his sentiment, feeling no closer to resolving the issue in a way that was theologically and morally sound and definite.[78]

The dilemma is exemplified by Luis de Molina's observations on the matter. A commonwealth (or its agents), he says, may depose a legitimate king ruling tyrannically by 'passing sentence on him if his excesses and the common good demand it, and punishing him once he is deposed.'[79] What Molina did not spell out was who exactly the agent pronouncing judgement was, and what kind of procedure should be followed. His fellow Jesuit Leonard Lessius thought that a legitimate ruler who governed tyrannically had to be declared a public enemy and deposed by the commonwealth or a council of the kingdom, 'or someone else having that authority, so that it would become legitimate to attempt something against his person'.[80] Who that someone was, however, he did not say. The upshot was that the prince, in Lessius's words, would have 'to cease to be a prince' before he could be sentenced and punished by the commonwealth.

---

tyrannicide in Höpfl, *Jesuit Political Thought*, pp. 317-19.

77   H. Höpfl (1982), *The Christian Polity of Jean Calvin*, Cambridge University Press, Cambridge, pp. 170-71 and fns. 109 and 111, p. 210, p. 213, p. 216.

78   See Francisco Suárez (1613), *Defensio fidei Catholicae et apostolicae aduersus Anglicanae sectae errors (…)*, n.p., Coimbra, VI.4.4.

79   Molina, *De iustitia et iure*, tract. III, disp. VI.2.

80   Leonard Lessius (1605), *De iustitia et iure caeterisque virtutibus cardinalibus libri IV*, Johannes Masij, Leuven, II, chapter IX, 2. Translation in Höpfl, *Jesuit Political Thought*, p. 318.

The supreme authority of the prince had to remain untouched in principle, which was to say, the commonwealth was not to be given *suprema potestas*. Otherwise, the charge of tyranny would be all too easily brought against any prince, royal authority challenged in an apparently lawful manner by any group of disgruntled nobles or a religious minority. There was far too much scope for upsetting established yet inherently unstable perceptions of the 'right' order of society, and for causing disturbance right across political and confessional divides. This dilemma led more conservative characters like the moral theologian Francisco de Toledo to state that the 'tyrant with a title' must not be killed, and require subjects to suffer him even to the point of their own destruction.[81]

Mariana on Tyrannicide: Humanist Teaching with a Cruel Edge

Do Mariana's writings bear out 'legitimate suspicions of unconventionality' against this background, as has been claimed?[82] In many respects, he delivers the staple treatment of tyranny found in the standard textbooks of theology, law and in *Summae* of cases of conscience.[83] Mariana agrees with the vast majority of Catholic theologians that the usurper or tyrant 'without a title' may be slain by any subject.[84] The usual vague restriction that tyrannicide must not lead to greater evil applies. More often than not, he says, echoing the sentiment expressed by Toledo, a people actually deserve the prince who oppresses them. His discussion of the 'tyrant with a title', on the other hand, does court controversy in several respects.

Mariana presents his discussion of the topic as a running commentary on the decline and sad demise of Henry III of France (1574-1589). Once a warlike prince defending the true faith, Henry came to embody the 'character and habits of the tyrant, hated equally by Heaven and men'.[85] Undoubtedly his worst crime is the way he violated the Catholic faith. Intent on installing the heretic Henry of Navarre as heir to the throne, he has the main opponents to his scheme murdered. The cowardly murder of the cardinal and duke of Guise makes any thought of settling disputes by means of council and assembly futile. Soon, most of France is up in arms against its legitimate king. The result of Henry's actions is the complete breakdown of communication between prince and people. His death at the hands of Jacques Clément merely concludes the harrowing tale of a royal life wasted in depraved and tyrannical acts.

Comparing a king of France with denatured 'monsters from antiquity' was always likely to raise hackles in a country which had only just started to recover from decades of religious civil war enmeshed with aristocratic feud. French *politiques*,

---

81   Francisco de Toledo (1596), *Summa casuum conscientiae*, Johannes Gymnici, Cologne, pp. 652-53.

82   Höpfl, *Jesuit Political Thought*, p. 315.

83   On topological discussions of tyrannicide in early modern theology, law and political polemics, see Turchetti, *Tyrannie et tyrannicide*.

84   See *De rege*, pp. 73-75.

85   Ibid., p. 65.

however, felt that *De rege* contained even more infuriating statements. Not only does Mariana appear to eulogize Henry's murderer. He seems keen to outline a quasi-juridical way in which the private individual may deal with a 'tyrant with a title'. Such a prince, Mariana says, must be admonished, and, if he complies, the people must be satisfied. If the prince refuses to change his ways and persists in his crimes, the commonwealth may meet to discuss, decide and publicly announce his deposition. War is likely to follow, and the commonwealth may prepare for it by raising taxes. The law of *vim vi repellere* entitles the *respublica* to declare the king a 'public enemy', and thus entitle private persons to kill him. This is not that far off Molina's or Lessius's pronouncements on the matter. Going on from there, however, Mariana explains that if the prince consistently prevents legitimate assemblies from gathering and proceeding against him in an orderly fashion, private individuals may well resolve to kill him on their own initiative.[86] This is where he clearly deviates from mainstream Catholic doctrine. He defines specific circumstances in which the private individual has the right to take action without having sought permission of cortes, estates or magistrates. To encourage the private individual to kill a king is problematic enough. To turn the private individual into both executioner *and* jury is stupendously dangerous.

Mariana appears to have been aware of the implications of what he is saying. He seeks to support his stance by claiming that the conciliar decree condemning the opinions of Jean Petit had never actually been approved by either Martin V or any of his successors.[87] He even distorts the actual wording of the conciliar decree. Allegedly, it only condemned the opinion that 'a tyrant may and ought to be killed by any subject, not only openly with violence but also through conspiracy and plots'. Mariana simply omits the council's reference to a private person acting 'without waiting for a sentence or a command from any judge'. He then goes on to insinuate that Orleans's assassin would be vindicated if it could be shown that the tyranny of Louis prevented him from obtaining the permission of a superior.[88]

In doubting the validity of conciliar decrees issued prior to the election of Martin V (11 November 1417), Mariana is not alone. Cardinal Bellarmine, determined to deny the right of appeal from Pope to council, argued in a similar vein. Bellarmine stated that the decree with which the Fathers had wished to establish the superiority of the general council over the Pope (the decree *Haec sancta*, issued 30 March 1415) fell into the period when there was no unquestioned Pope, and that it had never received papal approbation.[89] Still, a theologian of Mariana's training and calibre could not but have been aware of the precise wording of the actual decree. Here is an instance exemplifying the limits and potential pitfalls of the way in which Mariana interprets legal idiom in terms of political prudence.

---

86 Ibid., p. 76.
87 Ibid., p. 79.
88 Ibid., p. 80.
89 See Oakley, *The Conciliarist Tradition*, p. 162.

Mariana does make a determined effort to defuse his words, adding that there is 'no danger that many, because of this theory, will make mad attempts against the lives of princes on the pretext that they are tyrants.'[90] Apparently contradicting himself, he now claims not to have left the power to decide on the fate of the 'tyrant with a title' to either the individual or the 'multitude'. The sentence will be pronounced, he says, either by the 'public voice of the people' (*publica vox populi*), or else by 'learned and serious men'. Yet, how exactly is the 'public voice of the people' to express itself legitimately if not through a *publicus conventus*? And who are the 'serious and learned men' alternatively involved? Molina and Lessius had hesitated to go any further at this point, while Toledo, along with many others had resolved not to go there at all.

There is a legal fiction that could shed light on the vague reference to the *vox populi* expressing itself publicly, albeit not through established institutional channels. Mariana may have been inspired by the only doctrine concerning the lawful deposition of a Pope unanimously endorsed by scholastic thinkers: the doctrine of *excommunicatio latae sententiae*.[91] This tenet from canon law dealt with the case of a Pope who had fallen into heresy. If the latter refused to see the error of his ways and if his heresy was 'notorious' (i.e. public knowledge), he *ipso facto* ceased to be Pope.[92] The fact that his deviation from the faith was generally known came to replace proper legal procedure, that is, trial and deposition by a council of the Church. The heretical Pope in fact deposed himself. This doctrine had been put to good use in the deposition of John XXII at the Council of Constance (1415).[93] Its great advantage in the view of papalist thinkers was that it sidestepped the question of whether or not *suprema potestas* ultimately resided in the Pope or the general council. Mariana is likely to have thought along similar lines. A ruler who consistently obstructs the convocation of a *publicus conventus* earns himself such notoriety that he in fact deposes himself. Mariana certainly describes the situation in which Henry III was assassinated as one in which normal judicial procedures and institutions had long ceased to function, and where the 'tyranny' of the legitimate

---

90   *De rege*, p. 77.

91   The doctrine of *excommunicatio latae sententiae* is based upon D.40 c.6. See Huguccio's gloss on D.40 c.6, 'Dico quod gratia exempli hoc posuit vel forte in eo est differentia inter heresim et alia crimina notoria, scilicet quod de crimine heresis potest papa accusari si heresim publice predicat et non vult desistere quamvis tale crimen non sit notorium. Sed de alio crimine non non potest accusari nisi sit notorium. Ergo de occulto crimine non potest accusari. (…) Ego autem credo quod idem sit de quolibet crimine notorio quod papa possit accusari et condemnari si admonitus non vult cessare.' Quoted in Tierney, *Foundations*, Appendix I, p. 228 [Appendix I, p. 249, in the 1955 edition].

92   On the notion of notoriety in canon law, see T. Schmidt (1989), *Der Bonifaz-Prozeß, Verfahren der Papstanklage in der Zeit Bonifaz VIII. und Clemens V*, Böhlau, Cologne and Vienna, especially pp. 1-12; and Tierney, *Foundations*, especially pp. 61-67.

93   Whether or not the general council had the right to depose the Pope was fiercely debated. See, for instance, G. Alberigo (1981), *Chiesa conciliare: identità e significato del conciliarismo*, Paideia, Brescia; and Oakley, *The Conciliarist Tradition*.

prince had become manifest. Once the 'tyrant with a title' ceases to be prince, he is just a criminal whom any private individual is free to deal with.

As to the 'learned and serious men' possibly passing judgement on the prince, the phrase can hardly be taken as Mariana's epithet for nobles or higher secular magistrates. His particular distrust of the laity as political actors (including the cortes) is tangible throughout *De rege*. The concluding chapters of the three books of his treatise allow for conjecture. There, he celebrates the bishops of Castile as 'true guardians of the realm'.[94] It is more than likely that Mariana thought of the higher clergy as the one group able to take things in hand, and act as impartial defenders of the interests of the people of Castile. The situation he describes is one of out-and-out civil war in which it is impossible to follow due procedure for convoking estates or cortes. Distinguished bishops of the realm assembling ad hoc would have to do. An avid historian rather than a lawyer, Mariana is interested in responding to what actually happens on the ground rather than providing legal sanction retrospectively.

Readers then and now, however, can be forgiven for taking the relevant passages in *De rege* as a justification of religiously motivated regicide. Generally loath to offer the explicit definition and differentiation of terms characteristic of the scholastic exposition, and eager to proffer ambiguous narratives, Mariana invites multiple interpretations. After all, he bases his observations on the way in which a people will, eventually, deal with a 'tyrant with a title' mainly on the life and death of Henry III of France. His account clearly resembled those provided by the polemicists of the Catholic League, accounts that were meant to condemn Henry and justify his assassination. Anti-Jesuit polemicists were naturally delighted with this opportunity to vent their spleen and their suspicions about the Society of Jesus. They filled in the gaps, and where Mariana spoke vaguely of 'learned and serious men', they claimed that he had conferred on to the Jesuit superior general or the Pope the right to judge legitimate princes.[95]

No Jesuit ever sought to replace a secular prince with the superior general, and claims to that extent mark the outer limits of anti-Jesuit invective. Much more tangible, however, was the charge that Mariana wanted to confer some kind of supreme temporal authority on the Pope. Catholic theologians did generally acknowledge a papal right to depose princes and prevent the accession of heretics. The Jesuits Suárez and Molina propounded it, and so did Mariana's famous pupil,

---

94 R. Krebs (1890), *Politische Publizistik der Jesuiten und ihrer Gegner in den letzten Jahrzehnten vor dem Ausbruch des Dreissigjährigen Krieges*, n.p., Halle, pp. 113-14, p. 118, proposed that Mariana wanted to see the clergy of the realm entitled with the right to pass judgement on the prince. In the light of what Mariana says in later chapters of *De rege*, it is likely that he had the bishops rather than the secular clergy as a whole in mind. I do not agree with Höpfl, *Jesuit Political Thought*, p. 319 fn. 27, that Krebs's suggestion is merely gratuitous.

95 A notable exception is Roussel, who acknowledges that Mariana refuses to discuss tyrannicide as a matter of papal authority over secular rulers, *Antimariana*, p. 451.

Saint Robert Bellarmine (1542-1621).[96] The cardinal and saint is representative for the general structure of the argument.[97] Bellarmine is poised both to maintain the position of the Pope as head of the *respublica Christiana*, and to decontaminate the complex relationship between the papacy and secular princes. He sought to achieve this in the first instance by asserting that the secular power of princes did not originate in the papal *plenitudo potestatis*. It followed that, although the Pope had direct and immediate power in spiritual matters, he merely enjoyed *potestas indirecta in temporalibus*. The distinction between direct spiritual and indirect temporal papal authority, however, did not rule out that the Pope could nonetheless directly intervene in temporal affairs. Bellarmine could not but maintain that a Christian prince was bound to defend the true, Catholic faith. If a ruler failed to do so, he put his subjects' souls into serious danger. His actions, according to Bellarmine, constituted a specific case of extreme necessity in which the papal cure of souls converted into supreme temporal authority. Once his indirect power in temporal matters was activated, the Pope could direct, correct and coerce rulers *ad finem spiritualem*.[98] As a last resort, the Pope could even depose a prince and transfer his title to another ruler.

Mariana, too, is adamant that the Pope has no *potestas directa* over secular rulers.[99] The contention that secular princes owe their authority to the Pope rather than the *populus* is rejected outright and without further discussion as baseless. Yet, unlike his fellow Jesuit theologians, Mariana does not contend that extreme peril to Catholic souls activates a supreme, albeit usually dormant temporal authority the Pope enjoys by virtue of his proper and immediate spiritual authority. Popes can neither coerce nor depose princes. Heretical princes are the responsibility of their subjects. Involving the Pope as a potential agent and defender of the *respublica*, really, is the one thing Mariana is least likely to do.

The author of *De rege* cannot therefore be called a papalist.[100] Nor, on the other hand, do his observations resemble the elaborate theoretical constructs of a Hotman, Languet and Rossaeus or their Catholic counterparts. This is not because Mariana would have lacked courage or intellect. As already discussed, the reasons lie within

96   Most prominently and, perhaps, comprehensively in chapter five of his *Tractatus de potestate summi pontificis in rebus temporalibus: adversus Gulielmum Barclaium*, first published in Rome in 1610. I refer to pp. 62-75 of the 1611 edition of the *Tractatus de potestate*, B. Gualter, Cologne. For a detailed discussion of the development of Bellarmine's doctrine of indirect power see J.C. Murray (1948), 'St. Robert Bellarmine on the Indirect Power', *Theological Studies*, Vol. 9, pp. 491-535; also J. Brodrick (1961), *Robert Bellarmine: Saint and Scholar*, Catholic Book Club, London.

97   See the instructive discussion in Höpfl, *Jesuit Political Thought*, pp. 344-57.

98   *Tractatus de potestate*, p. 65.

99   See, for instance, *De rege*, p. 94.

100 There is no evidence to support P. Springborg's notion that Mariana is 'an ardent supporter of papal absolutism', P. Springborg (1995), 'Thomas Hobbes and Cardinal Bellarmine: Leviathan and the Ghost of the Roman Empire', in *History of Political Thought*, Vol. 16, pp. 503-31, p. 518 fn. 54.

the context and specific objectives of his writing, the genre he chose, and his peculiar distrust of laws and laity as potential guarantors of public order. *De rege*, it is true, does tell the story of Henry's assassination as one of justifiable regicide. It is not, however, a story told to unravel the juridical mechanics of early modern government. The quasi-juridical narrative has a primarily educational objective. Its principal purpose is to shock princes, and Philip III in particular, into realizing that they will lose their power if they squander the trust and respect of the *populus*:

> Many examples, both ancient and modern, are available to demonstrate how great is the strength of a multitude angered with hatred for a ruler, and that the ill-will of the people results in the destruction of a prince. Lately in France a well-known example occurred, from which it may be seen how important it is that the minds of the people be pacified, which are ruled not in the same way as their bodies (...). (...) by this [example] princes are taught that impious attempts by no means go unpunished, and that the power of princes is weak once reverence has departed from the minds of the subjects.[101]

The assassination of Henry III highlights the fact that a people is likely to retain the 'greater power' whatever the particular constitutional arrangements. This does not take anything away from Mariana's distinctly low opinion of the *populus*. He is not talking about a definite and well organized body politic. Mariana remarks that Henry III had every reason to believe that he would continue his reign despite his many crimes. Once provoked into rebellion, 'the multitude is like a torrent that destroys everything in its path'.[102] However, 'it is swollen but for a short time'. Most men are cowards and wish to preserve their lives. Wise men are aware that a violent change of government is likely to bring utter destruction in its wake. There would not be much to this episode, then, were it not for the naïve young monk who resolved to sacrifice his life in order to kill Henry. Mariana does not ignore the fact that there is considerable disagreement about the lawfulness of Jacques Clément's action. Some consider Clément 'an eternal honour to France', others denounce him as a parricide. Whether or not Clément's decision can be justified on doctrinal or moral grounds, however, is not important. What matters is that Henry's assassination serves as a timely reminder to all princes of 'how important it is that the spirits of the people (...) be pacified' and that 'fortune, or a mightier force makes sport of human affairs.'[103]

---

101 *De rege*, p. 65, 'Irritatae multitudinis odio Principis quantae sint vires, populi invidiam rectoris exitium esse, multis exemplis tum antiquis tum recentibus explicare promptum est. Nuperque in Gallia monimentum nobile est constitutum: quo perspicitur quanti referat popularium animos pacatos esse, quibus non perinde ac corporibus imperatur, insigne ad memoriam atque miserabile. Henricus eo nomine tertius Galliae Rex iacet manu monachi peremptus, (...). Faedum spectaculum in paucis memorabile. sed quo Principes doceantur impios ausus haud impune cadere. Principum potentiam imbecillam esse: si reverentia ab animis subditorum semel abscesserit.'

102 Ibid., p. 392.

103 Ibid., p. 69.

This is a lesson from history valid in the face of the intimations of courtiers as well as the sophisticated theories of theologians and lawyers claiming the contrary. Biblical and classical history expose the legitimate prince consistently abusing his power as an anomaly. The tyrant is on a par with 'a beast, wild and monstrous, that (…) lays everything waste, burns, spreads carnage and grief with tooth, nail and horn.'[104] Such a prince has chosen 'to forget that he himself is a man and a member of the commonwealth'.[105] Mariana's tyrant is a 'monster arising from the books of ancient fables', a creature outside the rule and protection of divine, natural and human positive law. The primeval *ius societatis* which bound men from all social orders into a commonwealth in the first place no longer applies to him. The majority of Mariana's assertions are neither particularly novel, nor are they particularly radical in themselves. They merely represent a humanist appraisal of the principle *vim vi repellere*. A people pushed to the brink of destruction has the right to use violent means to protect itself against unnatural violence. Transgression of constitutional limits is merely the prime symptom of all-pervasive human corruption. Such transgressions, however, cannot be comprehended in constitutional terms, and nor can the remedies. Resistance and regicide are exceptional actions against a kind of excessive abuse of power with which a prince places himself outside the realms of positive, perhaps even natural law.

Henry III is an example of a prince who exposed himself to the peril of assassination by persistently violating the rules of political prudence. He is his own victim, hoist with his own petard. Restrained only by his prudence, the powerful prince is always in danger of exposing himself to censure, deposition and, ultimately, assassination should he decline into what his subjects perceive as notorious tyranny of the most excessive kind. Unsurprisingly, Mariana's focal point in his discussion of tyrannicide is the prudential management of the political ambitions and emotions of both prince and people. He believes that:

> it is a salutary reflection that princes have been persuaded that if they oppress the state, if they are unbearable on account of their vices and foulness, their position is such that they can be killed not only justly but with praise and glory. Perhaps this fear will give some pause lest they deliver themselves up to be deeply corrupted by vice and flattery; it will put reins on madness. This is the main point: that the prince should be persuaded that the authority of the commonwealth as a whole is greater than that of one man alone.[106]

The educational rationale of the discussion of regicide in *De rege* is that of a psychological deterrent. What makes a legitimate king a tyrant remains to some extent a subjective decision on the part of the *populus* or the individual subject. Mariana plays on the threat to legitimate rule arising from subjective perception. The prime purpose

---

104 Ibid., p. 74.
105 Ibid., p. 106.
106 Ibid., pp. 77-78.

of the passages on tyranny is to remind readers of the hazards of ruling without the consent of the *populus*, whatever form that consent may take.

Fear, Rewards and the Government of Empire

The stick does not come without a carrot. A prince anxious to fulfil his responsibilities may be able to utilize his subjects' fears and aspirations in turn. One of Mariana's favourite maxims of prudence is that kingdoms and empires are governed by 'hope and fear, reward and punishment'. They in fact represent the only means of exercising effective control over a *populus* or *multitudo* best characterized as a 'wild savage beast' as well as the motley crew of 'base men' making up the majority of the nobility and the prince's courtiers. The prince has to make it his priority to ensure that every single one of his subjects 'fears greater things than he presently suffers'.[107] This broadly 'Machiavellian' sentiment is somewhat toned down in that Mariana criticizes manipulation by 'fear and punishment' alone as generally counter-productive. The fear of punishment 'must always be complemented by the hope of reward'. Like their princes, subjects can always be relied upon to act according to what they perceive as expedient to the furtherance of their private interests. Fear alone will not move them. It is only by carefully administering fear *and* hope that a ruler can hope to 'fetter the wills of men'.

Botero had proclaimed that interest prevails in the minds and courts of princes. Mariana extends this adage to the minds of the *cives* and *subditi*. A bias towards the sole application of fear is particularly unhelpful to the ruler of a composite monarchy like Habsburg Spain. In what might be a slight against Machiavelli, Mariana points out that Romans as well as Spartans eventually lost their empires because they wished to control by fear alone rather than fear tempered by generosity, reward and goodwill.[108] This is a lesson from history that no Spanish Habsburg ruler can afford to ignore.

If the prince decides to rule by hope rather than fear, he will find it much easier to recruit and inspire virtue in his most able subjects. Mariana pleads for the implementation of a principle of strict meritocracy. Whatever their social status, men of virtue 'must never find the door shut to any honour or reward, however elevated these may be'.[109] Philip is to distribute honours and rewards in such a way as to set up a veritable competition for excellence in virtue and service among his subjects. Mariana quickly identifies two powerful groups among Philip III's subjects who have yet to be inspired by hope rather than fear. The first are the non-Castilian nobilities of the *monarquía española*. The second are his Castilian subjects of Jewish or Moorish ancestry, 'who are still today punished for the sins of their fathers'.[110]

---

107 Ibid., p. 394.
108 Ibid., p. 296.
109 Ibid., p. 295.
110 Ibid., p. 300.

Mariana is outspoken about Philip III's dependence upon the nobilities of Aragon, Italy and Flanders.[111] Without the active support and the vast resources of his subjects, Philip cannot hope to preserve and defend his vast empire. The unwavering loyalty of his exhausted and impoverished Castilian subjects will not suffice to sustain the monarchy. Honours and offices must not be distributed according to lineage and wealth alone. The nobility of Philip's non-Castilian dominions have to be stimulated into unceasing self-sacrificial service for the crown. No honour, no reward must be unattainable for outstanding men 'as far as the Spanish empire (*Hispanicum imperium*) extends', and irrespective of whether the candidate 'is a Spaniard, or an Italian, Sicilian or Belgian.'[112] Once the nobilities of Castile and Aragon, Naples and Flanders are united in the service of the king, the *monarchia Hispanica* will be prepared to survive the onslaughts of her many enemies. However, if the king is to depend on the integrated support of the various nobilities, he also has to keep their ambition and greed in check. The best way to accomplish this objective is to goad them with the hope of tangible rewards and the fear of losing the king's favour.

Mariana offers further instances of why fear of his own people should guide the prince, and such that are immediately relevant to the person and the circumstances of Philip III in 1599. He warns that prudence compels a prince to rule personally rather than through a favourite and his family and clients. Philip III is told that he must not rely on a *privado* or any small clique of courtiers. The power of the one or the few deprives the many of the 'hope for rewards of all kind'. Once powerful subjects feel that they cannot expect any more rewards for services rendered and duties fulfilled, once they feel permanently excluded from the arena of power, they will cease to serve the king, start hating him and his favourite, and may finally plot against both. In the light of subsequent developments during the *privanza* of the duke de Lerma, Mariana's comments appear more than apt. The hatred of Lerma in many quarters of the population, however, never led to a decisive challenge to Philip's authority.

The same principle of 'fear and hope, reward and punishment' applies to a specific group of Castilian citizens and nobles. In Chapter four of Book three Mariana focuses on the distribution of 'honours and rewards' as indispensable for the maintenance of peace and the smooth running of monarchical government.[113] Subjects who are consistently denied the 'hope of honour' cannot afford to be loyal to king and commonwealth. This is particularly true of those of Jewish or Moorish origin. Mariana pleads for the impartial implementation of the principle of merit:

> The prince must decide firmly not to allow whole families to be disgraced because of vague rumours among the people. The marks of infamy should not be eternal, and it is necessary to fix a limit beyond which descendants must not pay for the faults of their predecessors, carrying on their brow always the stain that marked these (…).[114]

---

111 See ibid., pp. 292-93, pp. 294-97.

112 Ibid., pp. 294-95.

113 Ibid., III:4, 'De honoribus & praemiis in commune' ('On honours and rewards in general'), pp. 292-301.

114 Ibid., p. 295.

To act differently and not apply the maxim of 'hope and fear, reward and punishment' as widely and inclusively as possible means to drive the commonwealth into civil war:

> Can one believe that it does no harm for the commonwealth to be split into factions, always harassed by the unbelievable hatred of the majority of its citizens, hatred from which at the very first opportunity civil war and discord must arise? One could possibly run no risk in depriving of all honours those who bear this stain, if they were few in number. But today, when the blood of all degrees in the commonwealth is confused and mixed, it would be highly dangerous, since we have in our country all those who are excluded from public office, not for their own fault, but for that of their forefathers.[115]

'New men of obscure and tainted ancestry' should be able to achieve the highest offices according to their individual virtue and merit. He 'who once seemed a *homo novus*, of obscure and blemished ancestry, will by merit of service (...) inevitably attain noble status and establish his own lineage.'[116] The 'New Christians', Mariana urges, are more than ripe for acceptance as 'Old Christians'. Failure to integrate this 'numerous' and 'powerful' group, on the other hand, means pushing the monarchy towards civil war.

Mariana's observations reflect the increasingly bitter struggle within the Society of Jesus after the General Congregation of 1593 accepted the doctrine of purity of blood (*limpieza de sangre*), and issued a decree excluding descendants of *moriscos and conversos* from entering the Society. The conflict seems to have escalated not least because the superior general, Claudio Aquaviva used *limpieza de sangre* to exclude members of the Society stubbornly opposed to the generalate of a non-Spaniard as 'false sons of Christ'. When the decree was finally revoked in February 1608, Mariana could congratulate himself on having contributed to the campaign against the imposition of *limpieza* directed, prominently, by his friend Pedro de Ribadeneira.[117]

Mariana's discussion also reflects developments in Spain during the last year of Philip II's reign. The king, for most of his life a strong supporter of the statutes of 'purity of blood', ordered a *junta* of theologians to discuss this matter. He agreed with the theologian's conclusion that the statutes should be limited to a 'hundred years of Christianity'. This decision meant that the absence of heresy in one's family would need to be demonstrated only for three generations past. Philip's imminent death, however, prevented the proposed reform from being undertaken. *De rege* urges Philip III to execute his father's decision.

---

115 Ibid., p. 300.

116 Ibid., pp. 300-301.

117 See H. Kamen (1993), 'A Crisis of Conscience in Golden Age Spain: The Inquisition against *Limpieza de Sangre*', in *Crisis and Change in Early Modern Spain* (Variorum Collected Studies Series; CS 415), Ashgate, Aldershot, VII, pp. 1-29 [rev. English version of (1986), 'Una crisis de conciencia en la Edad de Oro en Espana: Inquisicion contra *Limpieza de Sangre*', *Bulletin Hispanique*, Vol. 88, pp. 321-56]; and also J.A. Munitiz (2004), 'Francisco Suárez and the Exclusion of Men of Jewish or Moorish Descent from the Society of Jesus', *Archivum Historicum Societas Iesu*, Vol. 73, pp. 327-40.

Like his appeal for the integration of the nobility, Mariana's argument on the *limpieza de sangre* statutes is cast entirely in terms of reasons of state, untainted by equally current theological doctrine condemning the exclusion of the New Christians. Mariana concisely expresses the *prudential* rationale behind the campaign of the enemies of the statutes. To his mind, the principal consideration appears to be that the statutes threaten to marginalize important groups without whose active support the monarchy will not survive. Identical sentiments are found in Ribadeneira as well as the relevant writings of the Dominican Agustín Salucio.[118] Mateo López Bravo, a magistrate of the city of Madrid, incorporated the relevant passages of *De rege* in his own treatise titled *De rege* (Madrid, 1616), warning that the exclusion of *conversos* from political and social advancement would estrange a significant and powerful part of the population of Castile.[119] In Mariana's *De rege* the discussion on *limpieza de sangre* is made part of the overarching argument on 'fear and hope, reward and punishment' as a principle of integrating the various power blocs within the Spanish monarchy. The fact that no prince can afford to alienate important sections of the population, that he has to 'embrace virtue and industry wherever it will be found' is directly applied to the situation of a monarch ruling over an agglomerate of territories with diverse political and cultural identities and traditions.[120]

The Moderate Prince

Mariana further develops his vocabulary, making political counsel based to a large degree on the traduction of legal into prudential maxims both more comprehensible and more appealing to readers. The reasons why a prince ought not to think of himself as 'above the law' are cast in terms that seem to fuse Christian virtue with pragmatic management of the emotions, the fears and hopes of his subjects. Virtue as the measure of both legitimacy and political aptitude in a prince is encapsulated in a set of complementary terms: *moderatio, modestia* and *mediocritas*. Each a complex term in its own right, their meaning overlaps, and *moderatio* tends to absorb the meaning of its counterparts. Together they provide the most succinct

---

118 Ribadeneira, *Tratado*, p. 245; See Agustín Salucio (1975), *Discurso sobre los estatutos de limpieza de sangre*, ed. A. Pérez Gómez, El Ayre de la Almena, Cieza [facs. of the original edition (1599), n.p., Madrid], 6v-7. See I.S. Révah (1971), 'La controverse sur les statuts de pureté de sang: un document inédit. "Relación y consulta del Cardenal Guevara sobre el negocio de Fray Agustín Saluzio" (Madrid, 13 aout 1600)', *Bulletin Hispanique*, Vol. 73, pp. 263-316.

119 Mateo López Bravo (1616), *De rege, et regendi ratione libri duo*, n.p., Madrid, pp. 3-7, pp. 145-55.

120 *De rege*, p. 295. On Spain as a 'composite monarchy', see J.H. Elliott (1982), 'Spain and its Empire in the Sixteenth and Seventeenth Centuries', in D.B. Quinn (ed.), *Early Maryland in a WiderWorld*, Wayne State University Press, Detroit, pp. 58-83 [now reprinted in J.H. Elliott (1989), *Spain and its World, 1500-1700, Selected Essays*, Yale University Press, New Haven and London, pp. 7-26].

explanation of why a prince *ought to think of himself* as 'bound by the law'. *Modestia* is best translated as a carefully and constantly controlled appearance and manner. It denotes the self-restraint distinguishing the accomplished individual, especially the courtier, including the ability to do and say the right thing at the right time. *Moderatio* and *mediocritas* stress self-discipline in thought and action, that is virtue in the Aristotelian sense of choosing the mean between two extremes. The prince, Mariana suggests, will want to appear below rather than above the law because 'nothing indeed strengthens regal power more than *moderatio* (…).'[121] In doing so, he exploits and reiterates a line of argument widely disseminated throughout Europe, for instance in the works of Justus Lipsius.

Indeed, the introductory passage of Book one, Chapter nine of *De rege* reads like a paraphrase of Justus Lipsius's *Politicorum*, II, 15.[122] Like Lipsius, Mariana supports the notion of virtue as a political affect. Virtues are presented as emotions both appropriate and useful in a prince.[123] The ruler who conducts himself virtuously will incite complementary behaviour in his subjects. In all his actions and decisions, the prince must aspire to raise positive emotions in those upon whom his rule depends. In doing so, the prince displays the kind of self-restraint in the exercise of the royal prerogative that people commonly associate with legitimate rule. Subjects generally perceive monarchical government as legitimate only if it is government conducting itself 'within the bounds of *modestia* and *mediocritas*.'[124] Only power that visibly and manifestly restrains itself will be perceived as legitimate, and therefore count as real power. Enacting the virtues of *modestia* and *mediocritas*, the prince will not only confirm his personal probity and the legitimacy of his rule, he will also reap tangible benefits.[125]

Like Lipsius, again, Mariana grasps the moral force of *moderatio*, *modestia* and *mediocritas* in the complementary terms of authority (*auctoritas*) and benevolence

---

121 Ibid., p. 100, 'Nihil enim regias opes magis confirmat quam modestia: si fixum fuerit animo atque intimis medullis impressum, ita Principes imperare ut serviant, consiliorum et vitae posituri rationem, primum Deo, cuius nutu sola terrarum gubernantur, imperia stabiliuntur caduntque.'

122 Justus Lipsius (1589), *Politicorum sive civilis doctrinae libri sex*, Plantin, Leiden.

123 Lipsius, *Politicorum*, IV, 8, p. 127, 'Laudabilem utilemque imperio affectum, de rege, vel in regem.'

124 *De rege*, pp. 94-95, 'Qui tum demum regius est, si intra modestiae & mediocritatis fines se contineat: excessu potestatis, quam imprudentes indies augere satagunt, minuitur penitusque corrumpitur. Nos stulti maiores potentiae specie decepti dilabimur in contrarium, non satis considerantes eam demum tutam esse potentiam, quae viribus modum imponit. Neque enim ut in divitiis, quo amplius augentur, eo locupletiores cuadimus, ita in regio principatu contingit, sed contrarium. cum Princeps volentibus debeat imperare, civium benevolentiam colligere, eorum commodis serivire: imperio exacerbato & Regis benevolentiam exuet, & potestatem imbecillitate mutabit.'

125 Ibid., p. 100.

(*benevolentia*).[126] Both originate in the conduct of the ruler, but have their seats in the 'heart and mind of the people'. *Auctoritas* is defined as the reverence and reputation a king enjoys among his subjects. *Benevolentia* is understood as its direct result, namely subjects' emotional attachment to the person of the ruler and a generally supportive attitude towards his endeavours. Philip III is assured that, should he choose to follow the precepts expounded in *De rege*, he will be able to rely on receiving material support, military service and individual self-sacrifice far beyond anything the laws of Castile, or those of any other kingdom can ever afford him. It is the willingness of a people to support their king that, in the end, will decide the outcome of his most ambitious and risky adventures. A king of Castile is much more likely to succeed in his many undertakings if he publicly acknowledges that his subjects' enthusiasm to sacrifice their lives and goods on his behalf represents the true measure of his power and authority.[127] If Philip orders 'his life so that he permits neither himself nor anyone else to be mightier than the laws,'[128] he will invariably 'inspire men to serve him and defend his honour with their lives as they would defend their wives and children' and 'to assist him from public and private funds'.[129]

Mariana does not fail to weave the tricky topic of taxation into this discourse on prudent mobilization of human affection. The prudent urge to preserve and increase the good-will of his people will induce a prudent king to 'build up the public treasury without the groaning of the people', or so he claims.[130] Philip III, if he chooses to listen to the voice of prudence:

> will not impose heavy and unusual taxes on the people. And should adverse circumstances or a war forced upon him at some point coerce him to do so, he will do so with their consent. He will abstain from intimidation and threats, nor employ fraud (what kind of consent, indeed, would that be?), but use sound argument to convince them of the imminent peril, the necessity of war, and the weak treasury.'[131]

---

126 See ibid., IV.8, p. 127, 'Studiose sic discrimino. Nam duplex eiusmodi Virtus sit, Benevolentia & Auctoritas: nasci quidem utraque a rege & per regem debet, sed sedem tamen suam & domicilium in animis Populi habet. Atque illa, in regem Affectus est; haec Opinio de rege. (…) Nam benevolentia, quam hic quaero & suadeo, est subditorum in regem eius que statum prompta inclinatio et amor.' See also pp. 57-58, p. 60, pp. 100-103. Neither Lipsius nor Mariana discuss *benevolentia, amor* and *lenitas* in terms of Christian love.

127 Ibid., p. 93, 'Postremo, (…), Principis malo coercendi potestatem in republica residere (…) (: si vitiis & improbitate infectus sit, ignoransque verum iter gloriae, metui a civibus quam amari malit: metumque paventibus & periculis imperare, iniuriam facere pergat factus tyrannus.'

128 Ibid., p. 101. See also p. 106.

129 Ibid., p. 57-58.

130 See ibid., pp. 58-60.

131 Ibid., pp. 58-59, 'Ergo neque vectigalia magna & insolita imperare populis opus habebit. Et si quando res adversae, aut bellum illatum coget, eorum consensu ut opus est faciet. Quem neque terroribus neque minis exprimet, ne fraude quidem suorum (qualis enim consensus is esset?) sed explicatione periculi, bellique, instantis, aerarii extenuati.'

History, above all the history of medieval Castile, Mariana claims, clearly proves that a king will not be able to levy taxes against the will of the people in any case.

This is where the author of *De rege* enters his own humanist NeverNeverland populated by hero-kings of the *reconquista* and consuls of the early Roman republic winning wars and building the foundations of empire 'with slender taxes'.[132] Either blissfully oblivious or deliberately ignorant of the realities of governmental finance, he praises the Roman consul Lucius Aemilius Paulus and king Henry III of Castile for waging wars without raising taxes. Aemilius Paulus deposited the enormous booty from the Macedonian War in the *publicum aerarium*, ending the need to raise taxes from the *populus Romanus* once and for all.[133] Henry is celebrated as a king who acted according to the maxim that 'the only true resources are those which are made available inoffensively and without causing complaint.'[134] It is in brief discussions of matters of taxation and military organisation that the author of *De rege* frequently displays a wilful indifference to the reality of early modern statehood. His deliberations on the prudence and interest of the prince are shot through with snippets of humanist wisdom gratuitously and injudiciously applied to a Spanish government under constant pressure to adapt inherited fiscal and military systems to a state of constant global war. Mariana is by no means unique in this respect. We find a similar mix of wishful thinking and plain ignorance in Machiavelli. Like the Florentine, Mariana, cannot at times but retreat from the disappointing reality of politics into the realm of visions of a Golden Age of (in Mariana's case feudal) statehood. *De rege* is the work of a humanist historian prone to idolizing Roman consuls as well as medieval kings of Castile. Usually, Mariana is adamant that primeval monarchy is irretrievably lost to 'time and the wickedness of men'. In instances like these, his vision of ideal kingship infiltrates his presentation of contemporary political reality. The result is practical reasoning at its most impractical, highlighting the frequently limited nature of seemingly pragmatic and 'modern' conceptualizations of the political in early modern Europe.

Mariana is in no doubts as to how a ruler is brought to appreciate the benefits arising from exercising *moderatio*, *modestia* and *mediocritas*. His tutors and advisers will instruct him 'from an early age' to think of himself as being 'bound by the laws more than those who obey him'.[135] The ultimate goal of the education of the prince, and, indeed, of *De rege* as a whole is to bring up a prince who is 'persuaded that the sacrosanct laws, by which the public weal is maintained, will be stable only if ratified by his own example.'[136] Mariana adduces examples primarily from ancient history to illustrate that the prince must at all costs demonstrate his respect for the laws in order to secure his power. They can be ranked among the most excessive manifestations of virtue.

---

132 Ibid., p. 59.

133 Ibid., [Aemilius L. Paulus (consul 196 BC); Polybius, *Histories*, XVIII, 35; XXXI, 22].

134 Ibid.

135 Ibid., p. 107.

136 Ibid., p. 101, 'Postremo sit Principi persuasum, leges sacrosanctas, quibus publica salus stat, tum demum fore stabiles, si suo ipse eas exemplo sanciat.'

Punishing himself for a crime committed by his deviant son, the mythical lawgiver Zaleucus of Locri deprived himself of his eyesight. Zaleucus mutilated himself rather than his son, who reckoned he would escape punishment because of the rank and esteem in which his father was held. He did so against the express will of his people.[137] Another example of virtuous self-sacrifice is Charondas of Tyre, who threw himself on his sword when he realized that he had accidentally violated his own decree that no one on pain of death must bring arms to the popular assembly.[138] Again, his people did not want to see this law executed against a man who had clearly acted without any ill intent. Charondas took his life nonetheless, making sure, by means of his example, that the laws enjoyed a respect that far transcended the coercive powers available to government. Zaleucus and Charondas maimed and killed themselves not because laws had the power or people had the will to force them to do so, but because they were determined to exemplify the respect for the law required in ruler and citizen alike.[139]

Philip III, however, is hardly expected to emulate these examples. They embody the kind of practice of virtue which lesser mortals, even powerful kings, may never expect to emulate or surpass in their actions. This is one of many examples of Mariana's use of humanist teaching techniques, hoping to instil awe in García de Loaysa's pupil. Imbued with the examples of Zaleucus and Charondas, Philip III will show 'the same obedience to the laws that he exacts from his subjects (…)'.[140] The prince will also 'love the customs and institutions of his fatherland', ignore 'foreign and unusual rites' and 'enjoy the ancestral religion, costume and tongues.' Discussing strategies apt to ensure respect of the law, Mariana briefly mentions the Athenian practice of ostracism. The ancient Athenians routinely exiled renowned members of the *respublica* whose power they considered potentially disruptive to public peace. The Athenian polity is criticized for failing to see the benefits of early education. The citizens of Athens would have done better 'to accustom [their leaders] from an early age to live under the law on a level with others' and to imbue them with an awareness that the members of the commonwealth depend on one another.[141]

Laws, or practices of restraint and limitation are futile, unless they are backed up by a shrewdly devised educational programme that is implemented at an *early* stage. Humanist literatures, and the Roman historians of the late Republic and early Principate in particular are the guarantors of the peace and well-being of the commonwealth. The whole educational process is focused on what history suggests

---

137 Ibid., p. 102 [Valerius Maximus, *Memorable Doings and Sayings*, VI, 5, 3]

138 Ibid., p. 102 [Diodor, *The Library of History*, XII, 19].

139 Ibid., pp. 102-103.

140 Ibid., p. 103, '(…) Princeps, omnibus praestet probitas & modestiae specimen: et quam a subditis obedientiam exigit, legibus ipse exhibeat: patriae mores amet & instituta: haudquaquam in externos ritus & insolentes degeneret. Patrio cultu, vestituque & vocibus delectetur. (…) Neque sibi licere quidquam putet, quod si populares imitarentur, legum & patriae consequeretur interitus.'

141 Ibid., pp. 105-106.

a ruler *should* and *ought* to do. At this point in the argument of the treatise, readers will already have realized that the clerical preceptor steeped in humanist literatures has taken the place of cortes, nobles and magistrates. This emphasis on education and indoctrination allows Mariana to take tentative steps towards reconciliation with those who consider royal power 'above the law'.

Invoking the authority of Saint Thomas Aquinas, Mariana concedes that there exists a *duplex vis* or double force of directing and coercing those who do not obey the laws.[142] With regard to the prince, 'all the philosophers' agree that

> although the double force of ordering and coercing the disobedient exists, they subject the prince to the law only from the first of these, that is, by precept. Making it a matter for his conscience if he forsakes his obligation under the law. They claim that other people are subject to the law under both its aspects. This reasoning appeals to me.[143]

On the final pages of Book one, then, Mariana finally clarifies the meaning of his frequent and sometimes impassioned claims that the 'prince is not free from the law'. He accepts that different standards of moral obligation apply to *princeps* and *subditus* respectively. Like the vast majority of contemporary theologians, he adopts Saint Thomas Aquinas's distinction between *vis directiva* and *vis coactiva*.[144] The prince is guided by the law (*vis directiva*) rather than compelled to abide by it (*vis coactiva*). Domingo de Soto, for instance, states that the prince cannot be subject to the coercive force of laws since 'it is inconceivable that any force is constrained by itself.'[145] Like any other Jesuit, Mariana is loath to provide legal pretexts for challenges to royal power. At the same time, he is much more openly distrustful of the directive force of the law. He doubts that it will ever suffice to prevent a prince from abusing his rank. Mariana therefore blurs the distinction between the two forces. 'Directive' laws are transformed into more compelling precepts of reason of state. Prudence instructs the prince on why it is expedient to act as if he indeed was 'under the law'. Once fully integrated into a discourse on political prudence, laws gain a 'coercive force' they did not previously possess, or did not possess to the extent they do now. As will be discussed below, this coercive force is not rooted in and exercised by the conventional constitutional agents (cortes or magistrates), at least not primarily.

Mariana's explanations concerning the distinction between directive and coercive force complement his interpretation of the *lex regia*. The civilians' quandary concerning the absolute power of the prince is resolved by re-interpreting jurisprudential matters as issues of education in reason of state. His overwhelming concern is how best to instruct a young prince on establishing and maintaining the flexible, though invariably precarious balance of power between himself and his

---

142 Ibid., pp. 106-107.

143 Ibid., p. 106.

144 *ST*, 1a 2ae, Qu. 96, art. 5. Aquinas himself is inspired by the *lex digna vox*; see Kantorowicz, *King's Two Bodies*, p. 136.

145 Domingo de Soto, *De iustitia et iure libri decem*, C. Pesnot, Lyon, 1.6.7.

people. There is no better way to emphasize what lessons ought to be learned from history than investigating the question of 'whether it is right to destroy a tyrant'.

Conclusion

The way in which Mariana resolves the quandary of one who insists that power ought to be limited and absolute at the same time is bold, though not in a sense that would justify labelling him a scholastic or humanist precursor of modern constitutionalism. A humanist historian and moralist, not a lawyer, he does not aspire to develop the correlation *maior singulis*, *minor universis* and related legal *dicta* into cornerstones of a constitutional theory that is scholastic in its origins but modified for the age of confessionalism. He does not discuss the issue of limitation and resistance in straightforwardly juridical terms of superior jurisdiction on the part of either princes or peoples. The emphasis is firmly on what he considers the virtues of a prince and the principles of good government. The languages of law are ever present in *De rege*. However, they are made to help establish an ultimately non-juridical understanding of princely power.

In fact, legal terminology is demoted to the status of raw material for a set of doctrines of political prudence. Political prudence nourished on historical experience demands the conversion of legal issues and languages into a language of political prudence. This use or abuse of juridical terms and notions rather betrays his intention of advancing a political language which not only mixes legal and non-legal languages, but aims at absorbing juridical understanding of the nature and exercise of political power into one rooted in prudence. The idea of the contingent nature of human social and political life had always informed the theory and use of commonplaces. Now, it affects the epistemic status of law. Law is removed from discourses of natural law aiming at 'absolute' truth. In the case of *De rege*, it has become a way of reasoning best suited to accommodate a faltering sense of political and epistemological certainty.

The transformation of scholastic legal concepts into *monita* and *sententiae* always bearing the hallmarks of a dark Tacitist vision of political life is one of the main objectives, and one of the most striking features of the political language of Juan de Mariana. Governance as a whole is treated exclusively as a matter of princely prudence. Yet once scholastic reasoning and jurisprudence are absorbed into a carefully arranged humanist mode of speech, they promote a dynamic view of government. The prince is strongly encouraged to think of his office as a continual exercise in sustaining and expanding the legitimacy of his rule. Juridical tenets converted into maxims of prudence fit Mariana's objective of providing a comprehensive and coherent political manual for the ruler of a composite monarchy. If Book one of *De rege* has made a start by translating constitutional doctrine proper into maxims of reason of state, the second and third book go on to differentiate, interweave and add to his set of guiding principles of statecraft. Issues as diverse as the limits of royal power, the selection of bishops and magistrates, the use of deceit in politics and the question of religious unity are made to revolve around the personality and education of the prince.

CHAPTER FOUR

Prudence, History and Providence

Many early modern writers of political treatises raise questions about the compatibility of prudence or reason of state with moral, religious and juridical norms. Mariana is exceptional in that he examines constitutional doctrine primarily as a matter of practical reasoning on the part of the prince. The translation of legal into prudential maxims is the result of Mariana's refusal to rely on king, cortes and nobility of Castile as guarantors of peace and stability. Probably the fiercest critic of the institution of monarchy within the Society of Jesus, he can also be ranked among the most 'absolutist' Jesuit thinkers. Inspired by his deeply pessimistic stance on human nature, he continues to temper support for 'absolute monarchy' with expressions of doubt concerning the ability of monarchs to fulfil their duties. This polarity underlies whatever he has got to say about the conduct and ethical norms of government in Books two and three of his treatise. It is borne out in the first instance by his observations on *prudentia* as the cognitive and moral facility early modern thinkers generally considered indispensable in a prince.

The Virtue of Prudence

Mariana offers a detailed discussion of the concept of *prudentia* as such only in Chapter fourteen of Book three of his treatise.[1] Despite the importance he clearly attributes to prudence in the sense of practical reasoning that allows for shrewd and balanced assessment of human affairs, the actual term *prudentia*, therefore, does not at first appear as prominent in *De rege* as in other authors of the period. Justus Lipsius dedicates several chapters of his *Politicorum* to *prudentia*, and Pedro de Ribadeneira's *Tratado* can for the most part be read as a somewhat flawed attempt both to differentiate 'false' from 'true' reason of state and to equate prudence with the latter.[2] It is nonetheless safe to subsume everything Mariana says about the actions of princes and the government of monarchies under 'counsels of prudence'. Like Botero's *Della ragion di stato*, the treatise as a whole is concerned with the dispensation of practical advice and its judicious application to varied and

---

1   *De rege*, iii.14, *De prudentia* ('On prudence'), pp. 387-406; see also iii.16, *Multas in una provincia esse religiones non est verum* ('It is ill-advised to have many religions in one province'), pp. 420-46.

2   Lipsius, *Politicorum*, e.g. i, 7 and 8; iv, 1-3. Ribadeneira dedicates chapters 23 to 33 of the *Tratado* to the discussion of the *prudencia* required in the prince and his counsellors. On Ribadeneira's political thought see R. Bireley (1990), *The Counter-Reformation Prince, Anti-Machiavellianism or Catholic Statecraft in Early Modern Europe*, The University of North Carolina Press, Chapel Hill and London, chapter five, pp. 111-35, and Truman, *Spanish Treatises*, chapter thirteen, pp. 277-314.

changing circumstances.[3] By the time Mariana arrives at his discussion of *prudentia*, he has already given his readers plenty of opportunity to ponder on the meaning and practice of prudent government. Laws and the rule of law themselves are treated as a matter of practical reasoning. For instance, Mariana has explained why a ruler is to assume that he is below the law and act accordingly, even if the laws themselves and the institutions protecting them neither merit such respect nor are powerful enough to enforce compliance. The prince has been told that he should act in like manner not only to avoid suffering the inevitable fate of the tyrant, but because he will want to inspire his subjects' loyalty and with their help 'accomplish great deeds'. It is *prudentia* that enables the prince to pursue objectives much more ambitious than 'a depleted treasury and slender revenues would commonly allow'. Chapter fourteen takes up this thread of argument, starting out by suggesting that *prudentia* makes the prince aware of the actual limits of his power, personal wisdom and experience, and compels him to seek the counsel of other 'prudent men' throughout his reign.[4] Showing respect for his subjects' laws and customs, offering rewards and shrewdly taking advantage of their sense of honour and thirst for glory, the prince will achieve his goals without burdening and alienating his people with new and ever higher taxes. A sometimes agitated, but mostly pragmatic evaluation of the demands of empire and the machinations of princes and courtiers, the chapter on *prudentia* primarily serves to assert the pivotal role of political prudence as the only obstacle standing between the prince and the destruction he is always likely to bring upon himself and his people. Chapter fourteen also confirms that prudence is the sole intermediary a people can reasonably rely upon when it comes to defending constitutional limits. Prudence operates in the one place where legal, moral and religious boundaries can be implemented and enforced without the immediate risk of tearing the commonwealth apart: the mind of the prince.

Prudence had always stood for a competence in handling affairs that demanded more than the mere knowledge of (theoretical) principles. It had to be learned over a long period of time and be constantly nurtured and honed by practice and experience.[5] The term *prudentia* itself was a Ciceronian translation of Aristotle's *phronesis* or 'practical wisdom'. Aristotle's understanding of *phronesis* had already included the capability of acting and varying one's behaviour for one's own good or one's own preservation.[6] Unsurprisingly, prudence tended to be equated with the much more ambiguous term 'reason of state' (*ragion di stato*/*Staatsräson*/*razón de estado*).[7] A sixteenth-century Italian coinage that had quickly established itself in

---

3   A succint analysis of Botero's take on reason of state is available in Höpfl, *Jesuit Political Thought*, pp. 90-97.

4   *De rege*, pp. 388-89.

5   For instance, Francisco Suárez (1626), *Tractatus de religione Societatis Jesu*, in ibid. (1857), *Opera omnia*, ed. C. Berton, Vol. 16, L. Vivès, Paris, p. 1064, 'diuturnam experientiam, quae ad prudentem gubernationem maxime necessaria est, et brevi tempore acquiri non potest.'

6   Aristotle, *Metaphysics*, 960b.

7   On the meanings and uses of the term see P. Burke (1991), 'Tacitism, Scepticism, and Reason of State', in *CHPTh*, pp. 479-98; see also the helpful discussions in H. Münkler (1987), *Im*

the councils of princes, reason of state could simply refer to the practical ways in which princes conducted their business and the reasons which guided them when doing so. Already by the time Botero used it as a book title (1589), however, reason of state had become a synonym for everything associated with 'the perverse and diabolical doctrine of (…) the disciples of Machiavelli'.[8] It was frequently taken to denote the pursuit of power, wealth and glory without any regard whatsoever for legal, and especially traditional Christian moral or religious constraints. Machiavelli's many detractors regarded the fact that he had not been able even to conceive of the possibility that a prince might be truly pious as further confirmation of his wicked designs on Christianity. Though 'Machiavellianism' as a political concept or philosophical doctrine largely originated in the imagination of those who sought to establish or maintain the primacy of (true) religion in the courts and councils of princes, authors offering practical advice on 'matters of state' had to anticipate and respond to the suspicion attached to the use of the terms prudence and reason of state.[9] Jesuits particularly confident of the flexibility of moral theology were always in danger of being denounced as Machiavelli's paladins by their many enemies.

Catholic theologians and rhetoricians generally meant to think of *prudentia* as Christian or moral *virtus* in the sense of a virtue concerning itself only with what is 'truly good' for man as well as the rightful means to attain such 'good'. Though a virtue of the intellect rather than a moral virtue in the strict sense (unlike, for instance, 'justice'), it was the faculty of reason that had to make sure that the will and the passions were directed towards what is 'good', that 'good' also being understood in the sense of what is morally right (often denoted as *honestum*). That rules of moral conduct had to be handled flexibly and adapted to circumstances was generally acknowledged. Even the most conservative Catholic theologians accepted that the application of laws or moral norms had to be screened by equity (*aequitas*), so as to ensure that rules employed from the desire to live rightly did not yield ultimately counter-productive or perverse results. Reason of state, of course, exacerbated this problem, introducing a radical distinction between what circumstances or necessity demanded, and what the ordinary rules of law as well as Christian religion and

---

Namen des Staates: Die Begründung der Staatsraison in der Frühen Neuzeit, S. Fischer Verlag, Frankfurt, pp. 165-207, pp. 261-98, especially pp. 193-207, and H. Höpfl (2002), 'Orthodoxy and Reason of State', *History of Political Thought*, Vol. 23, pp. 211-37.

8   The term 'politician' (*politicus, politique*) suffered a very similar fate, see N. Rubinstein (1987), 'The History of the Word *politicus* in Early-Modern Europe', in A. Pagden (ed.), *The Languages of Political Theory in Early-Modern Europe*, Cambridge University Press, Cambridge, pp. 41-56.

9   Höpfl, *Jesuit Political Thought*, pp. 85-86, quite rightly points out that the vilification of political opponents as 'Machiavellians' frequently amounted to 'no more than employing the old stereotype of the scheming, fawning, duplicitous courtier, but giving it a more fashionable label.' One of the ablest architects of 'Machiavellianism' was Innocent Gentillet (1576), *Discours, sur les moyens de bien gouverner et maintenir en bonne paix un royaume ou autre principauté*, J. Stoer, Geneva. On the invention of the 'evil Machiavel' see, for instance, P. Donaldson (1988), *Machiavelli and Mystery of State*, Cambridge University Press, Cambridge; and T.F. Mayer (2000), *Reginald Pole, Prince and Prophet*, Cambridge University Press, Cambridge, especially pp. 78-90.

morality seemed to prescribe. Machiavelli's notion of *virtù* clearly suggested that virtue ought to be understood as the intellectual ability to define the means and ends of political conduct disregarding the values stipulated by traditional Christian political ethics.[10] In other words, reason of state threatened to divorce political ethics from Christian morality. Catholic moral theology in turn had to come clean about the exact boundary between the insinuations of the 'Machiavellians' and the sound methods and eminently practicable precepts of Christian political ethics. As reason of state was by and large equated with prudence, it became necessary to reconsider what the latter actually meant. What kind of knowledge of the ends and means of moral action did prudence make available, and did the way in which it enacted such knowledge make it a moral virtue?

This much was clear: if prudent action was to be action that was morally sound and certain, it had to result from the individual's *habitus* or profound moral disposition or desire to act justly and rightly in a Christian sense. The crux was that prudence simply could not be held to provide knowledge that enjoined anything like the epistemological certitude of first principles and necessary deductions discussed in speculative theology. Prudence extracted invariably vague principles from ephemeral, contingent and particular matters through sense, experience and memory. There was no moral certainty to be had concerning the nature and use of principles of political conduct.

Aristotle considered *phronesis* a 'rational disposition towards action' which was 'concerned with human things'. He also called it a virtue (*arete*) and delimited it against both *techne* (commonly translated into Latin as *ars*: for Aristotle the capacity to make something and the reason for making it in a particular way) and *sophia* (commonly equated with *scientia*: the kind of knowledge that was universal and unchangeable).[11] He then went on to separate theory or the highest kind of knowledge (*sophia*) from practical wisdom (*phronesis*).[12] Both also represent a very different kind of practice, the former being much superior to the latter: the practice of *sophia* is the only way to achieve the perfect human life (*eudaimonia*). Aristotle even goes so far as to attribute *phronesis* to the lower kind of animals.[13] Aristotle, in other words, separated the pursuit of the highest and 'truest' form of knowledge from practical

---

10   On Machiavelli's notion of virtue (*virtù*) see M. Viroli (1998), *Machiavelli* (Founders of Modern Political and Social Thought), Oxford University Press, Oxford, pp. 86-87, pp. 91-95; and E. Garver (1987), *Machiavelli and the History of Prudence*, University of Wisconsin Press, Madison.

11   For Aristotle, the capacity of reasoning terminating in a kind of product (*techne*) had to be distinguished from the capacity of reasoning that lead to an individual acting in a particular way within the *polis*. The latter form of reasoning leaves no 'product' in the strict sense. The outcome lies in the action itself. For Aristotle's differentiation of *phronesis*, *techne* and virtuous behaviour, see the very helpful discussion in J. Dunne (1993), *Back to the Rough Ground: 'Phronesis' and 'Techne' in Modern Philosophy and in Aristotle*, University of Notre Dame Press, Notre Dame and London, chapter eight, pp. 237-74, especially pp. 237-49.

12   *NE*, 10.7 and 10.8.

13   *NE*, 6.7. I follow Dunne, *Back to the Rough Ground*, pp. 241-42, in accepting that Aristotle did place a higher value on the exercise of the theoretical faculty than on *phronesis*.

involvement in the *polis*.[14] He thus left his scholastic counterparts with one of his most notorious and lasting conundrums. How to ensure that the contemplation of the 'other life' (*sophia*) exercised authoritative influence on the ethical framework within which practical reasoning and social and political interaction took place (the remit of *phronesis*)?

Saint Thomas Aquinas (the Jesuits' as well as Mariana's prime authority on theological matters) offers a composite understanding of prudence that effectively ignores Aristotle's demand to differentiate between prudence on the one hand, *ars* and *scientia* on the other. Aquinas conceived of prudence as intuitive knowledge of first principles, practical judgement and moral action. In doing so, his emphasis seems to have been on the 'practical side', that is, on prudence as a knowledge of how to apply principles of conduct rather than knowledge of those principles themselves.[15] Scholastic theologians laboured to resolve the quandary they believed they had inherited from Aquinas (or, ultimately, from Aristotle). They saw it as their remit to clarify the cognitive status of *phronesis/prudentia* by explaining both how knowledge drawn from contingent sources (senses, memory, experience) could render anything close to certain knowledge (*scientia*) immediately associated with the godly life, and how it could come to be considered a *moral* virtue at all.[16] If they wanted to arrive at a theologically and ethically satisfying definition of prudence, Catholic theologians not only had to allow prudence access to the kind of knowledge normally reserved for *scientia*. As indicated above, they also had to go through the trouble of delineating prudence as a *moral* virtue from the kind of *virtù* Machiavelli clearly had in mind.[17]

In fact, Catholic theologians never managed to arrive at a satisfactory agreement on the cognitive status of prudence that would have clearly delineated it against the reason of state of the Machiavellians. Some Catholic authors therefore decided to denounce immoral means straightforwardly. Among the members of the Society of Jesus concerning themselves with matters of reason of state, Francisco Suárez and cardinal Bellarmine expressed most clearly and methodically the conviction that immoral means apparently dictated by circumstances or necessity could never be conducive to the good of either the individual or society.[18] This, however, was

---

14   Aristotle, *NE*, 6, however, had also decreed that *phronesis* was needed to maintain a community in which the pursuit of *sophia* will be possible and fruitful.

15   Höpfl, *Jesuit Political Thought*, pp. 169-70.

16   I do not have the space to explore scholastic interpretations of Aquinas's epistemic terminology in the context of the early modern debate of reason of state. For a succinct introduction to the issues driving scholastic discussion of 'means' and 'ends' as well as the interpretative attempts to settle the relationship between *prudentia*, *ars* and *scientia* see Höpfl, *Jesuit Political Thought*, pp. 167-76. For a broader discussion of the complex ways in which scholastic theologians sought to clarify the relationship between human reason and principles of moral action see R. Schüssler (2002), *Moral im Zweifel*, Vol. 1, Mentis Verlag, Paderborn.

17   Incidentally, the Aristotelian term *arete* itself was part of the problem; it signified to be good at or for something rather than a *virtus* in the Christian sense.

18   Suárez, *De legibus*, III, xii, 5. Saint Robert Bellarmine (1619), *De officio principis Christiani libri tres*, Bernard Gualter, Cologne, 8, pp. 60-63.

not necessarily the kind of advice likely to fortify the hearts of Christian princes and counsellors invariably concerned with the preservation and expansion of their power. Nor was it in the interest of Catholic theologians to provide their princes with a political ethics that *de facto* equated eternal salvation with political suicide. Faced with this dilemma, academic theologians like Bellarmine, Suárez or Molina and humanist rhetoricians like Botero each in their own way nonetheless strove to establish *prudentia* as the intellectual *and* moral virtue able to tell 'right' and 'false' means apart. Pedro de Ribadeneira, too, aspired to redress the issue by producing a language of reason of state more immediate to the emotions and perceptions of a politically astute lay audience. His *Tratado* illuminates some of the strategies employed as well as the difficulties faced by those keen to exclude the idea that 'false means' can further 'good ends' from the repertoire of practical reasoning. It is a prime example of the kind of aggressive anti-Machiavellianism invariably coupled with the effective domestication of Machiavellian doctrines that many members of the Society of Jesus pursued.

Ribadeneira could not but acknowledge the immense appeal of the concept of reason of state. In the preface to the *Tratado*, he assures the 'Christian and Pious Reader' that he does not wish to disparage 'all reason of state (as if there were none) or these rules of prudence by which, after God, states are founded, grow, and are governed and conserved'.[19] However, he strongly rejects the notion that political expediency queries against the very foundations of Christian ethics. He makes it abundantly clear that he wrote his treatise to:

> undo the entanglements devised by the *políticos*, who teach men to govern states in such fashion as though the Lord did not cast his providence over them and as if the world were governed by chance or solely by human roguery and cunning.[20]

Ribadeneira promises to neutralize the *perversa y diabólica dotrina de los políticos y discípulos de Maquiavelo* by distinguishing between 'false' and 'true reason of state'. The former, is 'dangerous and diabolical', the latter 'certain and divine', the one 'turns the state into a religion', the other 'religion into a state'.[21] His explication of *verdadera razón de estado* is meant to prove one and one point only: that God will favour a people only 'if their prince loves religion for religion's sake' rather than treat Christian faith as a means to a political end. The *Tratado* offers a grand vision of a world of princes and subjects ruled by God's providence and omnipotence only. In the two books of his treatise, Ribadeneira reassures readers of the immediacy of God and the intelligibility and accountability of divine will in secular history, fastening *virtudes*

---

19   *Tratado*, preface, pp. 455-57, p. 456.

20   Ibid.

21   Ibid., 'Pero que esta razón de estado no es una sola, sino dos: una falsa y aparente, otra sólida y verdadera; una engañosa y diabólica, otra cierta y divina; una que del estado hace religion, otra que de la religion hace estado; una enseñada de los políticos y fundada en vana prudencia y en humanos y ruines medios, otra enseñada de Dios, que estriba en el mismo Dios y en los medios que Él, con su paternal providencia, descubre á los principes y les da fuerzas para usar bien dellos, como Señor de todos los estados.'

necessary 'to rule and conserve the dominions of princes' to total and subjective reliance on the grace of God. His treatise represents a bold and polemical attempt to subject the realm of politics in all its confusion and ambiguity into a supernatural order accessible to natural reason. Ribadeneira contends that reason of state is a mere function of divine providence. Such is Ribadeneira's providential optimism that he appears prepared to deny man the experience of historical contingency and moral ambiguity. Ribadeneira wants his distinction between true and false reason of state understood not as one between two systems of norms and practices that would depend on equal or at least similar notions of rationality and utility. *Verdadera razón de estado* encapsulates the complete reliance of both the individual and society on divine providence as the only relevant force in secular history. Saint Augustine is his witness when he calls upon the reader to acknowledge that 'no one can have true virtue without true piety and true worship of the true God', and that 'those virtues that have the appearance of being genuine but do not refer beyond themselves to God and are desired only on their own account are in truth not virtues but vices.'[22] Mary Queen of Scots and Henry III of France, among others, serve as examples of rulers who 'by God's judgement came to die' because they sought to preserve their kingdoms through schemes and stratagems rather than the observance of the 'the law of the Lord'.[23] 'True reason of state' is summed up as absolute dedication to the cause of the one true faith on the part of the individual prince. The personal faith of the prince in turn assumes an immediate eschatological dimension.[24] The ruler is in fact left with little more than the obligation to put absolute faith in spiritual advisers able to mediate between the law of God and the human conscience.

Effectively skirting the issue of 'means' and 'ends', Ribadeneira shows noticeable flexibility concerning the necessity of hiding secrets from foreign princes, and carefully defines the circumstances in which powerful heretical minorities may be tolerated so as to avoid civil war. While vociferously condemning the 'false' reasoning of the 'disciples of Machiavelli', he effectively sanctions many 'reglas de bueno gobierno' that he would point out as 'Machiavellian poison' in any writer of whose Catholic orthodoxy he was not fully assured. Ribadeneira might well have noticed that adjustments of moral and pious imperatives to the reality of foreign policy and domestic conflict that he felt bound to make brought him into danger of blurring the boundary between the two kinds of reason of state

---

22   Saint Augustine (1898-1900), *De civitate Dei libri XXIII*, Corpus scriptorum ecclesiasticorum latinorum, Vol. 40, Tempsky, Vienna, V, chapter 19; XIX, chapter 25. Though he uses the pagan scheme of the natural or cardinal virtues to organize the second book of the *Tratado*, Ribadeneira is at pains to subordinate them to the 'true royal (Christian) virtues' of faith, hope and charity. Confronted with what he perceives as the contaminating influence of *falsa razón de estado*, he is much more concerned to draw a clear line between the orders of nature and grace than either Aquinas or the theologians of the School of Salamanca. See Truman, *Spanish Treatises*, pp. 293-94, p. 308, p. 363, p. 373.

23   *Tratado*, Book one, Chapters fourteen to sixteen, pp. 476a-82a.

24   For instance, ibid., pp. 518a-526a.

himself.[25] Yet he nonetheless believes that his pious manipulation of human history would demonstrate the superiority of the one over the other. Natural reason, pagan historiography, Christian moral philosophy, and even Jean Bodin are said to agree with Holy Scripture and the writings of the Fathers of the Church that 'true reason of state' knows only one chief maxim: *summa ratio est, quae pro religione facit*.[26] Ultimately, the success of his argument depended on whether or not readers were prepared to follow Ribadeneira's assertion that the benefits of practising 'true reason of state' are evident from acts of divine providence recorded in history. His treatise requires an orthodox Christian reader who is willing to combine a providential interpretation of history with the resigned acceptance that not even the most pious ruler can rest assured of divine benevolence. What the *Tratado* demonstrates is that even one of the most skilful Catholic moral theologians and polemicists failed to find a way around the fact that prudence or practical moral reasoning does not tender the kind of certain knowledge necessary to distinguish 'right' from 'false means', or even to define 'good' ends.[27] Prudence as a moral virtue would never during the early modern period be clearly delineated against a notion of virtue (such as entertained by Machiavelli, among others) as the ability to be good *at* something rather than the notion of being morally good.[28]

Mariana's definition and use of the term *prudentia* reflect this dilemma. The way in which he approaches the matter, however, differs markedly from Ribadeneira's. Mariana sets out employing the familiar Thomist definition of *prudentia* as the one *virtus* that subsumes all the virtues and all the responsibilities of the prince.[29] Equally familiar is his description of prudence as 'the power of the mind that looks ahead into every aspect, remembering the past, appraising the present, divining the future, surmising secrets from what is manifest.'[30] Prudence is the intellectual facility

---

25   Höpfl, *Jesuit Political Thought*, p. 167.

26   *Tratado*, p. 458b, 'Y que por esto se debe tener gran cuidado que una cosa tan sacrosanta como la religion se guarde inviolablemente y no se ponga en disputa, porque della depende la conservacion o la ruina de la república. (…) *Summa ratio est, quae pro religione facit*, que la suma y más principal razon de todas es la que favorece a la religion. Todo esto dice Bodino, con ser autor no dada pío.'

27   On the stunning complexity of early modern Catholic moral theology see M.F.W. Stone (2003), 'Scrupulosity and Conscience: Probabilism in Early Modern Scholastic Ethics', in H. Braun and E. Vallance (eds), *Contexts of Conscience in Early Modern Europe, 1500-1700*, Palgrave, Basingstoke and New York, pp. 1-16; and ibid. (2006), 'Truth, Deception, and Lies. Lessons from the Casuistical Tradition', *Tijdschrift voor Filosofie*, Vol. 68, pp. 101-131.

28   Jesuit authors in particular seem to have struggled to define the moral and epistemological value of 'prudence'. See, for instance, Leonard Lessius (1605), *De iustitia et iure caeterisque virtutibus cardinalibus libri IV*, Johannes Masij, Leuven, I, chapter II ,13, who aspires to dissociate virtue as well as the knowledge of virtue defining the ends of actions from prudence. The latter represents merely the intellectual facility to determine appropriate means to those ends.

29   *De rege*, p. 388, echoing *ST*, 1a2æ, 57.5. See also Ribadeneira, *Tratado*, Book II, chapter 23, p. 552a; chapter 33, p. 566a. Aquinas's *ST*, especially 1a-2ae, 57-61; and 2a-2ae, 47-52, provides the prime *loci* for scholastic theologians' discussions of prudence.

30   *De rege*, p. 388.

providing princes with the knowledge necessary to make judgements appropriate to particular and constantly varying circumstances. Prudence also stands for the ability of the individual to apply such knowledge, representing the capacity to act with reason and discretion, foresight and circumspection.[31] Mariana presents *prudentia* as the shrewd understanding and manipulation of human nature and human affairs, an intellectual as well as practical capability that leads on to moral (including 'constitutional' or lawful) action. Speaking of prudence in terms of the knowledge and execution of principles of political conduct that engender moral action in that they serve the entirely pragmatic interests of the prince, however, he raises the troublesome question of exactly what kind of 'virtue' he has in mind.

Mariana starts out with an uncontroversial definition of prudence as a form of practical wisdom involving intellect (*ingenium*) and experience (*experientia*).[32] Bluntly and without further explanation he then goes on to state that prudence is both *virtus* and *ars*. Aristotle had made it clear that he wished to keep the two apart, and so had Aquinas.[33] Aquinas looked upon prudence as the virtue that had to take the lead in the moral perfection of man and thus one 'of the utmost necessity for human life'. Prudence 'not only helps us to be of good counsel, but also to judge and command well'.[34] It therefore has to be regarded as the only intellectual virtue that cannot exist without being a moral virtue at the same time.[35] Which is why, in this instance, Aquinas wishes to dispense with Aristotle's distinction between intellectual and moral virtues.[36] This twofold status of prudence as both intellectual and moral virtue, in turn, demanded that it be clearly distinct from *ars* as dependent not on the moral disposition of the agent but only on the eventual product. At the same time, neither Aquinas nor his many interpreters could avoid acknowledging the fact that *prudentia* as a kind of knowledge nurtured on a diet of personal and collective experience (as manifest in historiography) had to contain an aspect of *ars*.[37] After all, it had to enable man to appreciate, explain and apply what experience told. The awkward pairing of 'virtue' and 'art' remained deeply problematic: *ars* (in the sense of Aristotle's *techne* or craft) could hardly be expected to make a significant and reliable contribution to (morally) certain knowledge.

Apparently oblivious to the problems entailed, Mariana couples *ars* and *virtus* straightforwardly, and without making any qualifications as to prudence's superior status as both a moral and an intellectual virtue. Wittingly or unwittingly, with the first few sentences of his chapter he already conveys the notion of a limited cognitive

---

31   Mariana uses the term *ingenium* to denote intelligence understood as the ability to employ reason (*ratio*).

32   *De rege*, p. 388. Aristotle, *NE*, 6.5, 6.7.

33   *NE*, 6.3 (1139b16); *ST*, 1a2æ, 57.4, 5.

34   *ST*, 1a2æ, 58.5.

35   *ST*, 1a2æ, 57.5; 58.4 and 58.5.

36   *ST*, 1a2æ, 58.2, 3.

37   See *ST*, 1a2æ, 57.3. Aristotle himself had suggested as much; *NE*, 6.3. See E. Berti (1993), '*Phronesis* et science politique', in A. Tordesillas (ed.), *Aristote politique: études sur la Politique d'Aristote*, Presses Universitaires de France, Paris, pp. 435-60.

status of prudence. Though dismissing Aristotelian terminological boundaries, he at the same time shares Aristotle's lowly opinion of *phronesis*. Indirectly at least, Mariana accepts that prudence as the faculty involved with 'life in the *polis*' cannot, or cannot that easily, be related to the superior knowledge that points to the other life. Mariana muddles the issue of the cognitive and moral value of *prudentia* even further by using the epistemologically highly ambiguous terms *prudentia, ratio, sapientia* and even *scientia* synonymously. He is by no means alone in fusing terms and concepts the venerable *philosophus* had wanted to keep apart, of course. It is just that, unlike many contemporary Jesuit theologians dealing with reason of state, he steers well clear of discussing prudence in philosophical terms as a matter of the place of knowledge and intelligence in moral agency. While making veiled references to Machiavelli, he makes no effort to tell 'true' and 'false' prudence apart. Nowhere does Mariana actually discuss the question of how to ensure that habitual aspiration to pursue 'good' ends will not be contaminated by impure knowledge and the practice of immoral means.

If the boundary between moral action and the pragmatic application of some kind of knowledge is left unexplored and as blurred as it is in *De rege*, the result is a strong, albeit indirect emphasis on prudence as being good at extracting and applying 'lessons from history' rather than checking that the resulting action is 'moral'. Aquinas, too, put the emphasis firmly on the 'practical' aspect of prudence. In the first instance, though, the merger of Aristotelian concepts in *Summa Theologiae* was meant to assert that political and moral action were intrinsically inseparable. In any case, Aquinas had written long before Machiavelli started to circulate the manuscript of *Il principe*, and may be forgiven for not having described the relationship between prudence and moral action in terms both more definite and practical. In a sixteenth-century treatise on statecraft dedicated to the education of the Christian prince, on the other hand, the lack of any attempt to clarify the relation between prudence and moral action, or differentiate between 'true' and 'false' prudence amounts to an omission. The fact that Mariana assigns *phronesis/prudentia* to the transient and morally ambiguous realm of the *polis* requires further explanation.

The apparent indifference with which Mariana treats the issue of the cognitive and moral status of prudence can hardly be put down to ignorance. A more likely scenario is that he was as assured of his readers' piety and orthodoxy as was Ribadeneira. Jesuit moral reasoning, as long as it was persuaded that the moral objectives pursued by a prince were of the right and 'true' kind, provided 'a great deal of latitude for sanitizing otherwise objectionable maxims and practices endorsed by reason of state.'[38] Mariana is no exception to that rule. He may also have been less perceptive, or simply less concerned than Ribadeneira about the way in which Machiavelli bolstered his version of the 'effective truth of things' by contrasting it with his distorted view of Christian moral absolutism. Yet Mariana's frequent, scathing comments on the moral and intellectual capacity of princes to act prudently suggest that he harbours doubts that go far beyond the usual topoi

---

38   Höpfl, *Jesuit Political Thought*, p. 90.

for slamming deceitful and sycophantic courtiers. His altogether negative attitude towards a secular political order that he saw as deeply corrupted induced him to make unique proposals for the inclusion of the Church of Castile into the government of the monarchy.[39] Another possible explanation for the fact that Mariana does not engage more closely with the relationship between prudence and moral action is that he was quite conscious of the fact that the cognitive status of prudence proved so difficult to pin down. His terminological vagueness certainly allowed him to avoid tackling an issue that he might have considered ultimately irresolvable (and quite rightly so). Ribadeneira, too, for all his effort to disentangle Machiavellian and Christian prudence and his eagerness to assure his readers of the immediate relation between moral knowledge and political action, fails to discuss the epistemic value of prudence. He compensated for the lack of theoretical discussion with a vigorous attempt to tie history to providence. As a rule, Mariana seems much more prepared to acknowledge how little moral and epistemic certainty history affords those who scour it for abstract and universal rules of political conduct than many of his fellow Jesuits, including that bold trailblazer, Giovanni Botero. Dispensing himself of the need to tell prudence and reason of state apart, Mariana acknowledges how unreliable a moral and epistemic tool prudence is.[40]

The Historian's Prudence

That experience drawn from history is the nursery of prudence had been staple knowledge among those dealing with the subject from the time of Roman oratorians to that of Renaissance humanists. At first glance, Mariana seems fairly assured of the kind of lessons to be garnered from works of historiography. In entirely conventional humanist fashion he avows that a ruler 'who will always seek the counsel of history' is going to be well equipped for the challenges of his office.[41] History provides a convenient shortcut to the 'essence of prudence', teaching 'within a few years what has been confirmed by so many centuries of trial'.[42] Only prudence nurtured on history, he says, is able to digest historical change, political diversity and cultural variety into valuable counsel. Mariana is adamant that historical experience does not just complement, but enhance, and indeed far exceed 'pure human reason'. Though prudence evolves from both intellect (*ingenium*) and experience (*experientia*), they are not equally balanced. There is no doubt in his mind that 'only a few distinguish the good from the bad, and the useful from the harmful by reasoning only (*ex ratione*),

---

39   See below, chapter five.

40   I disagree with Höpfl, *Jesuit Political Thought*, p. 167, who suggests that Mariana decided not to mention reason of state so as not to be obliged to defend his concept of prudence, but nonetheless believed 'that he had done so in substance'. Mariana's sense of the epistemological fragility of prudence did not, I believe, permit him to think in such optimistic terms. His resigned acceptance of human corruption carries with it the recognition of the highly precarious cognitive status of prudence.

41   *De rege*, p. 390, p. 391.

42   Ibid., p. 192.

but that the majority of men learn from practical experience (*rerum eventis*). Mariana the *humanista* tirelessly repeats the old adage that 'men are taught by the examples of others and thus learn what to do and what to avoid in every area of life'.[43] Though fully aware what a treacherous guide history can be, he also acknowledges that there is no alternative teacher of practical wisdom.

History is crucial to the formation of prudence not least because of the splendour, flattery, and subservience rampant in princely courts notorious for suffocating the critical facilities of princes. What makes the study of history absolutely indispensable is the fact that tutors and counsellors will not always dare speak their minds. History is 'the mute teacher' of prudence who speaks 'where others do not even dare murmur a word.' Concerning the syllabus for grooming the mind of the prince, Mariana names Caesar, Sallust and Livy as the historians with whose works a young boy should be confronted in the first instance. They will afford the pupil a necessary, albeit merely general introduction to the dynamics and vagaries of power. As is usual, Mariana's verdict on princes, courts and courtiers is shot through with a healthy dose of criticism clearly inspired by Tacitus. It is Tacitus, too, who is singled out as the one author whose books 'a prince must never lay aside'. Despite his 'obscure style', Tacitus is the best source for information on the workings of a court and the deteriorating effects of tyrannical rule.[44] What he has to say about the alienation felt by even the most faithful of Nero's counsellors and military commanders concludes the chapter on tyrannicide as a stark warning from history.[45] If the study of history is to be a lifelong preoccupation, Tacitus, according to Mariana, is the focal point around which it ought to revolve. If the business of government is one of continual self-education on the part of the prince, Tacitus is the prime medium that translates historical experience into rules of prudent conduct in politics.

Mariana does not ignore more contemporary historians, and commends analysts of Renaissance political life like Guicciardini and especially the Frenchman Philipe de Commines (1447-1511).[46] The latter provides a detailed discussion and more

---

43   Ibid.

44   Ibid., p. 172.

45   Ibid., p. 80 (concluding chapter six, the chapter on tyrannicide). Mariana's use and representation of Tacitus indicates that the latter had a presence in sixteenth century Spanish political writing well before the publication of the first partial translation of his works in 1613, which was quickly followed by Álamos de Barrientos's influential commentary (1614). The preoccupation with 'Tacitism' as a clearly delineated ideology may have obscured the ways in which his works entered into pre-1600 Spanish literature. The matter invites further study. On the reception of Tacitus into European political thinking (excluding Spain), see K. Schellhase (1976), *Tacitus in Renaissance Political Thought*, University of Chicago Press, Chicago.

46   Philippe de Commines (also Comines or Commynes) (1969-73), *The Memoirs of Philippe de Commynes*, ed. S. Kinser, transl. I. Cazeaux, University of South Carolina Press, Columbia. On Commines's critical analysis of contemporary politics, see J. Dufournet (1994), *Philippe de Commynes. Un historien à l'aube des temps modernes* (Bibliothèque du Moyen Âge, Vol. 4), De Boeck, Brussels.

recent examples of how monarchs ought to conduct themselves and their business.[47] A long quote from his *Mémoirs* offers proof that meetings between royal heads ought to be avoided at all cost. Especially rulers lacking in physical and intellectual presence as well as the self-confidence demanded by such occasions are likely to disappoint and be disappointed. Although Mariana does not say so explicitly, his words are directed at the notoriously shy and unimpressive Philip III. Practising what he preaches, Mariana employs Commines as the 'mute teacher' who dares speak unpleasant truths.

He would not be true to himself, however, if he did not sow little seeds of doubt concerning the epistemic certainty of knowledge drawn from history. Commines's *Mémoirs*, for instance, in detailing the varying contemporary approaches to monarchical government also convey a strong sense of how unexpected, irreconcilable cultural differences can seriously hinder effective political communication. Mariana draws on Commines to point out that Philip III must avoid meeting other rulers in person not only because the personalities involved are likely to clash. The customs, languages and attitudes of nations, too, are far too dissimilar to allow meetings of this kind to further mutual understanding and political agreement. Instead, such gatherings are likely to introduce an unwelcome element of competition that will invariably lead to misunderstanding and mutual disapproval.

The long quote from the *Mémoirs* is not the only place where Mariana elaborates on the pitfalls involved in attempts to abstract from the particular to the general. Elsewhere, the late Philip II is in effect criticized for having pursued justice indiscriminately. The task of rulers is always made difficult by the fact that 'each nation has its own method of looking at things'.[48] Different peoples experience history and politics differently. If it is troublesome enough to identify rules of conduct that heed the fact that most individuals are unreliable in the extreme, it is even more difficult to filter definite principles of good government from varying historical circumstances, experience and attitudes. 'Some nations', Mariana remarks, 'think it cruel that the most famous men, though they more than merit extreme punishment, be subjected to the law'.[49] Though Mariana does not himself identify any historical event he may have in mind, any reader halfway familiar with contemporary European politics would have recognized the reference to the Dutch revolt. The rationale is that had Philip II been patient with the rebellious Dutch aristocracy early on and treated the counts of Egmont and Hoorn leniently rather then having them executed (however much they deserved it), decades of ruinous war might have been avoided. In other words, had Philip II listened to the 'mute teacher history', he would have remembered one of the prime maxims of political prudence transcending the application of particular principles of law: 'above all, the prince ought to rule only over willing subjects.'[50] Philip III cannot afford to

---

47 *De rege*, pp. 402-406. Quoting *Memoirs*, II, 8.
48 Ibid., p. 394.
49 Ibid.
50 Ibid.

repeat his father's mistakes. He must not ignore the distinct political traditions and mentality of the many and distinct peoples over which he rules.

While the young prince receives advice closely tailored to fit his personality and anticipate the challenges he is likely to meet as the ruler of a veritable hotchpotch of nations and traditions, he is at the same time reminded of the limits of generalizing from 'knowledge of the particular'. Mariana's tentative reservations raise a crucial question indicated already in his discussion of law and the law of nations in Book one of *De rege*. Are not the principles of 'good government' to be gleaned from the particular customs and laws of different peoples altogether too vague to be of use to the head of a composite monarchy?

Mariana's use and perception of history as a source of prudence is not as straightforward as his usually deft and confident handling of historiographical material suggests. His doubt about human rational faculties extends to historical experience itself. Clearly aware that historian and reader alike face the problem of deciding what degree of practical and moral certainty can be expected from historical examples in the first instance, he refrains from insinuating that prudence nurtured on history may illuminate the will of God. The mutability of time, the incalculability of events and the corruption and fickleness of human nature perpetually challenge the intellectual and moral faculties of even the most prudent of princes. Mariana accepts that *prudentia* is as contingent as the reality it confronts and endeavours to shape. He warns the reader that 'if it is already hard for the private citizens, in so great a variety of circumstances and with the will of men so uncertain, not to commit errors, it is even more difficult, almost impossible for the *summus rector* to do so'.[51] Quite possibly, he means to censure Botero, who had assured his readers to the contrary that 'what is hard and perhaps impossible for a private citizen, should be well within the reach of a prince.'[52] In a sequence of poignant rhetorical questions, Mariana presents the task of the prince as 'to prescribe for all, to please the many, draw together the opposing wills, and to hold all in peace to their duties'.[53] It is one that he considers virtually impossible to master. His summary line of argument echoes the kind of epistemic doubt also familiar to readers of Justus Lipsius's treatise on politics. Lipsius (drawing out Aristotle's delineation of *phronesis* and *scientia*) describes prudence as:

> vague, confused, and uncertain. Vague in the first instance. (…) But also confused. Which is why we call prudence a thing that is truly and wholly unstable and in flux. What is prudence but the range of those things which never remain the same? But if the things themselves are

---

51   Ibid., 388. 'Quod si privatis difficile est in tanta rerum varietate, tam incertis hominum voluntatibus non offendere: quid summo rectori contingat, cuius providentia res publicae & privatae continentur, & quasi in altissima specula constitutus, inde debet prospicere in omnes partes? (…) Omnibus praecipere, multis placere, dissidentes voluntates constringere, atque in pace & officio continere quantus labor? Quam difficilis est provincia ita severitatem cum benignitate miscere, ut neque facilitas aliquid de auctoritate detrahat, neque maiestate benevolentia in subditorum animis minuatur?'

52   *Della ragion di stato*, ii, 3.

53   *De rege*, p. 388.

uncertain, [prudence] itself must of necessity be so. (...) It looks at times, places, people. With every change they go through, however small, [prudence] changes too. It is nowhere and in no single instance the same.[54]

Mariana puts similar emphasis on the fact that prudence is as impaired by the forces of corruption, time and cultural diversity as any other aspect of human existence. Prudence, by definition, cannot provide anything like certain knowledge. Bearing this in mind, it comes as less of a surprise that he neither attempts to distinguish between 'true' and 'false' reason of state like Ribadeneira, nor, like his fellow Jesuit theologians Valentia and Laymann, tries to establish a link between *prudentia* as a kind of moral virtue and *synderesis* as the general knowledge of moral principles.[55] While Mariana is as bold as Botero in transcribing the dire reality of politics into rules of reason of state, he is far more pessimistic and clear-sighted with regard both to the feasibility of extracting universal principles from historical experience, and, as a result, with the degree to which a prudent prince can steer and control human affairs.

His position sets Mariana the humanist historian apart from humanist lawyer-historians like François Baudouin and Jean Bodin.[56] Baudouin had been one of the first to follow 'the trajectory of history as an approach to historical certainty and "integrity"'.[57] Bodin, inspired by the chaos of the French religious wars, pursued an even more universal understanding of the methods and results of historiography. He sought to 'to create a legal, ethical, historical science of politics', by rooting prudence in the critical assessment of legal and historical documents.[58] Political prudence would have to be based on the 'accurate assessment' of history as he defined it in his treatise on historical method.[59] The study of universal history would provide universal laws to guide princes and peoples. Mariana, in contrast, posits that history and consequently political prudence draw on a collective memory that

---

54   *Politicorum*, IV, 1, pp. 132-33, 'Diffusa nimis res est, confusa, obscura. Diffusa primum. (...) Iam confusa eadem. Quia re vera instabile totum et fluctuans est, quod prudentiam vocamus. Quid enim aliud ea, quam electio rerum quae aliter atque aliter sese habent? Quod si illae incertae, etiam ipsa. (...) Tempora, loca, homines adspicit. Et pro minima eorum mutatione ipsa se mutat: adeoque non ubique una, ut nec in una re una.'

55   Höpfl, *Jesuit Political Thought*, pp. 171-72.

56   On the marriage of law and history in Baudouin, see D.R. Kelley (1970), *Foundations of Modern Historical Scholarship: Language, Law and History in the French Renaissance*, Columbia University Press, London and New York, pp. 116-36.

57   Kelley, *Foundations*, p. 136.

58   J. Soll (2003), 'Empirical History and the Transformation of Political Criticism in France from Bodin to Bayle', *Journal of the History of Ideas*, Vol. 64, pp. 297-316, p. 299. See also Kelley, *Foundations*, pp. 136-38; Schellhase, *Tacitus*, pp. 110-26; and D. Engster (1996), 'Jean Bodin, Scepticism, and Absolute Sovereignty', *History of Political Thought*, Vol. 17, pp. 469-99. Though Bodin's politics shifted from the constitutionalism of the *Methodus ad facilem historiarum* (1566) to the legal absolutism of his *Six livres de la république* (1576), his historical methodology remained the same.

59   Kelley, *Foundations*, p. 114, and ibid. (1970), 'The Rise of Legal History in the Renaissance', *History and Theory*, Vol. 9(2), pp. 174-94, p. 180.

is the realm of variability and incalculability. The connection between prudence, pragmatic politics, and history is not one of 'accurate assessment'. The prudence with which the prince has to concern himself clearly belongs to the realm of the contingent and uncertain. Mariana is frequently at pains to stress that there are no safe principles to be had, and certainly not any that could be gleaned from the laws of nations. History will not always afford prior knowledge of the right and moral means by which to realize a particular end. The political situation will be fluid, and the prince will have to be involved in a continual process of interpretation, a process marked by plurality and contingency. Pervading and distinguishing his argument is a sense of the disturbing volatility of human affairs and how it is invariably reflected in historiographical records and historical interpretation.

Like Bodin, Mariana aspires to filter maxims from historical experience. Like the majority of European humanists at the time, he organizes his material in term of 'commonplaces' (*loci communes*). At the same time, he is much more prepared to acknowledge the treachery, bias, and ignorance of memory and the keepers of memory. While maintaining that the widely varying historical experience of peoples can still be summed up into some form of general principles, Mariana also displays a heightened sense of how precariously vague those principles are. Prudence forged from historical experience clearly has its limits.

The Making of a Prudent Prince

A product of 'intelligence, practice and experience' on the part of the individual, Mariana says, the frailty of man and the contingency of human existence make prudence a sort of 'knowledge' and 'virtue' difficult to obtain and cultivate. This is particularly true of courts, where factions vie for power in pursuit of their own petty advantage rather than the common good. To begin with, the intellectual and moral stamina of heirs to the throne varies considerably. In some cases, tutors and counsellors, despite their very best efforts, will be left with nothing but patient hope for a more gifted successor.[60] Incompetence, though, Mariana is quick to assert, provides no justification for a change of government. Not least because even seemingly hopeless cases can sometimes be improved upon, even the 'most serious defects of nature' can be 'corrected'.[61] The prince, to use one of *De rege*'s cutting metaphors, 'is to be pruned like a tree'.

This cautionary voice is a far cry from the Christian optimism, charitable language and homely anecdotes which characterize the *Enchiridion* or the *Institutio principis Christiani* of Desiderius Erasmus. In many respects, Erasmus set the humanist tone for the learned moral and practical instruction of prince and courtier at the beginning of the sixteenth century.[62] The *Institutio* was written in response to the

---

60 *De rege*, p. 389.

61 Ibid., pp. 390-91.

62 See C. Augustijn (1992), *Erasmus: His Life, Works and Influence*, University of Toronto Press, Toronto; and Q. Skinner (1988), 'Political Philosophy', in C.B. Schmitt, Q. Skinner and

turmoil caused by the dynastic and territorial ambitions of powerful European princes during the period. Erasmus sought to express his undaunted confidence that no prince could fail to see the necessity of virtuous conduct, that no prince could fail to realize that nothing makes a great ruler 'except the consent of his subjects'.[63] Mariana, Lipsius and Ribadeneira, each in their own way, acknowledge 'that effective government might have to depend after all on accepting "reasons of state"'.[64] Each in their own way mark the departure from the sanguine and practical piety of earlier humanist mirrors-of-princes. Pragmatic and deeply pessimistic at the same time, Mariana's treatise represents perhaps the most radical and significant break with humanist tradition. No playful scholarly irony or uplifting metaphors of Christian spiritual combat in De rege. The moral core of prince and people of which Erasmus was so assured has evaporated. As a result, a wary, sometimes bitter worldly realism pervades his treatise whenever Mariana comes to talk about lay folk and lay politics. The 'consent of the people' itself has become an altogether ambiguous and beleaguered concept. Virtuous conduct has to be differentiated, explained and marketed in terms of *realpolitik*.

A cynical pedagogue cum observer of politics, Mariana suggests that tutors ought to prefer a dim-witted prince to one possessing a quick and sharp mind.[65] The former is much more likely to be compliant and malleable, and his tutors therefore much more likely to succeed in setting his mind up for the continual pursuit of prudence. Remarks like these testify to Mariana's conviction that kings commonly enjoy power that has a deeply corrupting influence and is difficult to resist. Its boundaries are to be lodged and enforced in the mind of the prince rather than anywhere else. Friend and client of a royal tutor, Mariana avers that the father and the tutors of the prince will have to work jointly and tirelessly to create a good king. Accomplished humanist himself, he insists that humanist education is the key to pedagogical success. Whether or not a people will enjoy good government depends in the last instance on whether or not the royal tutors have managed to shape the mind of the heir to the throne at an early age.

Mariana does not hesitate to set out the various predicaments of a notion of government almost solely reliant on an individual's aptitude to practical reasoning. One of the issues he raises is that of how long an heir to the throne should depend on his tutors. The acid test of proper education of a prince is whether or not he will continue to develop his experience and make decisions relying on the judgement of tested counsellors after he has acceded to the throne. Sceptical of the mental faculties of princes in general as well as those of Philip III of Spain in particular, Mariana suggests that if his upbringing has rendered a young prince prepared to receive instruction and counsel, he will want to be guided by his old tutors while

---

E. Kessler (eds), *The Cambridge History of Renaissance Philosophy*, Cambridge University Press, Cambridge, pp. 389-452, pp. 441-45.

63   *Institutio*, chapter six.

64   Skinner, 'Political Philosophy', pp. 444-45.

65   *De rege*, p. 391.

taking his first tentative steps as a king. If this is the case, there is a good chance that even a feckless young prince will grow into a seasoned ruler.

Ever ready to cast doubt on his hopes and convictions, he goes on to offer one of his less conventional observations. It responds to what some contemporaries rightly perceived as a very real and very present danger to the Spanish monarchy, that is, the rule of the royal favourite or *privado*. The author of *De rege* is almost obsessed with the risk of the kingdom of Castile being saddled with a ruler who cannot be trusted and does not trust himself concerning his ability to receive counsel and acquire prudence with age and experience.[66] Such a ruler is most likely to replace his tutors and counsellors with a favourite. Contemporary readers familiar with the politics of the court in Madrid and the personality of Philip III will have had no difficulties understanding his remarks as a thinly veiled comment on Philip III's close relationship and indeed reliance upon his favourite Ruy Gómez da Silva (latterly count of Lerma).[67] Philip II had been unsuccessful in his attempt to coax his son away from a man in whose presence Philip III seemed to have enjoyed the rare pleasure of feeling comfortable with himself.

Mariana's observation that 'the mark of a great prince is to have great courtiers' is a reference not only to the quality of courtiers, but also to their number - many counsellors are to have the ear of the king, not just one. The royal court is the place where kings reconcile and balance warring factions among the nobility against one another. The text draws readers' attention to the fact that the court in Madrid is the monarchy's hub of integration. Prudence is to be enacted by a king *together* with his counsellors. The favourite will put himself between the king and his counsellors and thus between the king and his people, doing his utmost to prevent the prince from exercising and honing his prudence.

The rise of the *privado* must be avoided, in the first instance by appointing as royal tutor a *magister litterarum* 'conspicuous for his prudence' and 'outstanding in his reputation for erudition and virtue'.[68] There is no doubt whom Mariana has in mind. Topical though his remarks on the quality of the royal tutor are, references to his patron García de Loaysa shine through. Denouncing the rule of the favourite, Mariana employs ideas and images familiar from early modern critics of kings believed to defile and effectively renounce their title and office by delegating

---

66   Ibid., pp. 343-44.

67   On Philip III, his *privado* and the organization of government during his reign see now A. Feros (2000), *Kingship and Favouritism in the Spain of Philip III, 1598-1621* (Cambridge Studies in Early Modern History), Cambridge University Press, Cambridge. On the emergence of the minister-favourite as a distinct feature of early modern courts see also I.A.A. Thompson (1999), 'The Institutional Background to the Rise of the Minister-Favourite', in J.H. Elliott and L. Brockliss (eds), *The World of the Favourite*, Yale University Press, New Haven and London, pp. 13-25; and W. Paravicini (2004), 'Der Fall des Günstlings. Hofparteien in Europa vom 13. bis zum 17. Jahrhundert', in J. Hirschbiegel and W. Paravicini (eds), *Der Fall des Günstlings. Hofparteien in Europa vom 13. bis zum 17. Jahrhundert* (Residenzenforschung; Vol. 17), Thorbecke, Ostfildern, pp. 13-22.

68   *De rege*, pp. 148-50.

their power to a favourite. By no means exceptional in his condemnation of the powerful royal favourite, he is still among the first to put a veiled anticipation and condemnation of Lerma's rule into writing.[69] It is one of the ironies of history that the man who had commissioned *De rege* so as to remind Philip III that he must continue to rely on tutors after taking the throne, archbishop García de Loaysa, was to be among the first victims of the Count of Lerma's post-accession purge.

'The Prince shall never lie ...'

Even a wary prince exercising personal rule rather than being ruled by a favourite, however, will find plenty of opportunity to fail his people as well as his spiritual well-being. Especially when it comes to speaking, or not speaking the truth. Though the issue is addressed in varying contexts throughout Books two and three of *De rege*, Mariana dedicates a separate chapter to the investigation of the case for and against outright lying (*mendacium*).[70] At that point, he has already indicated his willingness to make generous allowances for *realpolitik*. Readers could nonetheless expect a straightforward refutation of any intimation that a Christian prince could be allowed to lie in order to protect himself and his kingdom from damage and destruction. Early modern Catholic doctrine is exceptionally unanimous in its condemnation of lying as inherently sinful and evil (*malum in se*).[71] It was one of the most common (yet nonetheless unjustified) charges against Machiavelli that he had presented lying as the essence of political prudence.[72] Catholic theologians concurred much less where other, seemingly different strategies of deception were concerned, especially those technically known as 'simulation' (*simulatio*) and 'dissimulation' (*dissimulatio*). The common understanding was that *simulatio* stood for pretending that something exists which in fact does not, and *dissimulatio* for claiming that something does not

---

69   Negative views of the favourite dominated early modern European political discourse. See A. Feros, 'Images of Evil, Images of Kings: The Contrasting Faces of the Royal Favourite and the Prime Minister in Early Modern European Political Literature, c. 1580–c. 1650', in Elliott and Brockliss, *World of the Favourite*, pp. 223-38.

70   *De rege*, II.10, *De mendacio* ('On Lies'), pp. 203-22; see also II.11, *De adulatoribus* ('On Flatterers'), pp. 211-22; and III.12, *De fide* ('On Good Faith'), pp. 373-80.

71   The authoritative texts are Saint Augustine's *De mendacio* ('On Lying') and *Contra mendacium* ('Against Lying'), together with several other of his works. Though Augustine made no exception to his wholehearted condemnation of lying (summarily defined as 'a false statement made with the intention to deceive'), he did concede that not every type of lie was equally culpable. This modest hint of latitude was exploited and expanded by subsequent generations of scholastics confronted with strong biblical precedents for deception, most notably perhaps Jacob swindling his brother Esau out of his inheritance (Genesis 27:19). See P. Zagorin (1990), *Ways of Lying: Dissimulation, Persecution, and Conformity in Early Modern Europe*, Harvard University Press, Cambridge (Mass.) and London, especially pp. 15-37; and J. Sommerville (1988), 'The "New Art of Lying": Equivocation, Mental Reservation, and Casuistry', in E. Leites (ed.), *Conscience and Casuistry in Early Modern Europe*, Cambridge University Press, Cambridge, pp. 159-84.

72   For instance, Ribadeneira, *Tratado*, p. 287.

exist which in fact does.[73] The two closely related terms were easily interchangeable. As a result, the boundary between simulation and lying, too, was embarrassingly fluid. The diversity of opinion among orthodox Catholic writers boils down to the fact that it proved so eminently difficult to pinpoint the exact difference between *simulatio* and *mendacium*.

The alleged Machiavellian endorsement of lying as the axiomatic core of political prudence was widely held to be encapsulated in the maxim: *Qui nescit (dis)simulare, nescit regnare* ('He who does not know how to (dis)simulate, does not know how to rule'). Commonly attributed to Louis XI of France (1461-83), it came to haunt early modern Catholic political writers confronting the issue of lying and deceit. Louis's political skills became immortalized in Commines's *Mémoires*, and his successful reign provided a much more clear-cut example of what a determined Machiavellian prince could achieve than any of Machiavelli's own, sometimes failing characters. Giovanni Botero was one of the few to break ranks openly, having no qualms whatsoever affirming that 'he who does not know how to dissimulate does not know how to rule'.[74] Though Botero does differentiate between dissimulation (feigning to be ignorant) and simulation (pretending and doing one thing in place of another), and thus appears to separate *dissimulation* from the much trickier *simulation/mendacium*, he does not seem to have attributed any significance to this distinction.[75] What probably amounts to *de facto* equation of lying, simulation and dissimulation, however, is not developed anywhere in *Della ragion di stato*.

Much more orthodox and representative for Catholic theologians' approach to the matter is Ribadeneira, who finds harsh words condemning a maxim that to his mind encapsulates the aggressive dynamic of Machiavellian thought.[76] Even Ribadeneira, however, has to concede that dissimulation is necessary. While he spills much ink on condemning Machiavelli's proposition that 'simulation [is] the most powerful resource and firmest foundation on which false reason of state rests',[77] he is disposed to qualify his censure to the extent that 'it is in fact not a lie to hide something by silence, and to conceal the secrets (*arcana*) of councils and actions'.[78] Even if the dissimulation and connivance of the prince lead his opponents to deceive themselves, this is to be regarded as prudence rather than lying. Ribadeneira finally distinguishes between two 'arts' of (dis)simulation. There are those who practise (dis)simulation without cause or necessity, and those who have a just claim to do so because they act from necessity or advantage (here: *commoditas*). Ribadeneira does not only fail to draw the line between lying, simulation and dissimulation that he promised to provide, he effectively blurs it.[79] This does not contribute to

---

73   See, for instance, Saint Thomas Aquinas, *ST*, 2a2æ, 111.1.

74   In the chapter dealing with secrecy, *Della ragion di stato*, II, 7.

75   Höpfl, *Jesuit Political Thought*, p. 151.

76   *Tratado,* p. 235, where Ribadeneira provides the usual references to Tacitus's, Tiberius's, and Seneca's endorsement of dissimulation.

77   *Tratado*, pp. 293-94.

78   Ibid., p. 235.

79   Ibid., pp. 524-26.

the clarity of his argument. Harro Höpfl rightly points out that the only difference between Ribadeneira's 'true' and 'godly' doctrines and the 'pernicious precepts' of Machiavelli 'seems to be that he makes the justifiability of (dis)simulation depend on the goodness of the prince's purposes and the pressing nature of the circumstances as well as the contention that if a prince succeeds in being misunderstood as he intends, this is not lying.'[80] Though Ribadeneira does not explicitly say so, his opinion appears to be that the pious prince may well use deceit because he will not consider deceit as a principally appropriate means of political conduct.

Where his friend distinguishes two 'artes', Mariana identifies two schools concerning the practice of (dis)simulation.[81] In doing so, he is even more ambiguous about the distinction between dissimulation, simulation and lying than Ribadeneira, not least because he embeds some of his own views with the views of scholars and practitioners he presents as of more or less 'Machiavellian' ilk. The first of the two sets of opinion is held by 'men of great and excellent character, of the very highest reputation for prudence'.[82] The latter argue that 'a king ought to cultivate vices and virtues equally, and measure everything by practicality (*utilitas*) with no regard whatsoever for honesty (*honestas*).' The prince will 'refer everything to the public convenience, the stability of the empire, discriminating not at all between truth and falsehood'.[83] These *prudenti* demand the 'protean prince' who is to 'change himself into every form, (...) assume various personalities, often contradictory, get everyone's approval of his words and deeds'. Still, even they acknowledge that the able practitioner of (dis)simulation must know its bounds. The prince must preserve a manifest 'zeal for equity' (*aequitas*). Conducting himself with kindness, benevolence and *humanitas* towards his subjects, he is allowed to conceive in his mind all kinds of deceits, whichever ones he deems necessary to check his subjects as well as his enemies at the same time.[84]

The position of the *prudenti* is more or less the one Catholic critics identified with the 'teachings of Machiavelli', the more ferocious detractors failing to mention the sense of equity palpable in *Il principe*. Mariana himself identifies the view of the *prudenti* with Louis XI of France's practice and appraisal of simulation.[85] He claims that Louis even secluded the Dauphin and refused to have him brought up

---

80 Höpfl, *Jesuit Political Thought*, p. 152. See ibid., pp. 150-55, for further examples of Jesuit theologians' struggle with the thorny issue of (dis)simulation.

81 For the following, see *De rege*, pp. 203-206.

82 Ibid., p. 203, 'Magno & excellenti ingenio viri, prudentiae opinione maxima, Principem ad regendem populi multitudinem, alta dissimulatione opus habere persuadent. (...) Vertat se in omnes formas Protei adinstar, varias personas assumat saepe contrarias, qui omnibus placere debet, cunctis dicta omnia & facta probare.'

83 Ibid., pp. 203-204, '(...) omnia ad publicum commodum referat, imperii stabilitatem, veritatis ac mendacii nullo discrimine.'

84 Ibid., p. 203, '(...) modo praese ferat aequitatis studium, benignum se & tractabilem civibus praebeat, singulari humanitate se adeuntes com;ectatur: posse in animo ingentes fraudes suscipere, vitia & proba, (...).'

85 Rendering the (in)famous maxim *Qui nescit (dis)simulare, nescit regnare*, Mariana decided to use *simulare*; as did Ribadeneira, for instance, *Tratado*, p. 287.

in *artes et scientia*, declaring that his son need know and practise nothing but the 'art of simulation'.[86] Mariana coolly states that those who adhere to this opinion prefer to practise rather than publicly speak or theorize about it because they feel ashamed of themselves. Still, he cannot bring himself to denounce them simply as 'pernicious Machiavellians'. Unlike Ribadeneira and many orthodox theologians, he feels compelled to concede and answer to the fact that 'there is no doubt that many princes have held this philosophy and have held onto their power, once they have gotten it, to the end of their lives, more by their facility of intellect than by real virtues'.[87] He is reluctant to anathematize the *prudenti* not least because they believe that the prince is compelled to act in the way they describe because he must control as well as ensure the peace and prosperity of a fickle, corrupt and ungrateful multitude. *De rege* proffers ample evidence that this is a sentiment very close to Mariana's heart.

Throughout Book two and three the prince is reminded that he 'should never attempt in the commonwealth what it would not be possible to get the citizens to approve'. The chapter on *prudentia* (III.14), for instance, brings together the issues of (dis)simulatio, respect for the laws of the realm, and the best way of dealing with rebellious subjects. Again, Mariana's treatment does not amount to a wholehearted endorsement of abstract constitutional principles. If the prince is advised that he had better 'follow the judgement of the crowd' when it comes to changing hallowed laws and traditions, the reason is that peoples proud of their customs, privileges and traditions tend to cling to them without due discrimination.[88] Using a medical analogy, Mariana compares outdated and obstructive privileges and traditions to 'rotten sores', and peoples of the *monarquía española* reluctant to accept reform to patients afraid of the pain likely to be caused by medical treatment. Harsh measures are likely to provoke a violent response, and Mariana's concern that the prince respects the laws of the realm is quickly overshadowed by his fear of the reckless irrationality of the people. He reminds Philip III that 'the prince ought not to oppose the multitude when it is upset'.[89] Once in motion, the *populus* turns into a 'torrent which destroys everything in its path'. The prince will need 'to break the assault of the mad multitude by skill rather than open force.'[90] The *ars* needed 'to calm the flood' is, again, that of hiding or dissimulating true intentions. Once a group of rebels has been indulged with promises of fulfilling their demands and exemptions from punishment, it will disperse. Subsequently, the prince will pick off the ringleaders one by one, whenever circumstances are favourable, and over a protracted period of time if necessary. Echoing Machiavelli, Mariana suggests that punishment of rebels and malcontents should be meted out by judges whom the

---

86   *De rege*, p. 204.

87   Ibid., p. 204, 'Neque dubium est multos saepe Principes eam rationem tenuisse, acceptamque potestatem ad vitae exitum magis dexteritate ingenii, quam veris virtutibus conservasse.'

88   Ibid., p. 394.

89   Ibid., p. 393.

90   Ibid., p. 394.

prince can hold to account if they 'did not use their authority properly'.[91] While, unlike Machiavelli, Mariana suggests that magistrates ordered to suppress restless subjects ought to be treated fairly, he also emphasizes that punishing and effectively sacrificing magistrates will help to reconcile the *populus* with the retribution meted out to enemies of the crown.

Quite in line with the general Catholic stance, Mariana acknowledges that princes must resort to (dis)simulation especially when dealing with foreign affairs. One of the examples illustrating his position is drawn from Aragonese diplomatic history.[92] Trying to conceal his preparations for the invasion of Angevin Sicily (1282), Peter III of Aragon ('The Great', 1276-85) was repeatedly challenged by papal envoys increasingly unwilling to believe his assertions that he was about to invade Muslim Africa (an act of dissimulation: pretending that something is in place which in fact is not). The emissaries, dissatisfied and quite rightly suspicious, continued to confront the king, demanding that he openly declare his intentions. Vexed by their insistence, Mariana says, Peter answered that he would burn his undershirt if he had any such plans (an act of simulation: pretending that something is not in place which in fact is). Mariana readily justifies the way in which the king responded to the annoying entreaties of the papal emissaries. Admonishing the reader that a prince is sometimes required 'to keep things to himself, to conceal his plans, for when they are hidden they gain in strength, and when they are blurted out they are weakened', he quite consciously blurs the distinction between lying, (dis)simulation and secrecy. Peter's answer is not just evasive or misleading in the sense that he would have invited listeners 'to deceive themselves'. The king produces a plain lie that makes it difficult to maintain any practicable distinction between lying and dissimulating.

Mariana's pronouncements on (dis)simulation and the virtue of *honestas* are ambiguous whenever fused with issues of legitimacy, political psychology and moral authenticity. Like Ribadeneira, he often appears to insist that the prince must practise and truly believe in the virtues and values he exhibits, or else he will fail to convince, educate and lead his subjects. He strongly denies that a prince can survive on deception in a world where 'the acts of the prince cannot stay hidden'.[93] The prudent prince will therefore relinquish 'any hope of secret actions and deliberations'. This apparently rigid stance on strategies of deception, personal credibility and moral authenticity, however, is undermined by Mariana's own rhetoric and by historical examples sending an altogether ambiguous and confusing message. He confronts the reader with extremes of virtue and vice. On the one hand, he eulogizes the prince 'who will show in every instance as much probity, modesty, equity (...) as he requires in others'. In doing so, Mariana in effect appears to demand what he himself had described as a very rare occurrence after the Fall: the Aristotelian 'superhuman' ruler.[94] On the other hand he refers to Domitian

---

91   Ibid., p. 394.

92   For the following, see ibid., pp. 211-12.

93   Ibid., p. 60.

94   *De rege*, pp. 25-26; Aristotle, *Nicomachean Ethics*, 8.10/1600ª31-1161ª10, and *Politics*, 3.5/1279ª.

(AD 81-96), one of the Roman emperors notorious among humanist authors for their 'inborn monstrousness' and indulgence in public outrage and scandal.[95] Such argument in the extreme opens space for manoeuvre. Mariana is careful not to fill that space with less equivocal pronouncements. Avid readers of *De rege* pursuing the theme of fear could not fail to come across historical *exempla* which cast serious doubt on his moralist stance.

In one of the chapters of his treatise elaborating on the close link between fear, the practice of religion, and the stability of government, for instance, Mariana cites approvingly the example of ancient Egyptian petty princes who cleverly invented *diversa sacra novosque Deos* in order to strengthen their rule and forestall every attempt at re-unifying Egypt.[96] Similarly, Moses, *qua erat sapientia*, reinforced the unity of the people of Israel by inventing sacred laws, rites, and ceremonies that would confirm them in their faith and assure them of its exclusivity.[97] With regard to the experience of classical antiquity, Mariana refers to princes and legislators who either assumed the office of high priest or publicly and solemnly conducted sacrifices and other religious rites. The Roman general and politician Scipio Africanus, for instance:

> was in the habit of frequenting the Capitol and temples of Rome. By this religious activity, *whether from a sincere spirit or one suited to the times* [my italics], the people were convinced of his probity, and he attained an immortal name for glorious deeds.[98]

The implication of this anecdote drawn from Plutarch's biography of Scipio Africanus is that what is important is not so much that the prince is truly pious, but that he puts in a credible performance of piety or virtue. The subversive influence of humanist appreciation of the classical past is demonstrated even more poignantly and ambiguously in Mariana's references to the legendary second king of Rome, Numa Pompilius.[99]

In the first instance, Mariana compares Numa to Christian heroes who put the service of God above everything else. The king is praised for his proverbial piety that made him trust in the will of God rather than the power of arms. Yet he is also commended for the cunning way in which he manipulated the piety and superstition of his people. Recognizing the need to stabilize his government, Numa Pompilius invented laws to that effect and had them hallowed by suggesting that they were the result of his inspired conversations with the nymph and prophetess

---

95   *De rege*, p. 62.

96   Mariana appears to refer to the semi-independent kingdoms into which Egypt disintegrated after the end of the twelfth dynasty in 1786 BC.

97   *De rege*, pp. 425-26.

98   Ibid., p. 259, 'Scipionem scimus, cui devicta Carthago Africani nomen fecit, consuevisse Capitolinum & templa Romana frequentare. Eo religionis officio, seu syncero animo suscepto seu assimulatio ad tempus, opinione in civium animis excitata de eius probitate, rebus praeclare gestis nomen immortale consecutus est.'

99   Mariana draws on one of his favourite sources, Plutarch's *Lives*, I, Numa, 15, 2-9. Numa is also Machiavelli's example of the possibly fraudulent use of religion in order to bolster secular authority. See *Discorsi*, I, 11.

Aegeria (also: Egeria).[100] Mariana concedes that the religious beliefs involved are 'blatantly absurd'. Numa's cunning use of superstitious fear of divine retribution, however, is not. The strong implication is that in the main truth is what the prince can make his subjects believe. Mariana tempers this message somewhat by adding that no prince should expect that mere affectations of piety will suffice to deceive his people in the long term.[101] The few and faint assertions that a prince who merely affects piety will endanger the salvation of his soul sound altogether hollow in comparison.[102] Mariana's discourse on deceit and truth is one conducted in terms of prudence first and foremost.

With regard to the message conveyed by his choice of examples from history, Mariana's exposition of the pros and cons of *mendacium* smack of sympathy for the views of what he serenely presents as the second, more 'cautious' or 'moderate' (his term is *modestius*) school of thought.[103] Its supporters believe that the prince 'will use deceit and lie, but rarely, and only as a remedy'. The ruler will still accept *aequitas* 'and all the other virtues' as his guides, and will not deviate from the path of truth 'unless pressed by necessity (*necessitas*)'. They, too, hold that a prince is compelled to practise deceit so as to be able to master the 'blind multitude'. They compare the prince to Hercules, who covered 'his body with the fur of both the lion and the fox', thus combining terrifying strength with soft slyness.[104] Like Hercules or the Spartan general Lysander in Plutarch, the prince has to use deceit 'lest if he be overly concerned about justice, he involve himself in danger and the *respublica* in many calamities'. Botero in his treatise openly agreed that Lysander ought to be praised for his 'cunning in military matters'.[105] However, he also chastises the Spartan for having used deceit indiscriminately, poisoning all his promises. 'Guile', Botero states, 'should only be used in warfare'.[106] Mariana, in his brief exposition

---

100 *De rege*, p. 254, p. 257.

101 Ibid., pp. 254-55.

102 Ibid., p. 254.

103 Ibid., p. 205, 'Modestius alii Principi aequitatis & virtutum praesidium adiugunt. Neque concedunt ut sponte peccet, ab aequitate discedat. Coactum tamen necessitate permittunt mendacio fallere, fraudem suscipere. Ni si nimium iusti tenax sit, se periculo, rempublica multis calamitatibus involuat. (…) Utetur ergo Princeps ex commodo, fraude & mendacio, sed raro & quasi medicamento'.

104 The metaphor of the lion and the fox can be traced back to Plutarch's account of the life of the Spartan general Lysander. Cicero, *De officiis*, 1.13.41 condemns rulers acting as both lion and fox. On Machiavelli's inversion of the classical adage in *Il principe*, XVIII, see M. Colish (1978), 'Cicero's *De Officiis* and Machiavelli's *Prince*', *Sixteenth Century Journal*, Vol. 9, pp. 80-93.

105 *Della Ragion di Stato*, IX, 22.

106 Especially where fighting the infidel was concerned. Botero argues in the vein of a long tradition of Christian thought. Rodrigo Sánchez de Arévalo (1404-70), bishop of Osorio, for instance, describes deception and cunning as legitimate practices in just war and therefore in accordance with the exigencies of the *reconquista*. See his (1944), *Suma de la política*, ed. J.B. Pérez, (Instituto Francisco de Vitoria: Seminario de Historia de las Doctrinas Políticas; 2), Consejo Superior de Investigaciones Científicas, Madrid, preface. For further examples from medieval and Renaissance Iberian political literatures see J.A. Maravall (1984), *Estudios de historia del pensiamento*

of pragmatic and circumspect use of deceit according to the demands of necessity, does not offer any such restrictions.

Mariana counts Plato among the *modesti*, and concedes that Scripture itself backs their stance on the practice of outright lying.[107] With the help of his mother, Jacob cheated his older brother Esau out of his inheritance. No reader could doubt that, in doing so, Jacob fulfilled the will of God. Nor could any reader ignore the fact that the means apparently justified by the end were clearly dishonest. The embarrassed reference to Scripture pinpoints, again, the dilemma of Catholic theologians writing against Machiavelli. Christian sources and traditions frequently obstructed clear distinctions between 'good' and 'bad' means. Ultimately, what counted was that the end was inspired by the will to serve God. If intention is what really counts, the only way to proceed is to ensure that it will not be contaminated by overly enthusiastic, indifferent or badly informed practice of deceit. Mariana coolly compares what he identifies as the two main schools of thought, and invokes impressive authorities in support of the moderate practitioners of *mendacium*. Though he never explicitly approves of their stance, his examples amount to as much. He effectively endorses the position of the 'moderates', and thus one close to what Machiavelli had actually taught in *Il principe*. The watchful reader of his treatise was able to discern an author much less concerned to impose limits on the *prudent* use of deceit than either Botero or the majority of Catholic theologians.

This is borne out by the fact that Mariana's historical examples undermine his infrequent assertions that 'it is never licit for princes to lie, but that there is need for dissimulation'. In the end, he takes the plunge and draws the appropriate conceptual conclusion from his ambiguous interpretations of classical and medieval history. He concludes the chapter 'On Lies' admitting that lying and (dis)simulation cannot really be told apart. What is commonly denounced as *simulatio* or *mendacium* in a prince, Mariana suggests, should properly be called *cautio* and *dissimulatio* proper.[108] Rather than following up and justifying this terminological merger by means of a differentiated explication of scholastic terminology, Mariana goes on to adduce more historical examples. The first one provided to support his bold resolution to a complex moral and epistemological problem is drawn from the reign of James II of Aragon (1291-1327). The king's wife Blanca saved the life of their ally Charles of Salerno by promising his captors to execute him as soon as he had been handed over to her.[109] It is clear from the narrative that Queen Blanca did not have the least intention of staying true to her word. She merely pretended to have an objective in her mind that clearly was not there. The queen simply lied to achieve her ends. This is as clear-cut an example of mendacious behaviour as one could wish for, yet Mariana insinuates that Blanca did not lie, but only concealed her true intentions. Previously, he seemed prepared at least to draw a line between *dissimulatio* (concealing

español, Vol. 2, *La epoca del renacimiento*, Ediciones Cultura Hispánica, Madrid, especially pp. 13-38, pp. 42-43.

107 *De rege*, p. 205.
108 Ibid., pp. 209-10.
109 Ibid., pp. 392-93.

your true intentions) as opposed to *simulatio* equated with *mendacium* (lying). His terminological observation and *exemplum* renders any such distinction wholly meaningless. *Mendacium* and *simulatio* are conceptually absorbed into dissimulation. Ribadeneira had suggested that there is 'no moral wrong in secrecy or concealment of intent when dealing with enemies who are owed no openness'.[110] Mariana, in contrast, disqualifies the terminology that allowed one to differentiate between legitimate and illegitimate practices of deceit. Calling established terminology in question, he also refuses to offer an alternative one.

It is not surprising that Mariana tries to balance his ambiguous explications of legitimate (dis)simulation with a spirited diatribe against *mendacium* extending over almost two pages.[111] Here, he demands that the prince be brought up to detest *mendacium* more than any other form of iniquity. He combines seemingly steadfast denunciations of 'princes of recent memory' who wreaked havoc on their people's fortunes by practising 'lying and deceiving' with the assertion 'that Heaven does not allow a faithless man to enjoy gains gotten by lies for long'. Mariana's firm pronouncements to that effect, however, undermined by preceding discussion and examples from history, do not ring quite true with the reader. He himself admits that Ferdinand the Catholic and especially Louis XI succeeded in their enterprises not despite, but because they were among the most cunning practitioners of (dis)simulation.[112] The only real qualification Mariana offers is the familiar point that once a prince has acquired a firm reputation for double-dealing, no one will trust or ally themselves to him.[113] Somewhat fraudulently attributing to contemporary Machiavellians the belief that deceit and fraud are the only viable means of politics, Mariana is able to recommend the Florentine's genuine position as a moderate and acceptable one.

The actual target of Mariana's occasional outbursts of pious indignation is not the practice of (dis)simulation as such. It hardly can be, given that his own definition and relevant *exempla* allow for no practical restrictions whatsoever. The objective of another chapter rich in rhetorical twists and turns, again, is to urge that a certain way of thinking be 'imprinted upon the mind of the prince' when he is young. Mariana puts more emphasis than Ribadeneira on early indoctrination of the prince as the means of ensuring religious orthodoxy. If the youngster is taught properly, there is every likelihood that the (dis)simulating prince will never actually become a Machiavellian in the sense of someone who subscribes to the practice of gross deceit as an autonomous and axiomatic political theorem.

---

110 Höpfl, *Jesuit Political Thought*, p. 153.

111 *De rege*, pp. 208-10.

112 See Mariana's *Historiae*, xxv.10 (Ferdinand's character); and xxvi.1 and 2 (Ferdinand's machinations concerning Isabella of Castile's illegitimate succession,. and how he gained mastership of the military orders). On Ferdinand's ways of thinking see J.A. Maravall (1956), *Pensamiento político, política internacional y religiosa de Ferdinand el Católico*, Institución 'Ferdinand el Católico', Zaragoza [reprint, (1984), *Estudios de historia del pensamiento español: La epoca del renacimiento*, Ediciones Cultura Hispánica, Madrid, xii, pp. 343-61].

113 *De rege*, pp. 207-208.

If Mariana is more outspoken, or rather more anxious about the possible impact of education than Ribadeneira, this is partly a matter of context. Mariana does write during a period of transition which will end with the accession of a pious but utterly inexperienced prince. It also springs from palpable exasperation with all other means of checking the powers of princes. He prefers to put the mind of a humanist historian rather than a theologian to the task of developing ideas on the practice of prudence. The reader is led towards a position that acknowledges the impracticality of using lies and other forms of deception as *the only means* to achieve certain political ends. In fact, the *systematic* practice of lying is represented as the epitome of imprudent behaviour. Rather than differentiating between uses and terminologies, Mariana repudiates the attitude that elevates deceit, fraud and disloyalty to universal and complementary principles of prudence. *Dissimulatio*, *simulatio* and *mendacium* are legitimate as long as they remain infrequently applied means of politics rather than its ends; as long as they are used by princes conscious of the contingency and frailty of the human mind and character, not by rulers who believe them to be the universal principles of political ethics.

Pious Kings and False Prophets: The Vagaries of Providence

If Mariana's pragmatic advice on the practice of lying and deceit draws near Machiavellian standards, what, then, about the role of Christianity in moulding a practicable and appealing ethics for the early modern statesman? Machiavelli was widely condemned for banning Christian ethics as detrimental to political conduct. Thus far, the way in which Mariana expatiated on the practice of politics has been pragmatic and secular in character, even compared to generally flexible Jesuit thinkers (though with the possible exception of Botero). The acid test has to be his stance on the manifest presence of providence in political history. Again, Mariana's stance is conspicuous, and far from unequivocal.

The positions of Catholic theologians on the presence and verifiability of divine intervention in history and contemporary politics differed widely. It seems to have varied not least according to the extent to which, and different contexts within which, individuals and religious communities actually involved themselves with the decisions and fortunes of the courts of Vienna, Paris or Madrid.[114] The Jesuit William Lamormaini, for instance, stands out for his fierce insistence that God could not but bestow victory upon the arms of his 'most pious prince'.[115] Confessor to the emperor Ferdinand II at the court of Vienna during some of the most

---

114 There was no agreement among Catholic theologians concerning the verification of divine intervention. Jesuit confessors involved in the politics of the Thirty Years War, for instance, disagreed violently regarding their personal ability to assure their pious lords of divine support, and of the positive outcome of 'godly enterprises'; see R. Bireley (2003), *Jesuits and the Thirty Years War: Kings, Courts and Confessors*, Cambridge University Press, Cambridge, especially chapters two and three.

115 On Lamormaini's 'militant providentialism' and his considerable, albeit highly controversial influence on the making of imperial policy, see R. Bireley (1981), *Religion and Politics*

turbulent periods of the Thirty Years War (from 1624 to 1637), Lamormaini never wavered in his conviction that the Catholic powers must wage a 'holy war' on the Protestant and Reformed enemies of the faith. A highly controversial figure, he faced and frequently saw down vocal opposition from lay counsellors, fellow Jesuits, and other religious and secular clergy. Many Catholic counsellors, lay and clerical, did not share his confidence that decisive divine intervention on behalf of Counter-Reformation princes was imminent, and favoured religious compromise and peace with the forces of Protestantism. Like Adam Contzen, his equally providentialist counterpart at Munich, Lamormaini felt deeply involved in what he saw as Catholicism's struggle for survival and eventual renascence in the empire.

Lamormaini's and Contzen's outlook compares to that of Pedro de Ribadeneira, who featured prominently in Philip II's ideological preparation for the invasion of England. In his *Tratado*, Ribadeneira assures 'all those kings and princes who excel in His service' of the benefits of His 'special and paternal providence.'[116] They will find 'that everything turns out well', and that God will preserve their kingdoms, and bless them both during 'this wretched life and in heaven'. Part of the tribulations of this 'wretched life' was, of course, that even the most pious prince could not be certain that even his actions amounted to zealous observance of God's will and laws. Nor could the 'good prince' really count on being rewarded in this life. If there was no doubt that the 'ecclesia triumphans' would eventually prove victorious, it was also clear that the road to final victory would be a (very) tough one, beset with many setbacks and disasters. Ribadeneira seeks to offer solace, proclaiming that 'what is lost for Him, is truly won, and what is won without Him, is truly lost'.[117] Throughout the history of early modern Catholic religious communities' political reflection, periods of elevated hope alternated with those of doom and gloom. The vast majority of Catholic authors (including Ribadeneira), pushed by unfortunate circumstances, felt bound to acknowledge that even the most pious prince and policies could not be totally assured of God's favour. Ribadeneira himself called up the usual explanations for divine displeasure when blaming the tragedy of the Armada of 1598 on the sins of both the people of Spain and their king. Mariana, in *De rege*, joins Ribadeneira in chastising Philip II for the defeat of the mightiest fleet Europe had seen thus far.[118]

If it is true, as Höpfl argues, that for Jesuits the 'salient point was that there is no such thing as fortune or fate',[119] Mariana breaks the mould. *De rege* is sprinkled with references of a more secular humanist vein, naming *fortuna* and *fatum* as uncontrollable powers wreaking havoc upon the most carefully conceived schemes of man.[120] More striking perhaps is the fact that the treatise contains not a single

---

in the Age of the Counterreformation. Emperor Ferdinand II, William Lamormaini, S.J., and the Formation of Imperial Policy, The University of North Carolina Press, Chapel Hill.

116 *Tratado*, p. 470.
117 Ibid., p. 472.
118 *De rege*, p. 123.
119 Höpfl, *Jesuit Political Thought*, p. 110.
120 For instance, *De rege*, pp. 87-88.

direct reference to the divine origin of kingdoms, commonwealths and princes. Secular societies clearly are the product of a post-lapsarian process of corruption. The relationship between natural law, divine will and secular power is never laid out, and no hierarchy established between prudence, providence and fortune. Which is not to say that providence is absent from Mariana's treatise. It is just that examples of divine benevolence are reserved mainly for rulers who establish their piety in terms of their fiscal relation with the Church of Castile. Ferdinand III of Castile is frequently hailed as the ideal Christian ruler, and as a prince favoured by providence mainly because of his submissive attitude towards clerical authority and the many favours he bestowed on the churches of Castile. Mariana approvingly relates how Ferdinand, running out of troops and supplies during the siege of Seville (1248), responded to pressure exerted by nobles urging him to put levies on the churches of Castile so as to bring to a successful conclusion an otherwise doomed campaign.[121] The king, the reader is told, refused outright even to consider this option, declaring himself prepared 'to put greater faith in the prayers of the priests than all their physical possessions and money'. John I of Castile (1379-90), on the other hand, who 'plundered and melted down' the treasures of the church at Guadalupe to fund his war, failed miserably in his attempt to conquer Portugal.[122] Miracles are said to confirm divine goodwill conferred upon a king who pointedly refused to put the interests of the state before the fiscal autonomy of the Church.

Another example of the rewards pious rulers can expect is Ferdinand Antolínez, a *reconquista* warlord who spent his time in prayer while his vassals fought a pitched battle, and was rewarded with a miraculous victory.[123] In presenting the reader with this example, however, Mariana runs the danger of undermining his own vindications of political prudence. The reader is never told how to reconcile the image of the *reconquista* warrior praying instead of fighting with Mariana's pronouncements concerning the need for a prince to conduct himself in a manly manner and lead his armies in battle.[124]

Antolínez's behaviour becomes even more difficult to categorize once the reader comes across Mariana's relation of the fate of Martin Yañez de Barbuda, Grand Master of the Order of Alcántara during the reign of John I of Castile (1379-90).[125] Acting on the visions and instructions of a hermit renowned for his sanctity, Yañez de Barbuda decided to break a recently concluded peace and invade Moorish Granada with hastily assembled, untrained troops. Fatally mistaking piety and prophetic vision for political acumen, he perished together with his whole army in battle. Eulogists of the military orders would nonetheless praise him as a martyr to the Christian cause comparable to the idolized heroes of the Counter-

---

121 Ibid., p. 119.

122 Ibid.

123 Ibid., pp. 257-58.

124 Inspired by pragmatic assessment of the specific circumstances and contexts within which they are placed, Jesuits tend to be anything but homogenous in their approach to matters of politics and political ethics. See Bireley, *Jesuits and the Thirty Years War, passim.*

125 *De rege*, pp. 250-51.

Reformation.[126] Mariana, in contrast, severely castigates the grandmaster for his foolish reliance on the visions of a holy man totally ignorant of military affairs. Like any other virtue, religion is to be exercised according to the rational maxims of political prudence. The prince cannot afford to get lost in his own piety and spirituality.[127] Mariana admonishes Philip III to trust in God rather than listen to astrologers, saints and visionaries.[128] He must not 'spend night and day in prayer and anxiety of mind'; in cases of illness he is to follow the advice of doctors and natural remedies rather than pin his hopes on charms and superstitious practices. In a word, the prince must fill his time with rational political *negotium*, not with pious *otium*.[129] Philip III, probably the most pious of all the kings who ruled the Spanish monarchy between 1469 and 1700, ought to have taken this advice to heart.[130]

Even though Mariana celebrates Ferdinand III as the incarnation of a truly Christian king, he makes no serious attempt to identify a rational, historiographically verifiable pattern of interaction between the prudence of princes and divine providence. Appeals to providence in *De rege* are few and far between, and restricted mainly to incidents involving the fiscal fortunes of the churches of Castile. Mariana is generally less confident than some of his fellow Jesuits in discerning signs of providence in the conduct of human affairs. Unlike Ribadeneira, he is not prepared to establish a clear link between 'true reason of state' and divine providence, and does not try to turn providence into a more tangible and reckonable force in human history. Nor is he prepared to put as much trust in an individual prince as William Lamormaini. Ferdinand III of Castile is the exception rather than the rule.

Undoubtedly, Mariana will have subscribed to the view that the salvation of their soul is what princes have to be concerned about in the first instance. It is noteworthy, therefore, that he nowhere says so. Hesitant to pander to readers' desire for assurance of secular success, he does not make divine reward a full part of the equation of prudence and politics. His examples of divine providence shaping human history remain un-reconciled with a political pragmatism imposed by human corruption. Prudence is identified as a moral virtue first and foremost in that it serves the well-understood self-interest of the prince.

If the early modern period is indeed the 'age of exemplarity', then Mariana is an author who wittingly or unwittingly calls the value of exemplarity into question. His *exempla* on (dis)simulation and lying are a case in point. They expand moral boundaries, encourage the reader to abandon familiar distinctions, and totally undermine infrequent passages of righteous anger. *De rege* is a work that allows the reader an unusual amount of autonomy. Yet it is not autonomy borne from any real desire to empower an audience, though. It springs from Mariana's helplessness

---

126 See, for instance, Francisco Caro de Torres (1629), *Historia de las Ordenes Militares de Santiago, Calatrava y Alcantara*, I. Gonzales, Madrid, chapter 62, pp. 74-75.

127 *De rege*, pp. 250-53.

128 Ibid., pp. 250-51.

129 Ibid., p. 251.

130 See F. Díaz-Playa (1997), *Felipe III* , Planeta, Barcelona, especially pp. 145-50.

when confronted with the task of extracting moral guidance from the recalcitrant and unchangeably corrupt reality of politics.

Conclusion

Mariana does not set up his argument in conventional terms of anti-Machiavellian rhetoric and terminology familiar from the writings of Antonio Possevino or Pedro de Ribadeneira. He ignores Machiavelli's provocative presentation of Christian ethics as a kind of primary-school morals, and subtly and surreptitiously integrates what would commonly have been regarded as Machiavellian precepts into Christian statecraft. What distinguishes Mariana is not that he domesticates reason of state, but that he is prepared to push the boundaries of moral theology to the extent that he is prepared to render familiar casuistic terminology meaningless. The resultant interpretation of what does and what does not constitute legitimate forms of deceit appears rather generous in comparison with a Catholic propagandist like Ribadeneira. Obviously, Mariana fully absorbed Botero's *dictum* that 'in the deliberations of princes interest triumphs over every other consideration.'[131] As it is power, wealth and status that princes crave above all, a language of prudence has to be coined that accommodates and at the same time assimilates their desires into a halfway acceptable Christian framework.

If Mariana does not stand out by speaking to the fool according to his folly, he does set himself apart by the mostly resigned, at times ferociously critical attitude with which he accepts all pervasive human corruption. Any Catholic theologian agreed that the *ecclesia triumphans* would experience many defeats on its road to eventual victory over the enemies of the faith, and that the wicked may well succeed in this life. Yet authors as different as Possevino, Ribadeneira, and even Botero subscribed to an altogether providentialist and ultimately optimistic outlook.[132] Mariana edges away from this optimistic epistemological and moral stance. Deeply conscious of the uncertainties and moral ambiguities of history and politics, Mariana is clearly much less assured of his ability to verify and translate divine providence into axiomatic rules of conduct than Ribadeneira. This makes it easier for him to move across and blur the boundaries of true or false reason of state than it was for the latter. He constantly vacillates between the various positions he presents, and, despite assuming the position of the learned *arbiter*, rarely if ever offers straightforward judgements. Instead, morally ambiguous and legally complex matters are dissolved into conveniently vague commonplaces.[133]

Mariana's rhetorical strategies betray a lack of epistemological and therefore, ultimately, moral confidence. Still feeling bound to recruit historical *exempla* for confirmation of what is true, his philological, philosophical and historical insights

---

131 Botero, *Della ragion di stato*, II.6.

132 See Höpfl, *Jesuit Political Thought*, pp. 109-11.

133 On the equivocal and subversive nature of Mariana's humanist rhetorical strategies see also Ferraro, *Tradizione e Ragione*, especially chapter nine, pp. 207-30.

prevent him from ironing out the diversity of historical circumstances and the ambiguity of lessons from history. The overall pessimistic assessment of the human ability to extract knowledge from history goes along with a discernible lack of confidence in the human ability to obtain something like moral certainty from practical reasoning. Studying history for the purpose of providing *reglas de buen gobierno* seems to have forced Mariana to loosen the link between practical wisdom and morality. It is no accident that the issue of whether or to what degree prudence can be considered a moral virtue is never raised in *De rege*. Prudence in Mariana is a kind of practical wisdom no longer firmly and confidently attached to the moral good as an end in itself.

Wittingly or unwittingly, Mariana has given the 'virtue of prudence' more than a touch of Machiavellian *virtù*, not least because of the degree to which he anchors the preservation of the *bonum commune* in the mind and heart of the prince. Indirectly urging the prince to communicate ideal images of rulership to his people as a corollary of maintaining healthy relations of power, Mariana instead implies that the appearance of virtue may take priority before substance. Governance and political prudence in *De rege* are a matter of maintaining a semblance of peace among human beings who are for the most part irredeemably corrupt and almost always misguided. The *bonum commune* itself can therefore presented largely as a means for princes to preserve and expand their power. Characteristically, and appropriately, Mariana's term for prudent government is *principatus civilis*. Terms like *civiliter vivere*, *communitas civilis* or even *scientia civilis* or *politica* would have indicated a stronger emphasis on communal government that is 'political' in the inherited Aristotelian sense. These terms are absent from *De rege*. Resigned in his acceptance of human corruption, and calmly investigating which are and which are not the true virtues in a prince, Mariana edges towards a Hobbesian understanding of politics and the political.

The author of *De rege* thus delivers what in pure terms of political-legal theory is an insurmountable polarity: the only really effective political institution is a ruler completely fulfilling the ideal of the prudent, virtuous philosopher-king. This ideal, on the other hand, can hardly be realized by corrupted man. Mariana has let Machiavelli slip in through the back door, and he cannot but be aware of it. It would be surprising, however, had Mariana, an astute theorist of the corruption of the politically active individual, simply ended his argument here. Deeply distrustful of the capability of laymen to cultivate and exercise prudence, he broaches new ideas concerning the future role of the clergy in the government of the monarchy. In the following chapter, we will meet the men Mariana felt happy to entrust with the care of the realm. Prudence and politics cannot be left to laws, magistrates, cortes or princes. The only remaining institution is the Church.

CHAPTER FIVE

Guardians of the Realm

Mariana's reading of history does not allow him to think of laws, cortes or magistrates as being able to check the power of the monarch. The power of kings may originate in the people as a whole, but rulers have come to wield powers vastly exceeding those first bestowed upon them by their people. The Castilian cortes are a prime example of a popular assembly commonly exercising its right to vote on taxes, but all too frequently succumbing to princely ambition and ruthlessness. Princes, on the other hand, are likely to be too ambitious or too weak to resist the entreaties of selfish courtiers urging them to push the limits of their power to the point where their actions become potentially self-destructive. Much depends on the integrity and capability of the individual prince, and few rulers bring the necessary moral and intellectual qualifications to their office. The limits of royal power cannot therefore be negotiated and implemented in terms other than those of prudence and self-interest on the part of the prince.

Whilst confirming that there is no real alternative to the rule of a strong *and* prudent monarch, Mariana identifies new ways in which the prudent conduct of government ought to be ensured. The ways to improve monarchical government are discussed in detail in the final chapters of each of the three books of *De rege*. All three chapters enhance the place of religion and the secular clergy in the government of Spain.[1] The ever present discourse on prudence is consciously intertwined with reflections on the national Church as the nucleus of the secular body politic. Interweaving individual chapters and focusing the treatise as a whole, the concluding chapters of *De rege* express most clearly Mariana's agenda and prime objective: to assure Philip III that if he is to preserve his many dominions, the secular clergy of Castile must become the keystone of Spanish Habsburg government.

Moving the Castilian clergy into the centre of a discourse on reason of state and the state of the Spanish monarchy, Mariana spotlights carefully selected aspects of the early modern Castilian experience of government. By the late 1590s, clerical advisers exerted influence over many parts of the royal administration, albeit often in narrowly defined roles. Theologians and canon lawyers teaching at the peninsular universities were required to provide memoranda feeding into decision-making processes at Madrid. Select theologians were called up to staff various *juntas* set up to

---

1   *De rege*, i.10, *De religione nihil Princeps statuat* ('The prince should not decide on religious matters'), pp. 108-24; ii.14, *De religione* ('On religion'), pp. 249-60; iii.16, *Multas in una provincia esse religiones non est verum* ('It is not practical to have several religions in one province'), pp. 419-46. On the clergy's responsibility for the preservation of the monarchy see also iii.2, *De episcopi* ('On bishops'), pp. 273-84.

deal with specific, and often the most controversial issues.[2] For instance, theologians were called up to counsel upon the taxation of the clergy and the legitimacy of the *limpieza de sangre* statutes. Ecclesiastics also sat as regular members on some of the permanent royal *consejos*. Confessors, almoners and chaplains attached to the royal court and the households of nobles and patricians, again, exerted various degrees of influence over the minds of their flock. The world of sixteenth- and seventeenth-century Spaniards was one 'in which theology enjoyed a central role in politics even as political thought was becoming increasingly secularized'.[3]

Some of the issues treated in the chapters on Church and religion are familiar from more conventional mirrors-of-princes as well as the generic debate on reason of state. Yet *De rege* is markedly distinct when Mariana comes to develop his ideas on the future relationship between Church and crown of Castile. The treatise epitomizes the aspirations of a secular clergy and episcopate confident of its contribution to the government of Philip II and at the same time anxious to maintain, possibly enhance its role and reputation under the new regime. It demonstrates how far a post-Tridentine humanist theologian keen to uphold politics as the 'bailiwick of theology' might go. At the same time, the chapters on religion illuminate the degree to which the secularizing language of reason of state could be adapted to serve the objectives of a highly politicized clergy.[4] Mariana pulls no punches in this respect. He chooses a contentious issue to start off what will amount to a call for theocratic reform of the Spanish monarchy: the question of religious toleration.

Religio Vinculum Societatis or the Fallacy of Toleration

The issue of religious toleration provided perhaps the most obvious starting point for an argument on the political role of the secular clergy. Readers could be expected to be fairly familiar with the general structure and course of the argument revolving around the problem of tolerating religious deviance.[5] Catholic theologians were divided on the issue, and Jesuits were no exception. In a nutshell, there were two lines of argument. Everyone agreed that heresy had to be extinguished whenever and wherever it showed its ugly face. As to the justification for suppressing heresy, Ignatius of Loyola himself had argued that the salvation of souls was a good enough reason for the rigorous and if necessary violent enforcement of religious unity.[6] His words are echoed in the advice issued by such stalwarts of the military

---

2   See the illuminating discussion and examples in A. Pagden (1981), 'The "School of Salamanca" and the "Affair of the Indies"', in C.B. Schmitt (ed.), *History of Universities*, Vol. 1, *Continuity and Change in Early Modern Universities*, Amersham, Avebury, pp. 71-112, especially pp. 72-78; and C. Jago (1995), 'Taxation and Political Culture in Castile, 1590-1640', in Kagan and Parker, *Spain, Europe and the Atlantic World*, pp. 48-72, pp. 48-54.

3   Jago, 'Taxation and Political Culture', p. 51.

4   Fernández-Santamaria, *Reason of State*, p. 169.

5   See the excellent analysis of Jesuits approaches in Höpfl, *Jesuit Political Thought*, pp. 112-39.

6   In his letters to Peter Canisius, see O'Malley, *The First Jesuits*, p. 273.

Counter-Reformation as Lamormaini or Contzen.[7] Other writers chose to highlight the political dangers of heresy, emphasizing that religion is the 'civic bond' par excellence and will remain strong only if Catholic orthodoxy persisted. Inevitably, religious toleration undermines not just the fabric of religion but that of society and government as well. History provided undisputable evidence that different denominations simply cannot coexist in the long term. This is the line taken, for instance, by cardinal Bellarmine, Botero, the Jesuits Possevino and Scribani as well as Mariana himself.[8] Ribadeneira, unsurprisingly, dedicates entire chapters to assert that heresy is 'the cause of the revolution and ruin of kingdoms', and that different religions simply cannot be made to live side by side peacefully for more than short periods of time.[9]

Where Catholic writers disagreed was whether or not prudence could advise a policy of toleration under specific circumstances. Ribadeneira advised that as long as heresy had not yet managed to get a foothold in society, especially among the nobility, the prince should nip it in the bud. However, it ought to be extirpated:

> without occasioning tumult and without detriment to Catholics, considering prudently and circumspectly the condition of his kingdom, and whether it is a few or many who suffer from the heretical leprosy. For when heretics occupy the whole kingdom, or the greater part of it, princes cannot uproot the tares without at the same time tearing out the wheat. Or, if there is a fear or danger of great upheavals or wars, Christian prudence teaches the use of dissimulation, lest more harm than good should come of it.[10]

Ribadeneira is one of a number of authors suggesting that necessity entitled princes to make allowances for a *limited* and *temporary* policy of toleration. Mariana vehemently disagrees. He is firmly in the camp of those who argue that political prudence invariably demands that religious uniformity be enforced at all cost.

The damage caused by negotiating peaceful coexistence of true believers and heretics far exceeds those of suppressing heresy. Even if the restoration of religious uniformity exacts a terrible price initially, a prospect so horrifying that toleration does appear to be an attractive option, heresy must be rooted out. The eventual and inevitable collapse of religious co-habitation will lead to even more suffering and put the monarchy at an even higher risk. Whatever the difficulties involved in confronting powerful heretical groups, toleration is simply *very* bad politics.

Refusing to justify toleration on the grounds of necessity, Mariana exclusively argues in terms of the humanist rationale of civic religion. Religion is a 'natural impulse' that 'cannot by any means or by any force be torn out of us, any more than

---

7   See Bireley, *Jesuits and the Thirty Years War*, especially pp. 63-99.

8   Höpfl, *Jesuit Political Thought*, p. 112.

9   *Tratado*, p. 500. See Book one, chapters 23-29.

10   Ibid., p. 499. Ribadeneira refers to Matt. 13, 24-30, frequently quoted in this context. See also Bellarmine (1965), *De laicis*, in J. Fèvre (ed.), *Roberti Bellarmini opera omnia, ex editione Veneta*, Vol. 11, Minerva, Frankfurt, p. 343. Höpfl, *Jesuit Political Thought*, pp. 133-34, suggests that Ribadeneira, and indeed Jesuits in general refer to *dissimulatio* as the practice of ignoring or suspending the laws and principles a Catholic prince does not currently have the power to enforce.

the other feelings, such as laughter, wonder, and deliberation, with which we are furnished from birth'.[11] It is *virtus* in the sense of a human quality that can and must be inspired, cultivated, and above all manipulated in order to shape the private and public lives of men.[12] The prince may manacle the bodies of his subjects, but:

> the spirit, free and untrammelled, is restrained by no chains unless bound by religion. And since there are such great hidden recesses in the soul of man it would be easy to promise and to fail when occasion offers itself, unless we are convinced and certain that crimes and frauds are a concern of Heaven.[13]

If we do not believe that God has a part in our lives, 'how will contracts, alliances and covenants among men by guaranteed?'.[14] Religion is the only reliable *vinculum societatis*. Only religion can forge a bond strong enough to prevent human society from breaking apart.[15] With the loss of religious unity, accordingly, all other bonds that tie men to one another will be dissolved. The very nature of religion and the mechanisms of religious practice prescribe that different religions cannot coexist in one commonwealth.[16] Not even tyrants, who always strive to manipulate their subjects, are able to devise a *ratio gubernandi* that could restrain a religiously divided people.[17]

The case against religious diversity as tantamount to the destruction of the commonwealth is argued in entirely prudential terms.[18] Elaborating on the civic

---

11   *De rege*, p. 273. See also ibid., pp. 17-18.

12   Ibid., pp. 249-50.

13   Ibid., p. 255. See also ibid., p. 273, p. 421.

14   Ibid., 255, 'Nam si nullum numen est, aut negotium neque habet neque exhibet aliis: qui comercia inter homines, foedera, conventaque sanciantur? (…) Quod consensus gentium omnium declarat, neque privata foedera firma credentium, nisi iurisiurandi religione vallata: neque publica conventa, nisi caesis de more hostiis'.

15   Ibid., p. 421.

16   Ibid., pp. 421-22, 'Est enim religio humanae societatis vinculum, cuius sanctitate foedera, commercia, societatesque sanciuntur. (…) Quae autem communio & societas inter eos esse potest, qui non ad eundem Deum certe non eadem caeremonia cultuque recurrunt? alii alios ut impios aversentur: iisque violandis divinum numen promereri sibi persuadeant. (…) Quare qui rebus humanis consentiunt, divinis dissentiunt: eorum amicitia claudicet potiori ex parte necesse est: atque inter quos amicos rerum divinarum consensio non est, neque humanarum plena erit & vera.'

17   Ibid., p. 426.

18   Ibid., p. 421, 'Paci autem nihil magis adversatur, quam si in eadem republica urbe aut provincia una plures religiones sint'; also p. 422, 'Nulla sanguinis propinquitas, nulla morum similitudo, vitae genus aut patria tantum constringunt voluntates benevolentia, quantum religionis diversitas labefactat: neque ulla foedera tam sancto iure vallata esse possunt, quae non disturbentur facile, si diversae de divinitate opiniones suscipiantur'; and p. 433, '(…) neque in una domo uxori cum concubina convenire unquam: neque in una civitate, aut provincia falsam religionem cum vera recte tolerari. Collidant inter se necesse est, quorum natura est contraria: longoque usu intellectum, novam religionem nunquam fuisse in aliquam urbem admissam sine magna civium & rerum calamitate. Circumfer mentis oculos per omnia tempora, veterem ac recentem memoriam explica: videbis profecto ubicunque id malum viguit, iure honestatis convulsa, caedibus & latrociniis misceri omnia: atque ea in veteris religionis cultores, & ministros edita crudelitatis exempla, quae ab hesternis hostibus nunquam extitissent;' see also p. 434, pp. 253-54, pp. 292-301.

function of religion, Mariana repeatedly urges readers to recognize that 'fear and hope, reward and punishment are (…) the foundations which sustain sociability and union among men'.[19] Fear is always the more powerful and therefore more reliable inspiration of loyalty. One of Mariana's typically hardnosed comments on the human ability to act virtuously assures readers that

> fear often restrains people where the splendour of virtue itself would have no effect. The prospect of reward often stimulates their souls, and they do not waste away in lethargy and idleness. Yet these bedrocks of salvation will be strong only insofar as they anticipate the verdict of divine providence in terms of future punishments and rewards. The fear of the power of judges might prevent open crimes, but what will hinder covert ones, if not awareness of the awful majesty of God?[20]

Fear of the kind of punishment secular authority is able to mete out may suffice to suppress open rebellion and public expression of discontent (*vis publica*), but it will not protect the ruler from secret treachery (*occultis fraus*). Mariana resolves that, unless restrained by the kind of fear which only religion can inspire, people will not abstain from crime. In turn, religion is also by far the best tool to gain the 'goodwill of the multitude' and arouse their zeal for the prince's causes.[21]

Mariana applauds the inventiveness of pagan rulers who exploited the religious feelings of their subjects and made proper use of elaborate and awe-inspiring religious ceremony.[22] Scipio Africanus had a policy of carefully construed public displays of personal piety which went a long way to persuade the people of Rome of his sincere piety.[23] Other princes and lawgivers assumed the office of high priest, or like the ancient kings Minos and Numa Pompilius pretended to converse with gods. Early Egyptian rulers, again, managed to stabilize their fragile rule by inventing new cults, traditions and ceremonies.[24] Like the Egyptians, Moses conceived religious laws and rituals which assured the people of Israel of the love of God, and held them together during periods of crisis and persecution.[25] Mariana in effect discusses

---

19   Ibid., pp. 253-55.

20   Ibid., pp. 253-54.

21   Ibid., pp. 258-59. Compare this assertion of the preventive force of religious beliefs with the far more sceptical view of Lipsius in *Politicorum*, IV, 10, pp. 154-58.

22   Höpfl, *Jesuit Political Thought*, p. 114 points out that no Jesuit noted the obvious theatricality of Catholic as opposed to Reformed religious ceremonies.

23   *De rege*, p. 259.

24   Ibid., p. 254, 'Hoc cum legislatores intelligerent viri prudentes, vanam sine religione omnem industriam fore, legibus sanciendis sacrorum ritus, reliquum religionis apparatum & caeremonias adiunxerunt: in eoque maxime laborarunt, ut populo persuaderent poenas scelerum aliquando feras, irritas esse nunquam: leges quas ipsi ferrent non humana prudentia excogitatas, sed acceptas divinitus fuisse comenti sunt.' Also ibid., pp. 254-55, 'Nimirum cives ad parendum non modo imperio, sed etiam religione constringere satagebant. (…) Inepte haec, inquis, omnia & aniliter. Fateor, quis enim id non videat? Sed in eo sapienter quod universi naturae impulsu excitari intellexerunt, quod res erat, neque congregari homines sine lege, neque leges sine religione constare.'

25   Ibid., pp. 425-26.

the law of the Old Testament as a design to secure political concord as much as an expression of divine truth.

Though he ridicules pagan religious doctrine as such, Mariana offers no way of distinguishing between pagan and orthodox Christian ways of manipulating the religious inclinations of 'the multitude'. Nor does he make any effort to argue that upholding the Catholic as opposed to pagan or Reformed faith pays particular civic or political dividends. Prudent strategies of religious manipulation easily transgress otherwise scrupulously maintained boundaries between different faiths or confessions. Only a few Catholic, especially German Jesuit authors seem to have claimed that the Lutheran abolishment of 'good works' undermined civic virtue, including the virtue of military valour.[26] Like many of his fellow Jesuits, Mariana is curiously disinterested in whether the Catholic or the Reformed faith is the 'better' civic religion. Did Mariana realize that this would have been a difficult point to make in the face of the military prowess and perseverance shown by Spain's Reformed enemies, above all the rebellious Dutch? Whatever the reasons, he seems to have been satisfied with a general condemnation of the corrosive effect that change and innovation in matters religious invariably have on society.[27] What is less surprising is that he does not remark upon Machiavelli's argument that the Christian faith is detrimental to martial virtue and that the loyalty of citizens must not be divided between their care for their souls and their *patria*.[28] Unlike Botero, he does not extol Christian religion as the one particularly suited to ruling the souls and bodies, affections and thoughts of subjects.[29] As a Castilian conscious and proud of the military achievements and glory of the *reconquista*, Mariana may have found Machiavelli's proposition so risible that it was not even worth mentioning. His friend Ribadeneira at least takes the time to make short shrift of one of the more notorious passages of the *Discorsi*.[30]

Mariana is much more concerned with the opposition to his inveterate indictment of even the most limited policy of toleration based on humanist thought. He brings into play the way in which the Byzantine emperor Justinian I (527-565) was reported to have handled the threat from monophysite heterodoxy. Mariana acknowledges that Justinian's treatment of the Eutychian heresy may be regarded as an illustration of the concession and prudent management of religious coexistence.[31] Once the emperor realized that the sect of the archimandrite Eutyches could no longer be extirpated without causing serious political disturbance, he continued to defend

---

26   See Höpfl, *Jesuit Political Thought*, pp. 120-21.

27   See Ferraro, *Tradizione e Ragione*, pp. 195-99, p. 353.

28   *Discorsi*, II.2; I.11-15.

29   *Della ragion di stato*, II.16. See W. Reinhard (1982), 'Confessionalizzazione forzata? Prolegomeni ad una teoria dell'età confessionale', *Annali dell'Istituto Storico Italo-Germanico in Trento*, Vol. 8, pp. 13-37, pp. 34-36.

30   Ribadeneira, *Tratado*, p. 567.

31   Ibid., pp. 426-28. The other example is the situation of the Early Church before and immediately after the conversion of Constantine.

orthodoxy, but had his wife support or at least pretend to support the sectarians.[32] Justinian and Theodora acted according to the rules of court politics: integrating political and religious factions into the general struggle for royal favour and playing them off against one another. Discussing a further example of toleration inspired by political expediency, Mariana even praises the Roman emperor Jovian (c. 363-364) for his refusal to let the Christian majority impose their faith upon the pagan followers of Julian the Apostate.[33] In a situation where the empire was under imminent threat from Persian invasion, Jovian managed to stifle civic strife and strengthen the defence of the empire by enforcing toleration.[34] Justinian and Jovian are favourably compared to emperor Zeno's (474-491) ill-advised and ill-timed attempt at reuniting monophysite and orthodox Christianity.[35] In trying to impose the flawed theological formula of the Henoticon (482) on the whole of Christianity, Zeno in fact provoked the first schism between the Eastern and Western Church. Mariana admits that, at first glance, *exempla* like these strongly suggest that a policy of toleration can reap political dividends. He quickly resolves to examine them in more detail. In doing so, he comes to query the value of humanist faith in the exemplarity of history as well as humanist strategies of historical comparison. In fact, Mariana comes to question whether examples from history can provide moral guidance for public action in present circumstances.[36]

The authenticity and validity of historical examples of toleration, and the exemplarity of history with it, are called into question on two counts. Firstly, Mariana insists that the idea that coexistence of diverse religions worked in the past is likely to be based on misinterpretation of the relevant sources. If the *memoria veteris temporis* were to be examined more carefully, he suggests, it could quickly become clear that it was Justinian's intention to convert the Eutychian heretics by *clementia* rather than force. In all likelihood, the Byzantine emperor's course of action merely represents a classic example of the failure of toleration apparently dictated by necessity. Mariana discards the kind of necessity advocated, among others, by Pedro de Ribadeneira.[37] Justinian, in any case, played with the fire of religious toleration only once. Otherwise, he prudently stuck to a policy of straightforward suppression and exclusion, thus truly earning his reputation as a 'shining light of civic prudence' (*clarus civilis prudentiae*).

---

32 Mariana appears to confuse the Byzantine archimandrite Eutyches (c.378-454), deposed and exiled by the Council of Chalcedon (451) for his monophysite heretical views, with the contemporary of Justinian I and orthodox Patriarch of Constantinople (552-565, again 577-582) of the same name.

33 Captain of Julian the Apostate's (361-363) bodyguard, he received the purple after Julian's death and supported Christian orthodoxy.

34 *De rege*, p. 427.

35 Ibid., p. 427.

36 On how uneasy awareness of historical contingency increasingly characterized humanist discourses see T. Hampton (1990), *Writing from History. The Rhetoric of Exemplarity in Renaissance Literature*, Cornell University Press, Ithaca and London.

37 *De rege*, pp. 429-31.

Secondly, and more importantly, both Justinian and Jovian were successful only within the very specific contexts of their time.[38] Mariana invokes the old adage that *varia et commutabilis temporum ratio est* in order to discredit the historical case for religious toleration.[39] The actions of Justinian and Jovian are deeply rooted in the particular circumstances within which they operated. Circumstances have changed profoundly since the days of these Roman and Byzantine emperors. Mariana accounts for the profundity of historical change with the fact that historical experience accumulates over long periods of time. This is an instance where he appears to modify his view that the progress of time since the Fall of Man is concomitant with decline and the progress of human corruption. Things were done differently in the past, Mariana says, because of the 'faults of the times and of men'. The faults of men in this particular respect being that they had not yet gathered and digested sufficient collective experience to be able to know better. Future generations had yet to have the opportunity to learn from the mistakes of their ancestors. Mariana uses this tentative notion of 'historical progress' to conclude that policies of religious toleration that worked well in times past will prove destructive if applied to the present situation of European-wide confessional conflict. The dynamic of historical time summarily disqualifies historical examples marshalled in support for a policy of religious toleration.[40] It brutally exposes the *exemplum Justiniani* as a 'cursed example that nonetheless in our time is imitated in the councils of princes.'[41]

Yet Mariana insists that the topos of the *malitia temporum* applies to the present as much as it applies to a distant past.[42] The fact that humankind increases its collective wisdom over time does not prepare nations for a religious and political crisis of previously unimaginable proportions. It is true, the consequences of religious diversity are, invariably, the same. The *status reipublicae* is turned upside down, external enemies reap the harvest of dissent and civil strife and public assemblies

---

38   Ibid., p. 427.

39   Ibid., p. 429, 'Nos quidem certe non quid fuerit factum quaerimus, qui sciamus multa perturbata olim temporum aut hominum culpa fuisse: ne licuisse quidem bonis Imperatoribus vitia omnia ab stirpe convellere. quid iure & ex ratione fieri debeat, quid ex republica futurum sit, inquirendum putabamus. Varia & commutabilis temporum ratio est. multaque aliquando tolerata in perniciem vertant, si nostro tempore condedantur. Dies & usus & maior rerum cognitio declaravit, rempublicam constare non posse, civibus in cultu religionis discrepantibus.'

40   On the 'temporalization of history' or 'dynamization of time' (*Verzeitlichung der Geschichte* or *Dynamisierung der historischen Zeit*) in European historical thought see R. Koselleck (1985), *Futures Past: on the Semantics of Historical Time* (Studies in contemporary German Social Thought), MIT Press, Cambridge, Mass. [transl. of R. Koselleck (1979), *Vergangene Zukunft: zur Semantik geschichtlicher Zeiten*, Suhrkamp, Frankfurt]. Koselleck identifies the period around 1800 as European 'Sattelzeit', the historical period during which a notion of dynamization of history became prevalent among bourgeois theorists. As a result of his focus on the post-1789s, he tends to undervalue the dynamic aspect in early modern notions of historical time.

41   *De rege*, p. 427.

42   Ibid., p. 431.

cease to function as places of deliberation and decision.[43] Yet the havoc Luther and Calvin have thus far wrought upon France and Germany already surpasses the damage done by Julian the Apostate, the Novatians and Donatists, the Arians and Circumcelliones, the Albigensians and the Hussites taken together.[44] Circumstances have not just changed. In fact, they have worsened dramatically. 'Time and the wickedness of men' have widened the gap between the past and the present, between historical models and contemporary norms of moral conduct and political savvy. 'Time and the wickedness of men' are always likely to reduce and disable the exemplarity of history.

The Enemy Within

Mariana's dogged insistence that his contemporaries are faced with a crisis of incomparable historical dimensions compels him to re-assess the relationship between historical change and the exemplarity of history. It also provides a further cornerstone for what has by now become evident as one of the main preoccupations of his argument as a whole: the indictment of the secular elite and of the nobility in particular. His claim that the Church is more than ever before the victim of the political fallout of heterodoxy is by no means unique, but *De rege* puts it forward with an uncommon slant. In the first instance, the European Catholic nobility are warned against misjudging the destructive force of heterodoxy.[45] They are reminded that the maelstrom of destruction initiated by toleration of heresy eventually devours all social classes. It may start with the clergy, but will invariably end up with the nobility. Historical evidence is provided by the wars of the peasants' 'against the nobility in Germany' and neighbouring regions in the 1520s and 1530s.[46] Mariana associates the Peasants' Wars with the prophesies of Karl Böheim, the 'Pfeifer of Niklashausen' (1476) and the eschatological visions and sermons of Luther's one-time partisan, Thomas Müntzer (1521-25). The former in his 'dreams' and the latter in his address to the Thuringian peasants on the eve of the battle of Frankenhausen (1525) denigrated the concept of *libertas Christianae* and turned it into a vengeful slogan for the destruction of churches and the complete abolition of any secular order.

Germania (alongside France) provides Mariana with what he proffers as indubitable evidence for the 'true reason' behind the religious conflict sweeping through contemporary Europe. In principle, princes like to put on a 'show of religion' so as to use demands for the reform of the clergy as a pretext to deprive

---

43   Ibid., pp. 437-39.

44   Ibid., pp. 431-34.

45   Ibid., p. 434, '(…) etsi parum dici non debet, quod societatis mutuae vincula dissolvit, Christi tunicam, cui milites pepercerunt, crudeliter lacerat in partes, quibus neutri tegantur. Populus enim vectigalium gravitate fessus, & multis difficultatibus implicitus in sacerdotum opimos reditus, templorum thesauros, quos maiores ad supremas reipublicae difficultates, quasi in sacrum aerarium construxerunt, involare oblata occasione non dubitabit.'

46   Ibid., pp. 436-37.

Catholic churches of their property.[47] Because religion is the most powerful of emotions affecting and governing man, it can also very easily be abused, and made to serve the greed of princes and satisfy aristocrats' thirst for wealth.[48] Under the present conditions, the attempt to restrain the destructive force of religious diversity by playing off court factions against one another will lead to the destruction of the commonwealth. Mariana backs up his point with acute observations of the pragmatic and ruthless, yet ultimately disastrous tactics employed by Charles VIII and Henry III of France:

> If [the prince] favours one party, the others will inevitably become alienated, he will have to consider them suspect and disloyal, and will have to ban them from offices in administration and military, in order to prevent them from abusing their arms, authority, and favour to overturn the commonwealth. Inevitably, they will suffer heavily from this, (…) will conceal their hurt at first, (…) will initially conspire among themselves so as to protect themselves against the faction favoured by the king, but once they feel strong enough they will wrest religious freedom from the prince, they will gain in pride, threaten the prince, finally try to seize power, and if they do so oppress and disinherit their opponents; the king, then, can either convert to their religion or be deprived of his crown and life.[49]

---

47   See Ibid., p. 435, 'Dux se temerariae multitudini dederit, praesertim religionis specie armatus, si in sacerdotum mores invehatur, facta seditione in republica pars infirmior, quales sacerdotes sunt, in praedam multitudini cedent, templis divitias & ornamenta detrahent tam multos accumulatas per annos. Quod malum nostro tempore accidisse scimus, ubicunque religionis dissidia viguere.'

48   Ibid., pp. 422-23, 'Nihil fallacius, nihil violentius, quam ubi divinum numen seditioni praetenditur. pars enim impune sibi peccare videtur excusante conscientia: caeteri coercere petulantiam non audent, primum subeunte metu ne fraudibus vindicandis divini iuris aliquid admistum violetur. Deinde exacerbatis voluntatibus, ubi malum semel invaluit, filii ipsi in parentes exurgunt: nullam fratribus humanitatem exhibent iisdem parentibus nati. Omnia dolis, sanguine, caedeque propinquorum redundare necesse est. discordia, civili sanguine imbuta homines reddit immanes ipsoque naturae sensu spoliat.' Also ibid., p. 425, 'Finge duas in una provincia, aut civitate eadem vigere religiones, nobilium favore, ferroque populi armatas, numero spectatorum non impares. quid Princepts faciet? quo se vertet? (…) quam rationem administrandae reipublicae explicabit? An consiliis regere populos, legibus astringere, emendare iudiciis possit?'. 'Est enim religionis amor caeteris affectibus potentior.'

49   Ibid., pp. 425-26, 'Si uni parti faverit, alios sentiet alienatos: quos ut suspectos, atque infideles me quidem arbitro a reipublica administratione, & militiae muneribus arcebit: ne armis, auctoritate, gratiaque ad reipublicae eversionem abutantur. Quae cautio necessario quamvis suscepta, magnam illis molestiam pariet (…). Sed tantisper tamen dissimulabunt dolorem, (…). Ac primum inter se conspirabunt, ut salutem tueantur contra vires factionis adversae. Ubi satis virium erit, religionis libertatem a Principe extorquebunt: precibus minas adiungent. Id si successerit superbia mox elati, correptisque, armis feroces in rempublicam impetum dabunt. Si vicerint, oppressos adversarios, bonisque eversos finibus deturbabunt. Deinde Regem suorum praesidio nudatum, atque in potestatem redactum, aut ad suam traducent religionem, aut de gradu deiectum caesumque, imperio spoliabunt.'

The Valois failed utterly in their attempts to offset the aspirations of aristocratic clans which had set themselves up against one another along religious lines merely for reasons of political convenience. Trying to utilize the apparently confessional divide, they unwittingly delivered their kingdom into the hands of the highly suspect convert Henry of Navarre. Those who revolt against royal authority, according to Mariana, will always hide the real reasons for their actions behind allegedly ulterior religious motives. Demands for the acceptance of religious diversity primarily serve to anticipate and hamper efforts the crown would make to suppress rebellion motivated solely by thirst for power.

Mariana's lucid developmental analysis of the secular mechanisms of internecine religious conflict identifies two likely causes for the escalation of heretical tendencies into open religious civil war. Firstly, a king who is inexperienced or overly ambitious and hopes to line his coffers with the riches of the Church, or use religious divisions to play off aristocratic factions against each other. Secondly, the aristocratic houses and cliques themselves, vying for lucrative offices and honours and ceaselessly struggling for the mastery of court and royal administration. Both the prince and the nobility involved in an unrelenting struggle for power will generally use religion merely as a pretext for their purely political aims. Heresy turns into a national calamity only if the king or parts of the nobility decide to use religious dissent as a political lever. The prevention of religious civil war in turn is a matter not so much of checking the spread of heretical opinions in the general populace as of indoctrinating the prince from an early age and curtailing aristocratic ambition.

His father and tutors must prepare the young prince for his office, trying to imbue him with an understanding of the political nature and potential uses of religious feelings. However, once the heir to the throne becomes king, especially if he is still young, it is always likely that even his tutors' best efforts turn out to have been in vain. The prince may succumb to the insinuations of fawning nobles eager to bring about a change of religion for no other reason than to satisfy unbridled lust for power. Mariana asks his reader to:

> imagine, that a prince is left by his father at an early and weak age, (…) imagine that he has low morals and is contaminated with new ideas about religion, with the result that he changes the established ancestral religious practices. (…) Imagine that a conspiracy is formed and civil war is stirred up by the nobles. Is it proper that the Church be without protection? (…) It has been my view all along that the present bad conditions are mere trifles in comparison with what I have in mind as possible (…).[50]

The contemporary reader did not need to boast great powers of imagination to understand that Mariana was referring to Philip III himself. That Spain may indeed

---

50 Ibid., pp. 112-13, 'Finge principem a patre in minori atque adeo imbecilla aetate relictum: qua occasione turbulenti homines abuti ad exagitandam rempublicam consuevere. Finge (…) pravis moribus esse, novis de religione opinionibus contaminatum, patria instituta & ceremonias movere. Finge a proceribus coniuratione facta bellum intestinum excitari: an ordinem sacratum conveniat praesidiis carere? Ego parvum quiddam instar eorum quae animo concipio, praesentia mala putabam (…).'

fall prey to the same fatal alliance of nascent religious diversity, Machiavellian royalty and aristocratic warlords that devastated France, Mariana asserts, is 'clearly in the range of possibilities'.[51] Neither the natural boundary of the Pyrenees, nor the Holy Inquisition, and certainly not the king or the nobility are to be trusted with barring the spectre of civil war from sweeping through the country. Certainly not at a time 'when the Christian commonwealth is vexed by many heresies, even to such an extent that since the time of the Arians never were there greater religious disputes.'[52] Spain, 'next to France and not very far from England', is in a dangerous geopolitical location.[53] The war in France is too close for comfort, and may spill over into Philip III's Iberian realms at any time. Mariana appears to be aware of and share the concern of a Holy Inquisition feeling almost powerless to prevent the influx of heretical literature across the Pyrenees and through the Basque ports. Like any nation riddled with ambitious aristocrats and ruled by a young and somewhat gormless prince, Castile is in very real danger of succumbing to religious division and civil war. The monarchy is left with no choice but to fall back on its one remaining line of defence: a secular clergy distinguished by patriotic ethos and designated by history to safeguard religious and political unity.

A Court like a Most Holy Church

The Church as a major player in secular government makes its first, tentative appearance towards the end of Book one, Chapter eight of *De rege*.[54] In its closing passages, Mariana considers how the precepts of prudence that ought to limit royal power are to be institutionally enforced. He takes this as an opportunity to introduce his agenda for a major realignment of political power in Habsburg Castile. Readers are confronted with yet another image of a Golden Age dwindling under the onslaught of ambitious princes and the indifference of meek and corrupt subjects. In medieval Castile, not only the heads of the major families of the nobility enjoyed great power and resources, not only did many towns hold far-reaching jurisdiction, but so did the bishops of the realm.[55] Historical experience had by then persuaded the people of Castile that only the 'order of priesthood' could be entrusted with the improvement of religion and the protection of the realm.[56] At the time, the bishop and even the simple parish priest rather than king or nobles

---

51   See, for instance, ibid., p. 97, 'Quid enim an in uno capite salus publica, religionis sanctitas, cunctorum fortunae periclitentur, inter continuous aulae plausus, assentatorum turbam, immodicas voluptates vix sui compote, certem obnoxio periculis multis ne corrumpatur vitiis atque pravitate? An sacrato ordine debilitato profanis hominibus, quales in aula Principis vivunt, rerum, religionis reipublicae arbitrium permittemus?'

52   Ibid., p. 279.

53   Ibid.

54   Ibid., pp. 96-99. This is the chapter establishing 'whether the power of the commonwealth or that of the king is greater'.

55   Ibid., pp. 96-97.

56   Ibid., p. 97.

were regarded 'as in effect the guardians of the public weal' (*quasi custodes publicae salutis*). The bishops of reconquista Spain acted as 'true princes', and 'the people' in turn acknowledged them willingly as the 'principal part of the commonwealth' (*primae reipublicae partes*).[57]

These past and, presumably, future 'guardians of the realm' resemble those formidable fifteenth-century princes of the Church with their own chains of fortresses and private armies. Mariana's ideal is fierce warriors and shrewd statesmen like archbishop Alfonso Caríllo of Toledo or archbishop Pedro González de Mendoza of Seville rather than the saintly Hernando de Talavera, protector of the Moors of Granada.[58] The Castilian episcopate, however, is not simply to be reinstated into those feudal positions of power and influence which it allegedly held in pre-Habsburg Spain. Mariana continues to argue from the vantage point of a situation of constant political crisis. With Castilian nobles as well as French and English heretics ready to plunge Spain into civil war, new ways of protecting the civic cohesion of the realm have to be explored. The examples of Germany and France show that only prince-bishops can be relied upon to defend religion and *respublica*.[59] The inevitable conclusion for any right-minded reader is that the towns as well as the royal fortresses and garrisons of Castile are to be placed under direct episcopal jurisdiction.[60] Mariana demands that the power that the *reyes Católicos* and their Habsburg successors had wrested from secular and ecclesiastical magnates be handed over to the bishops of the realm. In fact, he requires that Castile be turned into a compound of large ecclesiastical seigneuries.

The lionization of the Castilian prelate in the age of the *reconquista* ties in with the insidious contrast between upright, patriotic clergy and a secular elite always prone to conspire against king and religion that is maintained throughout the three books of *De rege*. A secular clergy whose loyalty to faith and monarchy transcends even that of the monarch himself is compared to a nobility whose outlook makes it a notoriously unreliable, conceited and selfish partner in government. The depiction of nobles as 'effeminate wastrels' departing from the ways of their illustrious fathers and giving themselves up to spending their days lounging on comfortable cushions is all too familiar from early modern moralists. It commonly appears as a topos of clerical critique of conspicuous consumption. Mariana's *De rege*, however, is one of the very few instances where such criticism is translated into a programme for actual political change at the highest level of monarchical government. The experience of fiscal crisis caused by continual involvement in confessional war adds a new layer to familiar moralist utterances. Characteristically, Mariana conceives of moral reform, and seeks to resolve conflicts of power exclusively in terms of

---

57   Ibid., p. 97; see also ibid., pp. 113-14.

58   One of the sources of Mariana's idolization of medieval Castilian bishops appears to be Rodrigo Jiménez de Rada, thirteenth-century archbishop of Toledo, chancellor of Castile, historian and ardent propagandist of the primacy of his see. See his (1987), *Historia de rebus Hispaniae sive Historia gothica*, ed. J. Fernández Valverde, Brepols, Turnholt.

59   *De rege*, pp. 112-113.

60   Ibid., pp. 87-99, p. 111.

individual moral integrity. In turn, he defines individual moral integrity mainly by means of a person's collective identity (the prince, the noble, the secular cleric). Juridical conceptualization of the state or the practical organization of administrative systems in themselves do not matter much. Government is a highly personal affair. The selection and conduct of the individuals to be involved depends on the social, cultural and educational factors which shaped their moral outlook. Accordingly, political reform is primarily a matter of recruiting and placing the right people from the right layer of society in positions of power. Potentially conflicting ideologies have to be reconciled, and body politics restructured on the level of personnel. Humanist myth-making and arresting proposals for the re-feudalization of the defence of Castile, however, are merely the opening salvo. What follows is a comprehensive and hard-hitting critique of the very foundations and exercise of royal power in late sixteenth century Castile.

Mariana's acerbic and bold demands for reform represent a less than veiled critique of what is commonly called *regalismo*.[61] This summary term describes the extensive ecclesiastical jurisdiction and rights over the revenue and property of the churches of Castile that her kings had managed to accumulate by the end of the sixteenth century. The rulers of Castile had always accepted that the divine order obliged them to recognize the authority of the Church. As anywhere in Europe, however, the actual political and ideological form that recognition ought to take was a matter of never diminishing controversy between crown and Church as well as among the clergy of Castile themselves. Since the later fifteenth century, the crown had become deeply involved in the reform of the clergy. In the process, it affirmed its grip on all branches of ecclesiastical jurisdiction.[62] A royal commissioner, always a lay person, presided over the provincial synods of the Church of Castile, and

---

61 M. Menéndez Pelayo (1956), *Historio de los heterodoxos españoles*, Vol. 2, Biblioteca de Autores Cristianos, Madrid, p. 394, suggests that *regalismo* ought to be generally understood as 'the intrusion of civil authority in ecclesiastical affairs'. S. Alonso (1973), *El pensamiento regalista de Francisco Salgado de Somoza (1595-1665)*, Consejo Superior de Investigaciones Científicas - Instituto San Raimundo de Peñafort, Salamanca, *passim*, offers a useful discussion of *regalismo* during the later sixteenth and seventeenth century. Note that Alonso regards *regalismo* as a form of 'abuse of royal power' invited by a fifteenth-century Castilian church unable or unwilling to subject itself to necessary reforms of ecclesiastical life. He finds it difficult to reconcile Charles I's and Philip II's evident piety with the way in which they accumulate the rights and privileges of the Church. See also A. Domínguez Ortiz (1979), 'Regalismo y relaciones Iglesia-Estado en el siglo XVII', in A. Mestre Sanchis (ed.), *La Iglesia en la España de los siglos XVII y XVIII* (Historia de la Iglesia en España; Vol. 4), Biblioteca de Autores Cristianos, Madrid, pp. 73-121.

62 On the piecemeal expansion of royal control over the churches of Castile see C. Hermann (1988), *L'Eglise d'Espagne sous le Patronage Royal (1476-1834), Essai d'ecclesiologie politique* (Bibliothèque de la Casa de Velázquez; 3), Casa de Velázquez, Madrid, especially pp. 26-39; and J.M. Nieto Soría (1988), *Fundamentos ideológicos del poder real en Castilla, siglos XII-XVI* (Publicaciones del gobierno de Castilla y Leon), Eudema, Madrid. See also the detailed study by A.M. Rouco-Varela, (1965), *Staat und Kirche im Spanien des XVI. Jahrhunderts*, Hueber, Munich, especially chapter eight, 'Die staatsrechtliche Beschränkung der kirchlichen Immunitäten', pp. 150-88; and chapter thirteen, 'Die formalrechtliche Grundlage der staatlichen Intervention in das Leben der Kirche', pp. 288-97.

synodal decrees were published only after securing royal approval. The papacy was not allowed to interfere decisively with royal control of ecclesiastical jurisdiction. The procedures of ecclesiastical tribunals were closely aligned to those of royal courts, and the crown managed to ensure that the latter rather than papal courts took over from ecclesiastical tribunals accused of abusing their jurisdiction (*recurso de fuerza*). Papal bulls in fact had to be referred to the council of Castile before being published (*retención de bulas*). Such pervasive royal control over the Church of Castile was facilitated by the king's right to present candidates for ecclesiastical offices from the bishop down to the local priest whose parish lay within the royal domain (referred to as the *patronato real* in the strict sense).

Political control over ecclesiastical jurisdiction was coextensive with considerable fiscal power. The king received ecclesiastical revenue in the form of the *tercias reales* (one-third of all the tithes collected by the Church of Castile), the *subsidio* (a tax on clerical rent and incomes of all the Spanish kingdoms), the *excusado* (consisting of the entire tithe of the wealthiest household in a parish), and the *cruzada* (raised through proclamation of papal indulgences from all subjects, not just the clergy).[63] Apart from the *excusado*, which had been conceded by Pius IV in 1567 to help finance the war in Flanders, direct taxation of the clergy dated from the thirteenth-century campaigns against the Moorish kingdoms. Originally, these levies had been specific amounts to be raised over limited periods of time. From the thirteenth century onwards, the kings of Castile managed to transform them into permanent taxes. Though it is difficult to give exact figures for the Church's contribution to royal finance, realistic estimates put it at about a third of the total income of the *real hacienda*, more than a match for the famous royal fifth taken from American bullion. No other European monarch of the period came close to obtaining as much revenue from ecclesiastical sources.[64] Martin de Azpilcueta was by no means the only contemporary observer who caustically yet accurately described Philip II as the 'the greatest prelate in ecclesiastical rents that there is in the world, after the Pope'.[65]

---

63   The *subsidio* was agreed between king and Pope, but had to be approved by the clergy of the ecclesiastical provinces. The Castilian clergy organized in the *Congregación del clero de Castilla y León* usually managed to negotiate a sizeable reduction. See Q. Aldea Vaquero (1990), 'Politica interior: Oposición y Resistencia: La Resistencia eclesiástica', in J.H. Elliott and A. García Sanz (eds), *La España del Conde Duque de Olivares: Encuentro Internacional sobre la España del Conde Duque de Olivares celebrado en Toro los días 15-18 de septiembre de 1987* (Historia y sociedad; Vol. 14), Universidad de Valladolid, Valladolid, pp. 399-414; and Thompson, 'Castile: Absolutism, Constitutionalism, and Liberty', pp. 207-208. Long-standing tensions between Philip and successive Popes were rooted in deep-seated disagreement about the scope and exercise of the royal power over the Church of Castile which by far transcended the personalities involved.

64   On early modern conceptualizations of state finance see M. Stolleis (1983), *Pecunia Nervus Rerum: Zur Staatsfinanzierung der frühen Neuzeit*, Vittorio Klostermann, Frankfurt.

65   Martin de Azpilcueta (1566), *Tractado de las rentas de los beneficios ecclesiasticos*, A. Ghemart, Valladolid, fo. 28v. On direct taxation of the Castilian clergy, see C. Hermann (1995), 'La fiscalité monarchique sur l'Eglise de'Espagne' in Association des Historiens Modernistes des Universites

So impressive is the sum of rights, privileges and concessions the kings of Castile obtained from successive Popes that contemporary observers and latterly historians frequently describe it as the Spanish version of caesaropapism.[66] The term is applied to the way in which the crown made use of its *regalia* even before Philip II further asserted himself as the actual head of the Church of Castile in the wake of the Council of Trent (closed in December 1563).[67] The king took the initiative, convoking the provincial synods entrusted with the application of conciliar decrees, and imposing his authority on prelates reluctant to accept the reforms as well as moderating the zeal of those altogether too keen to follow the royal lead. Trent provided the monarch with a prime opportunity to consolidate and rationalize royal power over the clergy of Castile. Philip was able to seize on the fact that the Fathers of the Council had dispersed without making up their minds on three areas generally considered in particular need of reform: the Roman curia, the question of episcopal residence and, last but by no means least, the patronage and ecclesiastical jurisdiction exercised by secular princes.[68] In other words, the most controversial issues concerning the exercise of ecclesiastical power had in fact been left unresolved. Trent's unwillingness to declare on the issue of secular involvement in ecclesiastical jurisdiction was to have grave and lasting consequences.

Strong-minded Popes like Pius V persisted in their attempts to reclaim ecclesiastical jurisdiction from secular princes. Clericalist authors like the Jesuit Juan Azor even went so far as to declare that the 'civil laws of princes' could bind clerics only if confirmed by natural, divine or canon law.[69] In vain, they wrestled with the creeping process of 'naturalization' or 'territorialization' of churches and religious orders.[70] European princes vigorously defended and continued to extend their authority in Church matters. Philip II, champion of the Counter-Reformation, was no exception. The monarch took the interpretation, application and emendation of

---

(ed.), *Les Eglises et l'argent: Actes du Colloque de 1988* (Bulletin no. 13), Presses de l'Université Paris-Sorbonne, Paris, pp. 9-19; and Rouco-Varela, *Staat und Kirche*, especially pp. 189-219.

66   Alonso, *Pensamiento regalista*, pp. 40-42.

67   On the ways in which Philip II increased his control of the regular clergy by means of selective implementation of the decrees of the Council of Trent see I. Fernández Terricabras (2000), *Felipe II y el clero secular: la aplicación del concilio de Trento*, Sociedad Estatal para la Conmemoración de los Centenarios de Felipe II y Carlos V, Madrid. See also F. Palomo (1995), 'La autoridad de los prelados postridentinos', *Hispania Sacra*, Vol. 47, pp. 587-624.

68   Very much to the dissatisfaction of Philip II, who had not wanted the council to dissolve before having dealt with these issues. See Fernández Terricabras, *Felipe II y el clero secular*, pp. 362-64.

69   Juan Azor (1601), *Institutionum moralium tomi III*, Michael Sonnius, Paris, I pp. 639-40. Azor's papalist propositions were rejected by his fellow Jesuits, see Höpfl, *Jesuit Political Thought*, p. 344, p. 348.

70   On the territorialization or naturalization of Church and religious orders in Castile see Hermann, *L'Eglise d'Espagne*; and Fernández Terricabras, *Felipe II y el clero secular*, especially chapters six to eight. Further European examples are discussed in D. Alden (1996), *The Making of an Enterprise: The Society of Jesus in Portugal, its Empire and Beyond*, Stanford University Press, Stanford, especially chapter four; and Nelson, *The Jesuits*, especially chapter five.

the conciliar decrees into his own hands, facing down opposition from the papal nuncios and the commission set up to enforce the papal monopoly of interpretation against secular and ecclesiastical authorities. This is not to say that the exercise of royal authority turned the diffusion of Tridentine reforms throughout the Iberian territories into anything like a linear and continual process.[71] Philip II generally dictated the decisions made by provincial synods across Spain. Once the bishops had finalized their decisions, the cortes were given the opportunity to discuss and emend prior to publication. Each party endeavoured to interpret and apply the conciliar decrees according to its specific agenda. Implementation of conciliar decrees went hand in hand with multi-layered and protracted debate about their meaning. The result was a remarkably uneven, controversial and creative process. Resistance to further integration of the Church into the governmental apparatus was offered not only by the papacy, but also by Castilian bishops both eager to preserve their autonomy and confident about their ability to reform their diocesan clergy without continual royal interference. Some may even have seen Trent as an opportunity to roll back the extensive package of royal jurisdiction and fiscal rights. The canons of the cathedral churches, on the other hand, tended to style themselves as the defenders of apostolic authority against bishops and crown equally prone to encroach on ecclesiastical liberty. Whether nominations, episcopal visitations or the convocation of provincial synods, every issue of jurisdiction was turned into a combat between the alleged defenders of papal authority and the episcopal lackeys of the crown. Though usually able to assert themselves within their dioceses, the Castilian episcopate had reason to lament loss of autonomy. For a prelate feeling stuck between the rock of papal centralism and the hard place of royal authoritarianism, the image of the ideal bishop envisioned by the Fathers of the Council could easily loose some of its allure.

This is where Mariana's argument on the place of religion in Castilian society comes into play. The fact that Pius V had not allowed for the conciliar decrees and debates to be published with annotations and commentaries other than those contained in the *editio Romana* impeded debate, but it did not stop it.[72] The debate simply relocated, sometimes to the most unlikely of places. *De rege* is one of these *loci*. Spanish Jesuits on many occasions eagerly offered their support for the royal drive for the reform of the clergy.[73] The author of *De rege*, quite to the contrary, acts as a spokesperson for that part of the Castilian episcopate increasingly concerned about the prospect of even higher degrees of interference in ecclesiastical affairs on the part of the crown. Trent had given *regalismo* a new dynamic, and there was every reason to suspect that Philip III and his secular advisers would wish to continue in the same path and expand his rights and jurisdiction even further. Neither a course

---

71   See Fernández Terricabras, *Felipe II y el clero secular*, especially chapters three to five; and the pioneering study by J. Caro Baroja (1985), *Las formas complejas de la vida religiosa (Siglos XVI y XVII)*, Sarpe, Madrid; also A.D. Wright (1991), *Catholicism and Spanish Society under the reign of Philip II and Philip III*, The Edwin Mellen Press, Lewiston.

72   Fernández Terricabras, *Felipe II y el clero secular*, pp. 361-62.

73   Ibid., preface by J.-P. Amalric, pp. 15-19, p. 19.

of mere obstruction nor a systematic policy of involving the papacy was an option. The decades immediately after Trent had shown that Philip II's iron grip on the system of ecclesiastical jurisdiction would be strengthened rather than released by direct resistance. Involving the papacy, on the other hand, would mean exchanging one centralist power with that of another (possibly worse) one. The 'nationalist' clergy of Castile was looking for a third way. *De rege* attempts to conceptualize such a solution.

Turning the chequered history of crown and Church in medieval Castile into an exalted and unwarranted view of a secular clergy possessed of moral standards and political minds invariably superior to that of the laity is only one part of a new mythology contrived to support Mariana's agenda for the reform of the relationship between Church and state. He goes on to revise the doctrinal foundations for the changes he envisions. He reproaches 'distinguished theologians' for upholding a flawed ideal of the primitive Church. These erudite but misled teachers of divinity wrongly 'determine that it is necessary to deprive the clergy of jurisdictions and towns on the grounds that these are an unprofitable burden and a responsibility inappropriate for the Church.'[74] Bearing in mind that civic religion is what holds society together in the first instance, men of the Church cannot merely be regarded merely as 'that part of the Christian people that is charged with religious duties'.[75] Throughout history, societies created those 'ministers whom we call priests' because people realized 'that religion could not be uprooted from the *respublica* without destroying both'.[76] Though nations generally took great care to ensure 'that ministers of religion, (...), lived most closely with the other magistrates in whose hands power rested', the forms of co-operation between spiritual and secular authority could vary. Moses was the first to break with the ancient tradition of the priest-king. His decision to transfer the office of high priest to his brother Aaron, however, was not motivated by a desire to separate the priesthood from worldly authority. He merely paid heed to the fact that extensive religious ceremonies and increasingly complex doctrine demanded a division of responsibilities.[77] When Jesus Christ decided to confirm the separation of secular and spiritual power in order to create a more holy Church, he did not mean to force bishops and priests to forsake secular wealth and jurisdiction:

> The Lord our Saviour (...) did not (...) want [the priesthood] to be disjoined from the government of the people nor to make them wholly unqualified for it. For we see and we are compelled to repeat here, that in many provinces very wide powers have been granted to the priests from ancient times, as well as great resources.[78]

---

74 *De rege*, p. 97.
75 Ibid., pp. 274-75.
76 Ibid., p. 274.
77 Ibid., p. 275.
78 Ibid. See also p. 110.

The division of secular and spiritual power was intended to liberate the Church from the disturbing influence that laymen had come to exert on purely spiritual matters. It was not supposed to release prelates from their role and responsibility as effective co-rulers. The principle lost along the way was that

> [r]esponsibility in government should be entrusted to the churchmen and places of honour and magistracies should be given them, so that, as becomes this order, they may look after the public weal, so that they may protect the rights and freedom of the church, (...).[79]

The demise of the priest-king should merely have inaugurated the age of the prince-bishop on a par with the secular prince. Princes and churchmen alike, however, failed to heed the intentions of Christ.

Mariana now wants king and clergy to review their relationship and open a new chapter in the history of the Church and monarchy of Castile. He exhorts ecclesiastical and secular magistrates to think of themselves as 'twin members of the same body [the Church of Castile] rather than [members] forming different bodies'.[80] At this point, readers might expect him to start discussing the integration of Church and monarchy in formal juridical terms. After all, the question of who was the sovereign partner in that 'twin relationship' of secular and spiritual authority had been a matter of theoretical debate as well as political and military conflict for the best part of the history of Christianity.[81] Again, Mariana refuses to do so. Then again, he hardly needs to. His proposals speak to a large degree for themselves. The ideal which informs his agenda and rhetoric is that of a court 'which is no longer discernible from a most holy church'.[82] The vision is that of an ideal court untainted by moral corruption where 'the cleric will be concerned with the public weal and princes with the protection of the established religion.'[83] The summary principle underlying the necessary reform of monarchical government is that 'the two orders are best bound together if each has access to the honours and duties of the other'.[84]

This is more than a cursory condemnation of notions of the relationship between secular and spiritual authority drawing on the ideal of the primitive Church. Mariana's propositions insinuate a decisive shift of power from the crown to the clergy. The individual steps that ought to be taken towards a merger of royal and episcopal authority and responsibilities add up to more than a restoration of

---

79   Ibid.

80   Ibid., p. 274.

81   For a view of the development of the respective positions in the later middle ages, see M. Wilks (1963), *The Problem of Sovereignty in the Later Middle Ages, The Papal Monarchy with Augustinus Triumphus and the Publicists*, Cambridge University Press, Cambridge; and J.A. Watt (1988), 'Spiritual and Temporal Powers', in *The Cambridge History of Medieval Political Thought*, pp. 367-423.

82   *De rege*, p. 265.

83   Ibid., p. 275, p. 277.

84   Ibid., p. 277.

the autonomy of the Church of Castile in all matters pertaining to ecclesiastical jurisdiction. In fact, the threat of heresy and the need to actualize the full protective force of civic religion require the crown to abandon the very privileges which comprise the patronato real. Mariana boldly adapts the biblical tradition of priest-kingship to bring together the conflicting agendas of Church and monarchy and assimilate the potentially subversive ideology of reason of state.

Mariana suggests major changes in four areas. Each of the changes would be momentous in its own right. Together they amount to a factual theocratization of the *monarquía española*. The fact that he requires key areas of military power and authority to be handed over to the bishops has been mentioned above. His next two proposals concern the legislative and executive authority of the episcopate. Least controversial, perhaps, is Mariana's insistence that the episcopate be re-admitted to the cortes of Castile.[85] After the Cortes of Toledo (1538) refused to grant Charles V a new tax (the *sisa*, essentially a precursor to the *millones* introduced in 1590), Castilian nobles and clergy were no longer summoned to meetings of the cortes. Before Charles, the first Habsburg on the throne of Castile, decided to exclude the clergy, Castilian rulers had wanted 'nothing of major importance to be done without the assent of the bishops'.[86] Readers of *De rege* would have noticed both the slight against the ruling House of Habsburg as well as the fact that Mariana does not even raise the issue of re-admitting not just the clergy but also the nobility. The proposal following on from this advertises an open break with tradition. The king ought to recruit the members of royal councils and committees *exclusively* from among priests and bishops.[87] The secular nobility is to be restricted to diplomatic and military service. Conceding that it will prove difficult to exclude the secular elite completely from the highest layer of the royal administration in the short term at least, Mariana suggests a compromise: the king and the lay members of the royal *consejos* and *juntas* ought to be made lay bishops and abbots instead.[88] They will thus be much more inclined to protect the rights and property of the churches, and desist from senseless exploitation of ecclesiastical resources. In other words, Mariana's idea of a temporary 'compromise' is that if the clergy cannot instantly and fully replace secular magistrates, the political mentality of the secular elite has got to be assimilated as far as possible to that of the clergy.

These proposals fly in the face of notions of papal and episcopal authority promoted since the time of Pope Gregory VII, and cannot easily be squared with the spirit and letter of Tridentine reform of pastoral care. Mariana is well aware of this fact. His response is to adopt an outright regalist stance in defence of his vision of a 'court like a most holy church'. He is quick to assure his readers that bishops

---

85   Ibid., pp. 110-11.

86   Ibid., p. 111.

87   Ibid., pp. 275-76.

88   Ibid., p. 277, 'Censeo (…) populi principibus & magistratibus reipublicae modo prudentiae & probitate conspicuis, honores ecclesiasticos tribuendos & sacratas opes participandas tum ipsis, tum eorum filiis & necessariis, ut cuiusque ingenium erit. Nam ea illecti spe praemiisque propositis, sacratum ordinem maiori benevolentia complectentur, ecclesiae iura opesque tuebuntur (…).'

are to prefer and perform their duty of teaching their flock to any other business. If necessary, they ought to delegate secular jurisdiction to *homini prudentes*, preferably ecclesiastics themselves. With characteristic frankness, he then goes on to criticize, again, the 'poor judgement of famous and indeed astute theologians' who wish to keep secular princes and magistrates 'completely away from ecclesiastical honours, because they are not able to teach the people.'[89] Does it not suffice 'to delegate these duties to priests of whom everywhere there is a large number'? If Popes and bishops are free to enjoy the rights and status of secular princes, secular rulers and magistrates cannot by right be excluded from exercising ecclesiastical jurisdiction. Mariana anticipates and indeed shrugs off protest from theologians prepared to subordinate royal to papal authority in matters of ecclesiastical jurisdiction. If secular princes and magistrates were to be excluded from ecclesiastical offices, would not Popes have to be reproached for having preferred for centuries to exercise the rights and responsibilities of secular rulers rather than teach their flock?[90] Not for the first time, one of his most sarcastic and double-edged comments is reserved for the papacy.

While Mariana is prepared to take royal and episcopal rule of ecclesiastical bodies essentially as two sides of the same coin, he assumes an astoundingly radical position with regard to the fiscal immunity of the clergy. Already in the *Historia*, Mariana had explained that contrary to the views of staunch defenders of *regalismo* it was only the *tercias* and not the full *diezmos* that had originally been granted for a limited period of time to the kings of Castile by a succession of 'spineless popes'.[91] His assumption is that the first papal grant of this nature had been that of Gregory X to Alfonso X in 1275. In *De rege*, he casts Alfonso's predecessor Ferdinand III in the role of 'the paradigmatically pious monarch who declined to tax the Church'.[92] During the victorious siege of Seville (1248), Ferdinand rejected the advice of those who urged him to raise the funds necessary for the continuation of the war from the churches of the kingdom.[93] The episode is reported neither in the thirteenth-century *Primera crónica general de España* commissioned at the court of Ferdinand's successor Alfonso X, nor in Mariana's own *Historia*. It was to acquire importance only when evidence was submitted to Rome in the 1620s to support the canonization of Ferdinand.[94] It appears that Mariana was the first to give this

---

89 Ibid., pp. 277-78, 'Inepte ergo mea quidem sententia id genus hominum, quidam acuti videlicet Theologi & praeclari, ab honoribus ecclesiasticis penitus arcent quasi ineptos, neque populum docere (...).'

90 Ibid., p. 278. Regalist authors tended to defend the royal jurisdiction over the Church of Castile with reference to the dual role of the Pope as spiritual head of the Church and secular prince ruling over a number of Italian and French territories.

91 On Mariana's historiographical treatment of the matter of clerical fiscal immunity see Linehan, *Spanish Church*, pp. 331-34.

92 Linehan, *Spanish Church*, p. 331.

93 *De rege*, pp. 122-23, p. 119.

94 *Primera crónica general de España* (1955), ed. R. Menéndez-Pidal, Vol. 2, Gredos, Madrid, cc. 1128-31; Linehan, *Spanish Church*, p. 331.

legend currency, and it may well be that he felt inspired to invent a saintly king in order to support his case against the *patronato real*. However, it was in fact the ever so pious Ferdinand III himself who had been granted the *tercias* by Innocent IV in April 1247 as a contribution to the Seville campaign.[95] Although it was not the first papal grant to the war-chest of Castilian monarchs, it exceeded everything that had been granted before.[96] It was exactly this privileged position of the king of Spain, however, which, according to Mariana, had brought the wrath of God upon Spain and destroyed Philip II's Armada.[97] Reading *De rege*, one could well be led to assume that by far the most likely case of inviting divine displeasure is to try and tax the clergy. Prudence provides the prince with the rationale for leaving the wealth of the Church untapped: only the clergy is competent enough to allocate the resources of the realm to the right purposes.[98]

Mariana distinguishes three sources of royal revenue: the royal domain, the ordinary taxes (he refers to the *alcabala* and the *millones*), and extraordinary contributions.[99] The first source, he says, is to maintain the royal household and court; the second for the administration of the commonwealth in times of peace; and the third for extraordinary expenses in the case of war or other emergencies. His resolution is that the Church ought not be compelled to pay ordinary taxes at all.[100] What is more, Mariana advises that any national economic surplus should be taken out of the hands of notoriously profligate monarchs and handed over to the Church. The bishops will collectively act as 'arch-treasurer' of the realm, and distribute funds whenever extraordinary circumstances require the king to ask for their assessment of the needs of the commonwealth.[101] Mariana is anxious that the future king of Castile will abstain from doing what his less pious and less well informed ancestors did: that is, negotiate the nature and extent of taxes and grants to be levied on the Church of Castile with the Pope. The king ought to negotiate *only* with the bishops. Mariana rounds off these astonishing proposals with exhortations to the clergy to give generously if approached by their king. If the bishops give, however, they will give because they want to, and not because the king received papal permission to order them to do so. Thus Philip III is advised to build the defence of his empire on the benevolence of a clergy well-disposed to answering his pleas for *mercedes* once they have convinced themselves that the cause justifies the expense. The clergy are practically invested with the power to decide over war and peace: directly through (eventual) dominance in the royal councils, practically by controlling the strings of the royal purse whenever foreign policy or

95   *Les registres de Innocent IV (1243-54)* (1881-1931), ed. É. Berger, (Bibliothèque des écoles françaises d'Athènes et de Rome; Series 2), Fontemoing, Paris, 2538 (a grant of the *tercias* for three years).

96   Linehan, *Spanish Church*, pp. 111-13.

97   *De rege*, p. 123.

98   Ibid., p. 123.

99   Ibid., pp. 261-62.

100 Ibid., p. 120.

101 Ibid., pp. 114-18, pp. 120-22.

defence is concerned. At the same time, the king is to serve as a bulwark against papal intervention in the affairs of the national Church of Castile.[102] If nothing else, Mariana's views on the taxation and status of the Castilian clergy more than justify Cirot calling *De rege* 'le livre le plus remarquable et le plus hardi que possède la litterature politique de l'Espagne'.[103]

Mariana does not argue along paradigmatically constitutionalist lines, and he effectively ignores the cortes as a political player. Like the papacy, the cortes of Castile are another source of unwelcome, and from his point of view, unjustified interference with royal-ecclesiastical co-rulership.[104] On the basis of historical evidence which is nothing if not biased, Mariana claims that it was not just the kings of Castile who obstructed ecclesiastical involvement in government, but also the cortes.[105] The historical background is provided by the fact that once the cortes of Castile had started to concern themselves with the fragile status of the royal finances, they quickly identified clerical fiscal immunity as one of the root problems.[106] Throughout the sixteenth century, the churches of Castile increased in wealth through donations and legacies. The result, in the view of the cortes, was that the taxable *pecheros* could no longer compensate the losses which clerical immunities inflicted upon the crown's revenue. The cortes also assumed, with good reason, that continuous growth of ecclesiastical wealth would shift the balance of power in the Church's favour.

From 1591 onwards, crown and cortes ensured that the fiscal immunity of the Church was reduced. Whereas the clergy had usually been exempt from paying the *alcabala* (a general sales tax), the Pope had authorized the king to require them to pay the new tax on essential foodstuffs, the so-called *millones*.[107] The clergy of Castile immediately started campaigning against this new form of direct taxation.[108] In 1598, Philip II responded by setting up a *junta* to decide whether and to what extent the claim to clerical fiscal immunity was to be upheld.[109] The committee concluded

---

102 With regard to Mariana, we could almost speak of episcopal nationalism.

103 Cirot, *Mariana historien*, p. 35. Mariana's thought cannot easily be brought into accordance with neo-Thomist economic theory. Theologians like Francisco Suárez, Luis Molina and Juan Lugo also defended clerical fiscal immunities. However, they also held that taxation was dictated by the same laws of nature that dictated the emergence of the commonwealth.

104 Helpful discussions of the conflict between the Church and cortes of Castile is offered by C. de la Fuente Cobos (1995), 'La documentacion sobre patronato eclesiástico de Castilla', *Hispania Sacra*, Vol. 47, pp. 625-79, especially 'estudio preliminar', pp. 625-55; and C. Hermann (1974), 'L'Eglise selon les Cortes de Castille: 1476-1598', *Hispania Sacra*, Vol. 27, pp. 1-35.

105 *De rege*, p. 274.

106 See Hermann, *L'Eglise d'Espagne*, pp. 27-32.

107 Elliott, *Imperial Spain*, pp. 202-203, pp. 285-86; C. Hermann (1994), 'Settlements: Spain's National Catholicism', in T.A. Brady, H. Oberman and J.D. Tracy (eds), *Handbook of European History, 1400-1600, Late Middle Ages, Renaissance, and Reformation*, Vol. 2: *Visions, Programs, and Outcomes*, Leiden, pp. 491-552, p. 509.

108 See Jago, 'Taxation and Political Culture', pp. 53-56.

109 Hermann, *L'Eglise d'Espagne*, p. 28. The *junta* appears to have decided the matter essentially in accordance with neo-Thomist theory of taxation; see Laures, *Political Economy*, pp. 171-75,

that the royal policy of imposing direct taxes on the clergy was legitimate. One of the leading regalist lawyers of the seventeenth century, Pedro Frasso (1630-93) pinpointed the underlying principle when he remarked that 'the prince taxes the clergy not as clergy, but as citizens'.[110]

In other respects, however, the cortes of Castile were much less successful. Two instruments of ecclesiastical financial policy continued to disconcert the cortes. One was the growing number of ecclesiastical properties held in mortmain. The other was the issue of the spiritualization of lay patrimonies. A lay person could choose to become a titular cleric. Such a conferment of orders upon a lay patron made it attractive for noble families to leave vast amounts of the family patrimony to the Church. The Church benefited from the establishment or support of existing religious institutions, while the family of the patron retained control and some amount of income from the property. The result was that the Castilian tax-payers were supposed to pay more and more taxes from diminishing lay patrimonies.[111] Although Philip II attempted to prohibit mortmain, it was not before the eighteenth century that the monarchy seriously attacked these practices.[112]

Mariana's project of an 'episcopal monarchy' may appear the rather curious manifestation of excessive Castilian patriotism paired with clerical hubris. Yet, though undoubtedly radical, it is the expression of widespread concerns over the ruinous cost that Philip II's wars had imposed on the Castilian economy and people. The king had to declare the monarchy bankrupt for the third time during his reign in 1596. Like many of his contemporaries, Mariana feared that Philip III would simply continue the policy of his father. The fiscal and military collapse of the Spanish empire and mortal danger to the Catholic faith were foreseen as the inevitable result. Like many Castilians alert to the continual crisis of the monarchy, he sought to remind the future king of his responsibilities and obligations towards his subjects. Invariably, such prompting of the royal mind focused on the mutually beneficial and reciprocal relationship between the monarchy and the many communities on which it had to rely - be they Castilian, Portuguese, Aragonese, Neapolitan or Creole.[113] Some authors, especially those thinking and writing within the political milieux of the crown of Aragon, would assume that this relationship was essentially

---

pp. 181-88.

110 Pedro Frasso (1775), *De regio patronatu Indiarum*, B. Roman, Madrid, I, 42, p. 8, 'Princeps, quando oeconomice procedit contra Ecclesiasticos, non id facit tamquam in Ecclesiasticos, sed tanquam in cives.' First published in two volumes in 1677 and 1679, Frasso's treatise was reprinted in 1775 so as to support the Bourbon policy of expanding this principle beyond the lands of the crown of Castile.

111 The extent to which the spiritualization of lay patrimonies was practised, and its actual effect on the fiscal and economic situation of Castile remains to be studied in more detail.

112 See, for instance, *Novisima Recopilación de las leyes de España* (1975), Boletín Oficial del Estado, Madrid, 1, 12, 1. Hermann, *L'Eglise D'Espagne*, p. 32.

113 See, for instance, R.L. Kagan (1995), 'Clio and the Crown: Writing History in Hapsburg Spain', in Kagan and Parker, *Spain, Europe and the Atlantic World*, pp. 73-99; and I.A.A. Thompson (1995), 'Castile, Spain and the Monarchy: The Political Community from *patria natural* to *patria nacional*', ibid., pp. 125-59.

contractual in nature.[114] Mariana is remarkable both for the purposeful way in which he re-interprets juridico-constitutional notions in the light of principles of political prudence, and for the boldness with which the latter are harnessed with the political aspirations of the Castilian episcopate.

In this context, Mariana's pretence of ignorance concerning the political renaissance of the Castilian cortes during the later sixteenth century comes as less of a surprise. Certainly, the cortes did resurge mainly as a result of the permanent fiscal crisis of a monarchy engaged in too many wars at the same time.[115] Yet whereas the Cortes of Toledo still thought of themselves in constitutionalist terms in 1538, they appear to have ceased doing so by the 1590s.[116] Again, Mariana proves himself to be an acute observer of the different history, role and power of representative institutions in Castile and Aragon.[117] His disregard for the Castilian cortes as a constitutional entity in their own right is not without reason, nor is he alone in thinking that the clergy is the only institution effectively able to represent the interests of the commonwealth as a whole against the king.[118] Mariana's defence of clerical rights and immunities is brazenly partial. Yet at the same time, replacing the letter of the law with practical and moral considerations, he aims at preserving more than just 'something of the reality of the kingdom's free consent to the granting of taxation'.[119]

---

114 How a skilful Aragonese politician sought to balance and reconcile the principles of absolute monarchy with those of limited sovereignty is shown by C. Álvarez de Toledo (2004), *Politics and Reform in Spain and Viceregal Mexico: The Life and Thought of Juan de Palafox 1600-1659*, Oxford University Press, Oxford. See also Rubiés, 'Reason of State and Constitutional Thought', and ibid., 'La idea del gobierno mixto'.

115 See the work by Charles Jago, Xavier Gil and I.A.A. Thompson quoted above, preface, fn. 2. For further discussion of the revisionist view that the cortes of Castile did not succumb to ascending Habsburg authoritarianism see S. Dios de Dios (1988), 'El estado moderno, ¿un cadáver historiográfico?', in A. Rucquoi (ed.), *Realidad e imágenes del poder. España fines de la Edad Media*, Ambito, Valladolid, pp. 389-408; also his (1990), 'La evolución de las Cortes de Castilla durante los siglos XVI y XVII', in B. Clavero, P. Grossi and F. Tomás y Valiente (eds), *Hispania: Entre derechos proprios y derechos nacionales* (Atti dell'incontro di studio; Firenze-Lucca, 25-27 maggio 1989), Giuffrè, Milan, Vol. 2, pp. 593-755.

116 See Thompson, 'Castile: Absolutism, Constitutionalism, and Liberty', pp. 201-207.

117 Though, like many of his contemporaries, he is oblivious to the fact that the crown of Aragon was by no means as wealthy as widely presumed, and that the expense of asking the cortes for a grant was likely to be much higher than the money eventually collected.

118 On the way in which late sixteenth- and early seventeenth-century Spanish clerical elites could perceive of themselves as guardians of the realm see Q. Aldea Vaquero, 'La resistencia', passim; also Thompson, 'Castile: Absolutism, Constitutionalism, and Liberty', especially pp. 208-13; and A. Domínguez-Ortiz, (1970), *La sociedad española en el siglo XVII*, Vol. 2, *El estamento eclesiástico* (Monografias Historico-Sociales; Vols. 7-8), Consejo Superior de Investigaciones Científicas, Madrid, chapter eight.

119 Thompson, 'Castile: Absolutism, Constitutionalism and Liberty', p. 208.

Conclusion

In the final chapters of Books one to three, then, Mariana ties up loose ends. Castile and Christendom are faced with a threat of internecine strife of unprecedented scale and nature. The fact that the unity of religion is paramount to the preservation of the monarchy demands that the *cultores religionis patriae* be elevated to unparalleled heights of power. The Church is to assume the role of treasurer of the realm, and operate as a 'constitutional court', thus guaranteeing the prudent conduct of government.[120] Dominating the decision-making process in the various royal *consejos*, the clergy is able to supervise the making and administration of statutory law. Religion is the primary tool of political control, and ecclesiastical institutions therefore are to be provided with the resources necessary to enable them to fulfil their responsibility for the commonwealth. The full implementation of Mariana's propositions would have practically ended the papal-royal co-government of the Hispanic churches (at least with regard to the Church of Castile) which had emerged between 1480 and 1520, and had been extended and stabilized in favour of the Crown during the sixteenth century. Ultimately, Mariana's mirror-of-princes reads as an ill-disguised pamphlet against the creeping expansion of early modern secular authority as well as papal government at the expense of the episcopate. Here is an author keen to manipulate the process of 'confessionalization' in favour of the episcopate.[121] The Pope is absent even in terms of ecclesiastical jurisdiction, and the bishops are to suffuse the whole of secular government with their benevolent authority. Protected from a centralist papal administration by an assertive crown, the Castilian episcopate would be free to regain its liberty by stepping inside the minds and mechanisms of secular power. In *De rege*, the post-Tridentine bishop steps forward to claim a status of power and authority that was never to be his.

The transformation of scholastic juridical language into one of political prudence serves a profoundly clerical, ultimately episcopal agenda. Mariana prefers to define the place of Christian faith and clergy in society mainly in terms of political prudence, occasionally in those of unfathomable divine providence. He discounts both the juridical thinking of the *regalistas* at the court of Philip II and the philosophical conceptualizations of the natural law theorists of the 'School of Salamanca'. Papal authority is tersely relegated from the Castilian political arena, and replaced with that of the bishops. The reader is told in no uncertain terms that in a political world as precarious and volatile as his, and in the face of likely failure of king and nobility to preserve the realm, the Castilian episcopate is the only mainstay of empire.

---

120 See Hermann, 'Settlements', p. 504.

121 For a concise formulation of the concept of 'confessionalization' see H. Schilling (1998), 'Confessionalisation in Europe: Causes and Effects for Church, State, Society, and Culture', in K. Bussmann and H. Schilling (eds), *1648: War and Peace in Europe*, Vol. 1, Veranstaltungsgesellschaft, Münster, pp. 219-28. See also Fernández Terricabras, *Felipe II y el clero secular*, pp. 377-79.

De rege and the History of Early Modern Spanish Political Thought

Mariana neither propagates a form of Castilian constitutionalism, nor is it proper to categorize him straightforwardly as either a Machiavellian or anti-Machiavellian thinker. Even such opportunely broad tags as scholastic or humanist thinker do not do justice to the context, detail and fullness of his thought as offered in *De rege*. The text is exceptional in that it strings together a curious scholastic theory of the origins of society, a conservative ideology of absolute monarchy and a breathtakingly radical vision of theocratic renewal.

These components do not sit easily with one another. Yet there is unity to Mariana's reasoning. A Catholic-Augustinian rather than neo-Thomist view of human nature informs the argument as a whole. This bleak, at times downright cynical view of man imparts focus and coherence to a text that frequently challenges well established terminological boundaries and political discourses. In the first instance, Mariana's deeply pessimistic appraisal of human virtue induces as well as justifies his disregard of positive law. He is thus able to mould the many and diverse elements extracted from Roman and canon law, scholastic theology and humanist literature into a complex and deliberately equivocal discourse of reason of state. Finally, this secular interpretation of the world of politics is cleverly yoked to a thoroughly clerical agenda of reform. In *De rege*, reason of state is made to propagate the theocratic transformation of the *monarquía española*.

The way in which Mariana says what he has got to say matters as much as the ideological content of his treatise. The manner in which he turns scholastic juridical terminology into a language of exhortative rhetoric is one of the most original aspects of the work. Mariana stands out for the liberties he takes making diverse theorems and terms serve his overall political agenda. He thus defies attempts to define his political language in narrow and seemingly clear-cut terms. *De rege* demonstrates that early modern political thinkers may well choose not to confine themselves to the one or other clearly distinguishable and almost hermetic political language.[1] Rather they will pick and mix their conceptual approaches and terminologies depending on the political agenda that drives their writing as well as

---

1   See Pagden, *Languages of Political Theory*, introduction, pp. 15-16; also J.G.A. Pocock (1987), 'The Concept of Language and the *métier d'historien*: Some Considerations on Practice', in A. Pagden (ed), *The Languages of Political Theory in Early-Modern Europe* (Ideas in Context), Cambridge University Press, Cambridge, pp. 19-38; and ibid. (1996), 'Concepts and Discourses: A Difference in Culture? Comments on a paper by Melvin Richter', in H. Lehmann and M. Richter (eds), *The Meaning of Historical Terms and Concepts. New Studies on Begriffsgeschichte*, German Historical Institute, Washington, D.C., pp. 47-58.

the generic tradition within which they articulate that agenda. *De rege* is exemplary for the way in which moral theology, humanist literatures and the laws cross-fertilize one another in early modern Spanish political thinking.[2] The reader of early modern Spanish political texts is bound to discover a world of political thinking that is made up of composite monarchies as well as confident city-states.

In many respects, Mariana does not represent the mainstream of late sixteenth- and early seventeenth-century Spanish political thinking. He stands for a line of Castilian ecclesiastical political thought and action that has so far escaped due attention. Yet his treatise is paradigmatic nonetheless. *De rege* exemplifies the highly differentiated and complex nature of political debate in the Spain of Philip II and Philip III. It helps revise the idea that the political reality of Habsburg Spain was mirrored in antagonistic languages of oppressive absolutism and classical or scholastic constitutionalism. Mariana's attempt to lodge ultimate authority in the secular clergy, for instance, straddles concerns and concepts familiar from absolutist as well as constitutionalist literatures. Recent research, especially the lively debate on the cortes of Castile, has dissolved the somewhat simplistic dichotomy between absolutism and liberty in Habsburg Spain. In its unique way, *De rege* confirms that political life in late sixteenth- and early seventeenth-century Spain is at least as complex as the linguistic constructs it generated.

The political language and objectives of *De rege* are inspired by Mariana's ambiguous appraisal of history as *magistra vitae*. At times, his unforgiving persuasion of the corrupting influence of time mingles nervously with an appreciation of a positive, though altogether ambivalent historical dynamic. However, Mariana doggedly insists on the transient and confused nature of political order. This view is particularly evident in his treatment of law. Mariana is as dismissive of Thomist-Aristotelian notions of the body politic as part of a universal system of natural law as he is of the endeavours of humanist jurists to extract metahistorical norms from customary laws. The author of *De rege*, too, contrasts, collates and summarizes constitutional principles manifest in the custom of diverse nations. He does not, however, share the epistemological optimism of Jean Bodin. The latter is eager to develop the study of history as a tool to distil and purify absolute standards from recalcitrant material. Mariana's concept of law, on the contrary, is unreservedly positivist. The corruption which he believes to characterize the origins and development of political authority and society clearly extends to customary laws. Rather than being revealed as 'second nature', customary law is deprived of much of its normative power. Human nature and history join forces, invalidating any attempt to derive timeless political doctrines with the help of logical analytical categories or juridico-historical semantics. Any juridical or constitutional order is an historical occurrence likely to be moulded, changed or distorted with the progress

---

2   Thus the conventional distinction between scholastic and humanist logic, for instance, has been called into question by E.J. Ashworth (1988), 'Traditional Logic', in C.B. Schmitt, Q. Skinner, E. Kessler and J. Kraye (eds), *The Cambridge History of Renaissance Philosophy*, Cambridge University Press, Cambridge, pp. 143-72; and L. Jardine (1988), 'Humanistic Logic', ibid., pp. 173-98.

of time. The often contrasting opinions and statements of the jurists are taken for what they are, that is, local and contingent approximations to transient political and social reality. To Mariana's mind, juridical principles filtered from history cannot claim to possess the universal and axiomatic value others attribute to them. He stands out for the honesty with which he concedes the failure of any such enterprise.[3]

Mariana thus construes an opposition between juridical and prudential conceptions of monarchical order. He is not interested in establishing a systematic theory of the state composed of axiomatic principles. The stress on temporality and depravity as defining features of human mind and action ensures that *prudentia* remains an *ars* in the sense of the Aristotelian *phronesis*. Prudence cannot produce sets of universal political principles. Prudence is not the concern of an autonomous *scientia politica*. There are general maxims of prudent conduct to be had and concessions to necessity to be made, but there are no axioms to be found that would exclude divine providence from secular history, society and politics. In *De rege*, early modern historicist capacities brutally collide, losing the desire to impose eternal or sempiternal principles on a far too intractable reality.

Like Tacitus, the author of *De rege* regards individuals, peoples, societies and constitutions as malleable.[4] Legislation is merely the expression of the (usually limited) political wisdom of the individuals and peoples involved. Concerned with personalities rather than principles, Mariana prefers to analyse the uses and abuses of power. History provides him with ample material for comparative analysis and practical advice. The result is a raw vision of society and politics, and one that stands out for its uncompromising acceptance of the moral ambiguities of political life. The political analysis in *De rege*, therefore, is best described in terms of *Herrschaftsinterpretation* (historical exposition of the workings of political power) rather than *Herrschaftsbegründung* (axiomatic legitimating of political power).[5] The distinct advantage of this conceptual opposition is that it helps to distinguish the contractual elements in the political thinking of Mariana from those found in the works of the Monarchomachs or the authors of the School of Salamanca. Mariana's place in the pantheon of early modern political thinkers is next to Justus Lipsius rather than Jean Bodin or Francisco Suárez.

---

3   On early modern historicist capacities clashing with the desire to establish eternal or sempiternal principles see S. Toulmin and J. Goodfield (1965), *The Discovery of Time* Harper and Row, New York; and J.G.A. Pocock (1993), 'A Discourse on Sovereignty', in N. Phillipson and Q. Skinner (eds), *Political Discourse in Early Modern Britain*, Cambridge University Press, Cambridge, pp. 377-428.

4   For Tacitus's vision of politics see R. Mellor (1993), *Tacitus*, Routledge, New York, especially pp. 88-91.

5   See W. Kersting (1990), 'Vertrag, Gesellschaftsvertrag, Herrschaftsvertrag', IV: 'Religiöser Bund und ständischer Herrschaftsvertrag bei Calvin und den Monarchomachen', and V: 'Frühe Zeugnisse des Gesellschaftsvertrages in der Neuzeit: Althusius', in *GG*, Vol. 6, pp. 910-14 and pp. 914-18.

Mariana's legacy is rich, and varied. Towards the end of Philip III's reign, Álamos de Barrientos, Saveedra Fajardo and, indeed, the playwright Lope de Vega would renew their efforts to press for a general overhaul of the political mentality of the court and a profound revision of the strategic aims of the monarchy.[6] The pragmatic mode of political thought known as *tacitismo* had by then become much more generally accepted as the vehicle for a desirable infusion of political realism into Spanish politics.[7] The atmosphere of crisis and expectation during the establishment of the regime of the count-duke of Olivares encouraged the free flow of ideas. Álamos de Barrientos would finally be heard, and end up as *protonotario* of the crown of Aragon. Mariana, now eighty-six years of age and ailing, was too weak to join the fray once more. Yet writers like Eugenio Narbona and Mateo López Bravo would keep referring to him, and the count-duke of Olivares himself appears to have borrowed his ideas. Wittingly as well as unwittingly, he had inspired this new way of political thinking. Juan de Mariana was in the vanguard of a profound change in early modern Spanish political culture.

---

6   On the political and mental world of the new regime under the leadership of the Conde-Duque de Olivares, see J.H. Elliott (1986), *The Count-Duke of Olivares, The Statesman in an Age of Decline*, Yale University Press, New Haven and London.

7   See, for instance, the contributions in Rus Rufino, *Razón de estado*; as well as X. Gil (2004), 'Las fuerzas del Rey. La generación que leyó a Botero', in M. Rizzo et al. (eds), *La forze del principe. Recursos instrumentos y límites en la práctica del poder soberano en los territorios de la monarquía hispánica*, Universidad de Murcia, Murcia, pp. 969-1022. Still useful is Maravall, *Estudios*, chapter two: 'Maquiavelo y maquiavelismo en España', pp. 39-76; chapter three: 'La corriente doctrinal del tacitismo político en España', pp. 77-106, and chapter four: 'La cuestión del maquiavelismo y el significado de la voz 'estadista'', pp. 107-24.

Bibliography

Primary Sources

Álamos de Barrientos, Baltasar (1598), *Discurso político al rey Felipe III al comienzo de su reinado* [modern edition: (1990), *Discurso político al rey Felipe III al comienzo de su reinado*, ed. M. Santos (Textos y Documentos, Vol. 7), Anthropos, Madrid].

—— (1614), *Tácito español, ilustrado con aforismos*, Luis Sa[n]chez, Madrid.

Añastro, Gaspar de (1590), *Los seis libros de la República de Iván Bodino, traducidos de lengua francesa y emmendados catholicamente*, Bevilacqua, Turin [modern edition: (1992), *Juan Bodino, Los seis libros de la Republica. Traducidos de lengua francesa y emmendados catholicamente*, ed. J.L. Bermejo, Centro de Estudios Constitutionales, Madrid].

Anonymous (1610), *Anticoton ou refutation de la lettre declaratoire du Père Coton*, n.p., Paris.

Anonymous (1610), *Aphorismes ou Sommaires de la Doctrine des Iesuites, & de quelques autres leurs Docteurs*, n.p., Paris.

Anonymous (1610), *Arrest de la cour du Parlement ensemble la censure de la Sorbonne contre le livre de Jean Maniana intitulé de Regis & Rege institutione* (…), n.p., Paris.

Anonymous (1610), *Remonstrance a Messieurs de la Cour de Parlement sur le parricide commis en la personne du Roy Henry le Grand*, n.p., Paris.

Antonio, Nícolas (1788), *Bibliotheca hispana nova: sive Hispanorum scriptorum qui ab anno MD. ad MDCLXXXIV floruere notitia*, J. de Ibarra, Madrid.

Aquinas, Saint Thomas (1964-81), *Summa Theologica*, ed. T. Gilby (the 'Blackfriars edition'), Eyre and Spottiswoode, London and McGraw-Hill, New York.

Augustine, Saint (1974), *Contra Julianum Pelagium*, Corpus scriptorum ecclesiasticorum latinorum, Vol. 85, Verlag der Österreichischen Akademie der Wissenschaften, Vienna.

—— (1898-1900), *De civitate Dei libri XXIII*, Corpus scriptorum ecclesiasticorum latinorum, Vol. 40, Tempsky, Vienna.

Azo, Portius (1566), *Summa*, n.p., Venice.

Azor, Juan (1601), *Institutionum moralium tomi III*, Michael Sonnius, Paris.

Azpilcueta, Martin de (1566), *Tractado de las rentas de los beneficios eclesiasticos*, A. Ghemart, Valladolid.

Barclay, William (1600), *De regno et regali potestate adversus Buchananum, Brutum, Boucherium et reliquos Monarchomachos libri VI*, Guillelmus Chaudière, Paris.

Bartholomew (Ptolemy) of Lucca and Saint Thomas Aquinas (1997), *On the government of rulers: De regimine principum*, transl. by J.M. Blythe, University of Pennsylvania Press, Philadelphia.

Bartolus of Sassoferrato (1471), *Super prima parte Codicis*, Vol. 1, Sixtus Riesinger, Naples.

Bayle, Pierre (1697), *Dictionaire historique et critique*, Reinier Leers, Rotterdam.

Bellarmine, Saint Robert, (1611), *Tractatus de potestate summi pontificis in rebus temporalibus: adversus Gulielmum Barclaium*, B. Gualter, Cologne.

—— (1619), *De officio principis Christiani libri tres*, B. Gualter, Cologne.

—— (1965), *De laicis*, in *Roberti Bellarmini opera omnia, ex editione Veneta*, ed. J. Fèvre, Vol. 11, Minerva, Frankfurt.

Bodin, Jean (1583), *Methodus ad facilem historiarum cognitionem*, I. Mareschall, Heidelberg.

—— (1583), *Six livres de la république*, Jacques Du Puys, Paris [facsimile reprint: (1961), Scientia Verlag, Aalen].

—— (1586), *De republica libri sex*, J. Du Puys, Lyons.

—— (1606), *The six books of a commonweale*, transl. R. Knolles, Adam Islip, London [facsimile reprint: (1962), ed. K.D. McRae, Harvard University Press, Cambridge, Mass.].

Botero, Giovanni (1589), *Della ragion di stato*, Gioliti, Venice [modern edition (1948), *Della ragion di stato*, ed. L. Firpo, Unione Tipografico, Turin].

Boucher, Jean (1589), *De iusta Henrici Tertii abdicatione*, n.p., Paris.

López Bravo, M. (1616), *De rege, et regendi ratione libri duo*, n.p., Madrid.

Buchanan, George (1579), *De iure regni apud Scotos*, I. Rosseus, Edinburgh.

—— (1582), *Rerum Scotiarum Historia*, n.p., Edinburgh.

Burnet, Gilbert (1897), *History of my own Time*, Clarendon Press, Oxford.

Cabrera de Córdoba, Luis de (1611), *De historia para entenderla y escrivirla*, n.p., Madrid.

—— (1619), *Filipe segundo, rey de España*, n.p., Madrid.

—— (1857), *Relaciones de las cosas sucedidas en la corte de España desde 1599 hasta 1614*, n.p., Madrid.

Calvin, Jean (1568), *Institutio Christianae religionis*, Franciscus Perrinus, Geneva.

Caro de Torres, Francisco (1629), *Historia de las Ordenes Militares de Santiago, Calatrava y Alcantara*, I. Gonzales, Madrid.

Cartularios de Toledo: catálogo documental (1985), ed. F.J. Hernández (Monumenta Ecclesiae Toletanae historica. Series I: Regesta et inventaria historica; Vol. 1), Fundación Ramón Areces, Madrid.

Castillo, Baltasar Pérez de (1564), *El Theatro del mundo de las miserias y de la dignidad del hombre*, Andres de Angulo, Alcalá [a translation from the French into Castillian of Pierre Boaistuau's (called Launay) *Le theatre du monde*].

Cicero (1976), *De inventione; De optimo genere oratorum; Topica*, with an English translation by H.M. Hubbell, Loeb classical library, Cambridge, Mass. and London.

—— (1961), *De officiis*, with an English translation by W. Miller, Loeb classical library, London and New York.

—— (1942), *De oratore*, Books I-II, with an English translation by E.W. Sutton, completed, with an introduction by H. Rackham, Loeb classical library, Cambridge, Mass. and London.

—— (1977), *De re publica, De legibus*, with an English translation by C.W. Keyes, Loeb classical library, Cambridge, Mass. and London.

Commines, Philippe de (also Comines or Commynes) (1969-73), *The Memoirs of Philippe de Commynes*, ed. S. Kinser, transl. I. Cazeaux, University of South Carolina Press, Columbia.

Conciliorum Oecumenicorum Decreta (1962), ed. Istituto per le scienze religiose die Bologna, cura di G. Alberigo, Herder, Basle.

Corpus Iuris Canonici, (1879-1881), Vol. 1: *Decretum Magistri Gratiani*, Vol. 2: *Decretalium Collectiones*, ed. E. Friedberg, 2nd edn, Tauchnitz, Leipzig.

Corpus Iuris Civilis (1973), *Institutiones*, ed. P. Krüger; *Digesta*, ed. T. Mommsen and P. Krüger, Weidmann, Zurich.

Correspondencia privada de Felipe II con su Secretario Mateo Vázquez, 1567-1591 (1959), ed. C. Riba Garcia, Vol.1 (1567-1586), Consejo Superior de Investigaciones Constitucionales, Madrid.

Covarrubias y Leyva, Diego de (1604), *Opera omnia*, Vol. 2: *Practicarum quaestionum*, n.p., Venice.

Covarrubias, Sebastián de (1611), *Tesoro de la Lengua Castellana o Española*, Luis Sánchez, Madrid.

Decrees of the Ecumenical Councils, Reprinted with an English Translation (1990), ed. N.P. Tanner, 2 vols., Georgetown University Press, London and Washington

De Soto, Domingo (1582), *Libri decem de iustitia et iure libri decem*, C. Pesnot, Lyon.

Duhr, B. SJ (1921), *Geschichte der Jesuiten in den Ländern deutscher Zunge*, Vol. 3, G.J. Manz, Munich and Regensburg.

Epistolario de Justo Lipsio y los Españoles (1577-1606) (1966), ed. A. Ramírez, Castalia, Madrid.

Erasmus, *Institutio principis Christiani* (1516), Johann Froben, Basle.

—— (1521), *Enchiridion militis Christiani*, Knobloch, Strasbourg.

Fontes iuris romani antiqui (1909), ed. C.G. Bruns, 7th edn, I.C.B. Mohr, Tübingen.

Fox Morcillo, Sebastian (1556), *De regni regisque institutione libri III*, Gerard Speelman, Antwerp.

Frasso, Pedro (1775), *De regio patronatu Indiarum*, B. Roman, Madrid.

Fuero viejo de Castilla: sacado, y comprobado con el exemplar de la misma obra, que existe en la Real Biblioteca de esta corte, y con otros mss (1964), ed. I.J. Asso y del Rio and M. de Manuel y Rodríguez, Editorial 'Lex Nova', Valladolid [reprint of the 1771 edition published by J. de Ibarra, Madrid].

Gentillet, Innocent (1576), *Discours, sur les moyens de bien gouverner et maintenir en bonne paix un royaume ou autre principauté*, J. Stoer, Geneva.

Gerson, Jean (1963), *Oportet haereses esse*, in *Oeuvres complètes*, ed P. Glorieux, Vol. 5, Desclée, Paris and New York, pp. 420-35.

González de Ávila, Gil (1638), *Historia de la vida y hechos del rey don Henrique tercero de Castilla, inclito en religion y justicia*, F. Martinez, Madrid.

Gretser, J. SJ (1610), *De imperatorum, regum ac principum Christianorum in Sedem Apostolicam munificentia*, Adam Sartorius, Ingolstadt.

Gudiel, Jerónimo (1577), *Compendio de algunas historias de España, donde setratan muchas antiguedades dignas de memoria: y especialmente se da noticia de la antigua familia de los Girones, y de otros muchos linajes. Dirigido al excellentissimo Señor don Pedro Giron quarto deste nombre, Duque primero de Ossuna, y quinto Conde de Ureña*, Juan Iniguez de Lecqueríca, Alcalá.

Hinojosa, R. de (1896), *Los despachos de la diplomacia pontificia en España*, Vol. 1, B.A. de la Fuente, Madrid.

Hobbes, Thomas (1670), *Leviathan, sive de materia, forma, & potestate civitatis ecclesiasticae et civilis*, n.p., Amsterdam.

Hotman, François (1972), *Francogallia*, ed. R.E. Giesey, transl. by J.H.M. Salmon, Cambridge University Press, Cambridge.

James I (1918), *The Political Works of James I*, ed. C.H. McIlwain, Harvard University Press, Cambridge, Mass.

Jiménez de Rada, Rodrigo (1987), *Historia de rebus Hispaniae sive Historia gothica*, ed. J. Fernández Valverde, Brepols, Turnholt.

Jouvancy, J. SJ (1710), *Historia Societatis Jesu pars quinta*, Vol. 2: 1515-1616, San Marco, Rome.

Las siete partidas del sabio rey don Alonso (1974), ed. G. Lopez, Boletín Oficial del Estado, Madrid.

Leclerc, Antoine (1610), *La defense des puissances de la terre*, n.p., Paris.

Les registres d'Innocent IV (1243-54) (1881-1931), ed. É. Berger, (Bibliothèque des écoles françaises d'Athènes et de Rome; Series 2), Fontemoing, Paris.

Lessius, Leonard (1605), *De iustitia et iure caeterisque virtutibus cardinalibus libri IV*, Johannes Masij, Leuven.

Lipsius, Justus (1584), *De constantia libri duo*, Plantin, Leiden.

—— (1589), *Politicorum sive civilis doctrinae libri sex*, Plantin, Leiden.

—— (1594), *Sixe Bookes of Politickes or Civil Doctrine*, transl. W. Jones, Richard Field for William Ponsonby, London.

—— (1605), *Monita et exempla politica libri duo*, Plantin-Moret, Antwerp.

Loaysa, García de (1593), *Isidori Hispalensis episcopi sententiarum libri III, emendati et notis illustrati* , Johannes Baptist Bevilaqua, Turin.

—— (1593), *Collectio Conciliorum Hispaniae*, n.p., Madrid.

Lopez, Gregorio (1597), *Excellencias de la Monarchia y Reyno de España*, Diego Fernandez de Cordoba, Valladolid.

López Bravo, Mateo (1616), *De rege, et regendi ratione*, n.p., Madrid.

Louis I [de Bourbon, Prince de Condé] (1743), *Mémoires de Condé ou Recueil pour servir à l'histoire de France (…) où l'on trouvera des preuves de l'histoire de M. de Thou*, Vol. 6, n.p., The Hague.

Macedo, Duarte Ribeiro de (1669), *Advertencias aludicionador de la historia del Padre Juan de Mariana*, n.p., Madrid.

Machiavelli, Niccolò (1968), *Opere di Niccolò Machiavelli*, ed. S. Bertelli, Vol. 1: *Il principe; Discorsi sopra la prima deca di Tito Livio*, Giovanni Salerno, Milan.

Mantuano, Pedro (1611), *Advertencias a la historia del Padre Juan de Mariana de la Compania de Iesus*, n.p., Milan..

Mariana, Juan de (1592), *Historiae de rebus Hispaniae libri XXV* [XX], Pedro Rodríguez, Toledo.

—— (1599), *De rege et regis institutione libri III*, Pedro Rodríguez, Toledo [reprint: (1969), Scientia Verlag, Aalen]. Spanish translation: Juan de Mariana (1981), *La dignidad real y la educación del rey (De rege et regis institutione)*, ed. L. Sanchez-

Agesta, Centro de Estudios Constitucionales, Madrid; English translation: Juan de Mariana (1948), *The King and the Education of the King*, transl. G.A. Moore, The Country Dollar Press, Chevvy Chase.

—— (1601), *Historia general de España, Compuesta primero en Latin, despues buelta en Castellano por Iuan de Mariana*, Pedro Rodríguez, Toledo.

—— (1605), *Historiae de rebus Hispaniae libri XXX*, Balthasar Lipp, Mayence.

—— (1609), *Tractatus VII*, Anton Hierat, Cologne.

—— (1620), *Scholia in Vetus et Novum Testamentum*, Sonnius(?), Paris.

—— (1625), *Discours du Père Jean Mariana Iesuite Espagnol, Des grands defauts qui sont en la forme du governement des Iesuites*, transl. J. de Cordes, n.p.

—— (1699), *The General History of Spain, from the First Peopling of it by Tubal till the Death of King Ferdinand (…) with a Continuation to the Death of King Philip III. With Two Supplements, by Friar Ferdinand de Salcedo [and] Friar Basil Varen de Soto*, trans. J. Stevens, Richard Sare, Francis Saunders and Thomas Bennet, London.

—— (1768), *Discurso de las enfermedades de la Compañia: Con una disertacion sobre el Autor y la legitimidad de la obra y un apendice de varios testimonios de Jesuitas Españolas que concuerdan con Mariana*, D. Gabriel Ramirez, Madrid.

—— (1783-1796), *Historia general de España, que escribió el P. Juan de Mariana ilustrada en esta nueva impresion de tablas cronologicas notas y observaciones criticas con la vida del autor*, B. Monfort, Valencia.

Marnix, Jean de (Baron de Potes) (1624), *Resolutions politiques, et maximes d'estat*, Jean Pain, Rouen.

Márquez, Juan (1612), *El Governador Christiano, deducido de las Vidas de Moysen, y Iosue, Principes del Pueblo de Dios*, F. de Cea Tesa, Salamanca.

Memoriales y cartas del conde duque de Olivares (1980), Tomo II: *Política interior: 1628 a 1645*, ed. J.H. Elliott and J.F. de la Pena, Ediciones Alfaguara, Madrid.

Molina, Luis de (1615), *De iustitia et iure*, Johannes Keerbergius, Antwerp.

Narbona, Eugenio (1621), *Doctrina política civil, escrita en aphorismos: sacados de la doctrina de los Sabios, y exemplos de la experiencia*, n.p., Toledo. Expurgated version of the first edition published in Toledo in 1604.

Novisima Recopilación de las leyes de España (1975), Boletín Oficial del Estado, Madrid.

Pachtler, M. SJ (1887-94), *Ratio studiorum et institutiones scholasticae Societas Jesu per Germaniam* (Monumenta Germaniae pedagogica), Vol. 9, A. Hofmann, Berlin.

Pliny, *Historia naturalis* (1999), transl. H. Rackham, Vol. 2: Books 3-7, Loeb classical library, Cambridge, Mass. and London.

Possevino, Antonio (1593), *Iudicium, de Nuae militis Galli, Ioannis Bodini, Philippi Mornaei, & Nicolai Machiavelli quibusdam scriptis. Item defensio veritatis adversus assertiones Catholicae fidei repugnantes eiusdem Nuae libris aspersas, auctore Petro Coreto*, I.B. Buysson, Lyon.

Primera crónica general de España (1955), ed. R. Menéndez-Pidal, Gredos, Madrid.

Pufendorf, Samuel (1688), *De iure naturae et gentium libri octo*, n.p., Amsterdam.

Reynolds, William (or Rainolds, or Gulielmus Rossaeus) (1592), *De justa reipublicae Christianae in reges impios et haereticos authoritate*, Johannes Kerbergius, Antwerp.

Ribadeneira, Pedro de (1588), *Historia ecclesiastica del scisma del reino de Inglaterra (…)*, P. Madrigal, Madrid.

—— (1597), *Tratado de la religion y virtudes que deve tener el principe christiano, para governar y conservar sus estados, contra lo que Nicolas Machiavelo y los politicos deste tiempo enseñan*, Plantin-Moret, Antwerp [references to the 1605 edition, reproduced in: (1899), *Obras escogidas del Padre Pedro de Ribadeneira*, ed. V. de la Fuente, (Biblioteca de autores españoles; Vol. 60), Hernando y Compañia, Madrid, pp. 449-587].

—— (1609), *Illustrium scriptorum religionis Societatis Iesu catalogus*, 2nd edn, n.p., Lyon.

—— (1613), *Catalogus Scriptorum Religionis Societatis Jesu*, Plantin-Moret, Antwerp.

Roussel, Michel (1610), *Antimariana ou refutation des propositions de Mariana*, n.p., Paris.

Saavedra Fajardo, Diego (1649), *Idea principis christiano-politici, centum symbolis expressa*, I. Mommartius, Brussels.

Salucio, Agustín (1975), *Discurso sobre los estatutos de limpieza de sangre*, ed. A. Pérez Gómez, El Ayre de la Almena, Cieza [facs. of the original edition: (1599), n.p., Madrid].

Sánches, Francisco (1581), *Quod nihil scitur*, Antonius Gryphius, Lyons [engl. transl.: (1988), *That nothing is known = quod nihil scitur*, ed. E. Limbrick and D.F.S. Thompson, Cambridge University Press, Cambridge].

Sánchez de Arévalo, Rodrigo, *Suma de la política* (1944), ed. J.B. Pérez (Consejo Superior de Investigaciones Científicas – Instituto Francisco de Vitoria – Seminario de Historia de las Doctrinas Políticas, Vol. 2), Consejo Superior de Investigaciones Científicas, Madrid.

Scotus, John Duns (1497), *Quaestiones in quattuor libros Sententiarum*, Bonetus Locatellus for Octavianus Scotus, Venice.

—— *Reportata Parisiensia* (1930), in *Doctrina Philosophica et Theologica*, ed. from the manuscript of P. Migne, 2 vols., Collegium St Bonaventurae, Quarachi.

Sotomayor, Antonio Valladares de (1640), *Novissimus librorum prohibitorum et expurgandorum index*, Diaz, Madrid.

Suárez, Francisco (1612), *De legibus, ac Deo legislatore*, D. Gomez de Loureyo, Coimbra.

—— (1615), *Defensio fidei Catholicae aduersus Anglicanae sectae errors (…)*, n.p., Coimbra.

—— (1626), *Tractatus de religione Societatis Jesu*, in – (1857), *Opera omnia*, ed. C. Berton, Vol. 16, L. Vivès, Paris.

Tamayo de Vargas, Tomás (1616), *Historia general de España del P. D. Iuan de Mariana defendida*, Diego Rodriguez, Toledo.

Thou, Jacques Auguste (1609), *Historiarum sui temporis*, 3 vols, Conrad Nebenius, Offenbach.

Toledo, Francisco de (1596), *Summa casuum conscientiae*, Johannes Gymnici, Cologne.

Vindiciae contra tyrannos (1994), ed. and transl. by G. Garnett, Cambridge University Press, Cambridge.

Virgil (1982), *Georgics*, transl. L.P. Wilkinson, Penguin, London.

Yáñez Fajardo y Montroy, Juan Isidro (1723), *Memorias para la historia de don Felipe III. Rey de España*, Officina Real: Nicolás Rodriguez Franco, Madrid.

Secondary Literature

Abel, G. (1978), *Stoizismus und Frühe Neuzeit: zur Entstehungsgeschichte modernen Denkens im Felde von Ethik und Politik*, De Gruyter, Berlin and New York

Abellán, L. (1979), *Historia crítica del pensamiento español*, Vol. 2, Espasa-Calpe, Madrid.

Aitken, J.M. (1939), *The Trial of George Buchanan before the Lisbon Inquisition, The Text of Buchanan's Defences along with a Translation and Commentary*, Oliver and Boyd, Edinburgh.

Alberigo, G. (1981), *Chiesa conciliare: identità e significato del conciliarismo*, Paideia, Brescia.

Aldea Vaquero, Q. (1990), 'Politica interior: Oposición y Resistencia: La Resistencia Eclesiástica', in J.H. Elliott and A. García Sanz (eds), *La España del Conde Duque de Olivares: Encuentro Internacional sobre la España del Conde Duque de Olivares celebrado en Toro los días 15-18 de septiembre de 1987* (Historia y sociedad; Vol. 14), Universidad de Valladolid, Valladolid, pp. 399-414.

Alden, D. (1996), *The Making of an Enterprise: The Society of Jesus in Portugal, its Empire and Beyond*, Stanford University Press, Stanford.

Allen, J.W. (1961), *A History of Political Thought in the Sixteenth Century*, repr. with revisions, Methuen, London.

Alonso, S. (1973), *El pensamiento regalista de Francisco Salgado de Somoza (1595-1665)*, Consejo Superior de Investigaciones Científicas – Instituto San Raimundo de Peñafort, Salamanca.

Álvarez de Toledo, C. (2004), *Politics and Reform in Spain and Viceregal Mexico: The Life and Thought of Juan de Palafox 1600-1659*, Oxford University Press, Oxford.

Alves, A.A. (1994), 'Complicated Cosmos: Astrology and Anti-Machiavellianism in Saavedra's European Politics', *Sixteenth Century Journal*, Vol. 25, pp. 67-84.

Ascheri, M., Baumgärtner, I. and Kirshner J. (eds) (1999), *Legal Consulting in the Civil Law Tradition*, Robbins Collection Publication, Berkeley.

Asensio, F. (1953), 'El profesorado de Juan de Mariana y su influjo en la vida del escritor, *Hispania*, Vol. 13, pp. 581-639.

—— (1972), 'Juan de Mariana ante el Indice quiroguiano de 1583-84', *Estudios Bíblicos*, Vol. 31, pp. 135-78.

Ashworth, E.J. (1988), 'Traditional Logic', in C.B. Schmitt, Q. Skinner, E. Kessler, and J. Kraye (eds), *The Cambridge History of Renaissance Philosophy*, Cambridge University Press, Cambridge, pp. 143-72.

Astraín, A. SJ (1923), *Historia de la Compañia de Jesús en la asistencia de España*, Vol. 3, Razón y Fe, Madrid.

Augustijn, C. (1992), *Erasmus: His Life, Works and Influence*, University of Toronto Press, Toronto.

Backer, A. de (1890-1932), *Bibliotèque de la Compagnie de Jésus*, ed. C. Sommervogel, 12 vols, Schepens, Brussels.

Bataillon, M. (1991), *Érasme et l'Espagne, Nouvelle édition en trois volumes, Texte établi par D. Devoto*, Droz, Geneva [first edition: (1937), Droz, Paris].

Baumgarten, P.M. (1927), 'García de Loaysa de Girón', in P.M. Baumgarten and G. Buschbell (eds), *Hispanica, Untersuchungen zur Geschichte und Kultur des 16. und 17. Jahrhunderts*, Vol. 1, n.p., Traunstein, pp. 18-33.

—— (1932), *Ordenszucht und Ordensstrafrecht, Beiträge zur Geschichte der Gesellschaft Jesu besonders in Spanien*, n.p., Traunstein.

Belda Plans, J. (2000), *La Escuela de Salamanca y la renovación de la teología en el siglo XVI* (Biblioteca de autores cristianos maior; Vol. 63), Biblioteca de Autores Cristianos, Madrid.

Beltrán de Heredia, V. (1971-73), *Miscelánea Beltrán de Heredia: colección de artículos sobre historia de teología española* (Biblioteca de teólogos españoles; Vols. 25-28), 4 vols, n.p., Salamanca.

Berti, E. (1993), '*Phronesis* et science politique', in A. Tordesillas (ed.), *Aristote politique: études sur la Politique d'Aristote*, Presses Universitaires de France, Paris, pp. 435-60.

Bireley, R. SJ (1981), *Religion and Politics in the Age of the Counterreformation. Emperor Ferdinand II, William Lamormaini, S.J., and the Formation of Imperial Policy*, The University of North Carolina Press, Chapel Hill.

—— (1990), *The Counter-Reformation Prince, Anti-Machiavellianism or Catholic Statecraft in Early Modern Europe*, University of North Carolina Press, Chapel Hill.

—— (2003), *The Jesuits and the Thirty Years War: Kings, Courts, and Confessors*, Cambridge University Press, Cambridge.

Black, A. (1993), 'The Juristic Origins of Social Contract Theory', *History of Political Thought*, Vol. 14, pp. 57-76.

Blüher, K.A. (1969), *Seneca in Spanien, Untersuchungen zur Geschichte der Seneca Rezeption in Spanien vom 13. bis 17. Jahrhundert*, Francke, Munich.

Borrelli, G. (1996), 'Obligation juridique et obéissance politique: le temps de la discipline moderne pour Jean Bodin, Giovanni Botero et Thomas Hobbes', in Y.C. Zarka (ed.), *Jean Bodin: Nature, Histoire, Droit et Politique*, Presses Universitaires de France, Paris, pp. 11-26.

Boucher, D. (1993), 'Histories of Political Thought in the Post-Methodological Age', *History of Political Thought*, Vol. 14, pp. 301-16.

Bouwsma, W.J. (1975), 'The Two Faces of Humanism: Stoicism and Augustinianism in Renaissance Thought', in H.A. Oberman and T.A. Brady (eds), *Itinerarium Italicum: The Profile of the Italian Renaissance in the Mirror of its European Transformations*, Brill Publishers, Leiden, pp. 3-60.

Bouza Álvarez, F.J. (ed.) (1994), *La corte de Felipe II*, Alianza Editorial, Madrid.

Boyden, J.M. (1995), *The (C)courtier and the (K)king: Ruy Gómez da Silva, Philip II, and the c(C)ourt of Spain*, University of California Press, London and Berkeley.

Braun, H.E. (2004), 'Conscience, Counsel and Theocracy at the Spanish Habsburg Court', in H.E. Braun and E. Vallance (eds), *Contexts of Conscience in Early Modern Europe, 1500-1700*, Palgrave-Macmillan, Basingstoke, pp. 56-66.

Breen, Q. (1968), 'Renaissance Humanism and the Roman Law', in *Christianity and Humanism, Studies in the History of Ideas*, W.B. Eerdmans, Grand Rapids, Michigan, pp. 183-99.

Brett, A. (1997), *Liberty, Right and Nature. Individual Rights in Later Scholastic Thought*, Cambridge University Press, Cambridge.

Brodrick, J. (1961), *Robert Bellarmine: Saint and Scholar*, Catholic Book Club, London.

Buck, A. (1957), *Das Geschichtsdenken der Renaissance*, Scherpe, Krefeld.

—— (1968), *Die humanistische Tradition in der Romana*, Gehlen, Bad Homburg.

Buckland, W.W. (1963), *A Textbook of Roman Law from Augustus to Justinian*, 3rd edn, rev. by P. Stein, Cambridge University Press, Cambridge.

Bujanda, J.M. de (1993), *Index des livres interdits*, Vol. 6: *Index d'l'inquisition Espagnole, 1583, 1584*, Sherbrooke: Centre d'études de la Renaissance, Quebec.

Burgess, G. (1996), *Absolute Monarchy and the Stuart Constitution*, Yale University Press, New Haven and London.

Burke, P. (1991), 'Tacitism, Scepticism, and Reason of State', in J.H. Burns (ed.), *Cambridge History of Political Thought, 1450-1700*, Cambridge University Press, Cambridge, pp. 479-98.

Burns, J.H. (1986), *Absolutism: The History of an Idea* (The Creighton Trust Lecture), University of London, London.

—— (1990), 'The Idea of Absolutism', in J. Miller (ed.), *Absolutism in Seventeenth-Century Europe*, Macmillan, Basingstoke, pp. 21-42.

—— (1991), 'Conciliarism, Papalism, and Power, 1511-1518', in D. Wood (ed.), *The Church and Sovereignty, c.590-1918*, Essays in Honour of Michael Wilks, Basil Blackwell, Oxford, pp. 409-28.

—— (1991), 'Scholasticism: Survival and Revival', in *Cambridge History of Political Thought, 1450-1700*, pp. 132-55, pp. 140-46.

—— (1992), *Lordship, Kingship, and Empire: The Idea of Monarchy, 1400-1525*, Clarendon Press, Oxford.

—— (1994), 'George Buchanan and the anti-Monarchomachs', in R.A. Mason (ed.), *Scots and Britons: Scottish Political Thought and the Union of 1603*, Cambridge University Press, Cambridge, pp. 138-57.

—— (1996), *The True Law of Kingship, Concepts of Monarchy in Early-Modern Scotland*, Oxford University Press, Oxford.

Canning, J. (1987), *The political thought of Baldus de Ubaldis* (Cambridge studies in medieval life and thought; 4th ser.; 6), Cambridge University Press, Cambridge.

Carlyle, R.W and Carlyle, A.J. (1936), *A History of Medieval Political Theory in the West*, Vol. 6: *Political Theory from 1300 to 1600*, Blackwood, Edinburgh and London.

Caro Baroja, J. (1985), *Las formas complejas de la vida religiosa (Siglos XVI y XXVII)*, Sarpe, Madrid.

Castillo Cáceres, F. (1990), 'El arte de la guerra en "El principe cristiano" de Pedro de Rivadeneyra', *Boletín de Información del Ministerio de Reforma*, Vol. 218, pp. 61-70.

Cepeda Adán, J. (1953), 'Una vision de America a fines del siglo XVI: las Indias en la *Historia* del P. Mariana', *Estudios Americanos*, Vol. 6, pp. 397-421.

Chambert, F. (1983), 'Juan de Mariana et la Doctrine du Tyrannicide (de la Théologie politique à la politique Théologique)', unpublished PhD Thesis, Université de Paris I.

Cirot, G. (1905), *Études sur l'historiographie espagnole: Mariana historien* (Bibliothèque de la Fondazion Thiers; Vol. 8), Feret et Fils, Bordeaux.

—— (1904), 'La famille de Juan de Mariana', *Bulletin Hispanique*, Vol. 6, pp. 309-31.

—— (1907), 'Quelques remarques sur les archaismes de Mariana et la langue des prosateurs de son temps: Conjugaison', *Romanische Forschungen*, Vol. 23, pp. 883-904.

—— (1908), 'A propos du *De rege*, des *Septem tractatus* de Mariana et de son ou de ses proces', *Bulletin hispanique*, Vol. 10, pp. 95-99.

—— (1936), 'Mariana jesuite: la jeunesse', *Bulletin Hispanique*, Vol. 38, pp. 295-352.

Clavero, B. (1984), *Evolución histórica del constitucionalismo español*, Temas clave de la Constitución española, Tecnos, Madrid.

—— (1991), *Razón de estado, razón de individuo, razón de historia*, Centro de Estudios Constitucionales, Madrid.

Colás Latorre, G. and Salas Ausens, J.A. (1982), *Aragón en el siglo XVI, Alteraciones sociales y conflictos políticos*, Departamento de Historia Moderna, Universidad de Zaragoza, Zaragoza.

Coleman, J. (1988), 'Property and (P)poverty', in *The Cambridge History of Medieval Political Thought, c.350-1450*, ed. J.H. Burns, Cambridge University Press, Cambridge, pp. 607-48.

Colish, M. (1978), 'Cicero's *De Officiis* and Machiavelli's *Prince*', *Sixteenth Century Journal*, Vol. 9, pp. 81-93.

—— (1985), *The Stoic Tradition from Antiquity to the Early Middle Ages*, Vol. 1: *Stoicism in Classical Latin Literature*, Vol. 2: *Stoicism in Christian Latin Thought through the Sixth Century* (*Studies in the History of Christian Thought*, Vol. 34/35), Brill, Leiden.

Congar, Y. (1958), 'Quod omnes tangit ab omnibus tractari et approbari debet', *Revue historique de droit français et étranger*, Vol. 36, pp. 210-59.

—— (1971), *Die Lehre von der Kirche: Vom Abendländischen Schisma bis zur Gegenwart* (Handbuch der Dogmengeschichte, Vol. 3: Christologie, Soteriologie, Ekklesiologie, Mariologie, Gnadenlehre; fasc. 3d), Herder, Freiburg.

Coujou, J.-P. (1999), *Suárez et la refondation de la métaphysique comme ontologie: étude et traduction de l'Index détaillé de la métaphysique d'Aristote de F. Suárez*, Editions Peeters, Louvain and Paris.

Couzinet, M.-D. (1996), *Histoire et méthode à la renaissance: une lecture de la Methodus ad facilem historiarum cognitionem de Jean Bodin*, J. Vrin, Paris.

Coville, A. (1932), *Jean Petit: la question du tyrannicide au commencement du XVe siècle*, A. Picard, Paris.

D'Addio, M. (1987), 'Il Tirannicidio', in L. Firpo (ed.), *Storia delle idee politiche, economiche e sociali*, Vol. 3, *Umanesimo e Rinascimento*, Unione Tipografico, Turin, pp. 511-610.

Davies, C. (2001), 'Baltasar Álamos de Barrientos and the Nature of Spanish Tacitism', in N. Griffin, C. Griffin, E. Southworth and C. Thompson (eds), *Culture and Society in Habsburg Spain*, Tamesis, London, pp. 57-78.

Dessens, R. (1995), *La pensée politique de Juan de Mariana dans le mouvement monarchomaque catholique*, unpublished PhD Thesis, Paris.

Díaz-Plaja, F. (1997), *Felipe III*, Planeta, Barcelona.

Di Camillo, O. (1988), 'Humanism in Spain', in A. Rabil (ed.), *Renaissance Humanism, Foundations: Forms, and Legacy*, Vol. 2: *Humanism beyond Italy*, University of Pennsylvania Press, Philadelphia, pp. 55-108.

Dios de Dios, S. (1988), 'El estado moderno, ¿un cadáver historiográfico?', in A. Rucquoi (ed.), *Realidad e imágenes del poder: España fines de la Edad Media*, Ambito, Valladolid, pp. 389-408.

—— (1990), 'La evolución de las Cortes de Castilla durante los siglos XVI y XVII', in B. Clavero, P. Grossi and F. Tomás y Valiente (eds), *Hispania: Entre derechos proprios y derechos nacionales* (Atti dell'incontro di studio; Firenze-Lucca, 25-27 maggio 1989), Giuffrè, Milan., Vol. 2, pp. 593-755.

Döllinger, I. von and Reusch, H. (1889), *Geschichte der Moralstreitigkeiten in der römisch-katholischen Kirche seit dem sechzehnten Jahrhundert*, 2 vols., C.H. Beck, Nördlingen.

Doerig, J.A. (1972; 1973), 'Juan de Mariana (1535-1624), relevante pensador político del clasicismo español', *Folia Humanística*, Vol. 10, pp. 637-48; Vol. 11, pp. 259-65.

Domínguez Carretero, E. (1956), 'La Escuela teológica Agustiniana de Salamanca', *La Ciudad de Dios*, Vol. 169, pp. 638-85.

Domínguez Ortiz, A. (1970), *La sociedad española en el siglo XVII*, Vol. 2: *El estamento eclesiástico* (Monografias Historico-Sociales; Vols 7-8), Consejo Superior de Investigaciones Científicas, Madrid.

—— (1979), 'Regalismo y relaciones Iglesia-Estado en el siglo XVII', in A. Mestre Sanchis (ed.), *La Iglesia en la España de los siglos XVII y XVIII* (Historia de la Iglesia en España; Vol. 4), Biblioteca de Autores Cristianos, Madrid, pp. 73-121.

Donaldson, P. (1988), *Machiavelli and Mystery of State*, Cambridge University Press, Cambridge

Dufournet, J. (1994), *Philippe de Commynes. Un historien à l'aube des temps modernes* (Bibliothèque du Moyen Âge, Vol. 4), De Boeck, Brussels.

Dumeril, A. (1885), 'Un publiciste de l'Ordre des Jesuites calomnie: le Père Mariana', *Memoires de l'Academie des Sciences, Inscriptions et Belles Lettres de Toulouse*, Vol. 7, pp. 83-146.

Dunne, J. (1993), *Back to the Rough Ground: 'Phronesis' and 'Techne' in Modern Philosophy and in Aristotle*, University of Notre Dame Press, Notre Dame and London.

Eire, C.M. (1995), *From Madrid to Purgatory, The Art and Craft of Dying in Sixteenth-Century Spain*, Cambridge University Press, Cambridge.

Elliott, J.H. (1963), *The Revolt of the Catalans: a Study in the Decline of Spain*, Cambridge University Press, Cambridge.

—— (1969),'Revolution and continuity in early modern Europe', *Past and Present*, Vol. 42, pp. 35-56 [reprinted: – (1989), *Spain and its World, 1500-1700*, Yale University Press, New Haven and London, pp. 92-113].

—— (1977), 'Self-Perception and Decline in Early Seventeenth-Century Spain', *Past and Present*, Vol. 74, pp. 41-61 [reprinted: as above, pp. 241-62].

—— (1982), 'Spain and its Empire in the Sixteenth and Seventeenth Centuries', in D.B. Quinn (ed.), *Early Maryland in a Wider World*, Wayne State University Press, Detroit, pp. 58-83 [reprinted: as above, pp. 7-26].

—— (1985), 'Yet another Crisis?', in P. Clark (ed.), *The European Crisis of the 1590s: Essays in Comparative History*, Allen and Unwin, London, pp. 3-32.

—— (1986), *The Count-Duke of Olivares, The Statesman in an Age of Decline*, Yale University Press, New Haven and London.

—— (ed.), *Krieg und Politik, 1618-1648* (Schriften des Historischen Kollegs, Kolloquien; Vol. 8), Munich, pp. 185-202 [reprinted: *Spain and its World, 1500-1700*, pp. 114-36].

—— (1992), 'A Europe of Composite Monarchies', *Past and Present*, Vol. 137, pp. 48-71.

—— (2002), *Imperial Spain, 1469-1716*, Penguin, London.

Engster, D. (1996), 'Jean Bodin, Scepticism, and Absolute Sovereignty', *History of Political Thought*, Vol. 17, pp. 469-99.

Etter, E.-L. (1966), *Tacitus in der Geistesgeschichte des 16. und 17. Jahrunderts* (Basler Beiträge zur Geschichtswissenschaft; Vol. 103), Helbing und Lichtenhahn, Stuttgart and Basle.

Ettinghausen, H. (1972), *Francisco de Quevedo and the Neostoic Movement*, Oxford University Press, Oxford.

Exum, F. (1974), 'Lope's King Pedro: The Divine Right of Kings vs. the Right of Resistance', *Hispania*, Vol. 57, pp. 428-33.

Ezquerra Revilla, I. (2000), *El consejo real de Castilla bajo Felipe II: grupos de poder y luchas faccionales*, Sociedad Estatal para la Conmemoración de los Centenarios de Felipe II y Carlos V, Madrid.

Fasolt, C. (1995), 'Visions of Order in the Canonists and Civilians', in T.A. Brady, H.A. Oberman and J.D. Tracy (eds), *Handbook of European History, 1400-1600*, Vol. 2, Brill, Leiden, pp. 31-60.

Feist-Hirsch, E. (1967), *Damião de Góis: The Life and Thought of a Portuguese Humanist, 1502-1574* (International Archives of the History of Ideas; Vol. 19), M. Nijhoff, The Hague.

Fernández, L.G. (1981), *Panorama social del humanismo español (1500-1800)*, Alhambra, Madrid.

Fernández Albaladejo, P. (1984), 'Monarquía, cortes y 'cuestión constitutional' en Castilla durante la Edad Moderna', *Revista de las Cortes Generales*, Vol. 1, pp. 11-34.

—— (1994), 'Cities and the State in Spain', in C. Tilly and W.P. Blockmans (eds), *Cities & the Rise of States in Europe, 1000-1800*, Westview Press, Boulder, Col., pp. 168-83.

Fernández de la Mora, G. (1993), 'El Proceso contra el Padre Mariana', *Revista de Éstudios Políticos*, Vol. 79, pp. 47-99.

Fernández-Santamaria, J.A. (1977), *The State, War, and Peace: Spanish Political Thought in the Renaissance, 1516-1559* (Cambridge Studies in Early Modern History), Cambridge University Press, Cambridge.

—— (1983), *Reason of State and Statecraft in Spanish Political Thought*, University Press of America, Lanham, Md.

—— (1997), 'Juan de Mariana y el constitucionalismo', in –, *La formación de la sociedad y el origen del Estado: ensayos sobre el pensamiento político en el Siglo de Oro*, Centro de Estudios Constitucionales, Madrid, pp. 213-60.

—— (1998), *The Theater of Man: J.L. Vives on Society* (Transactions of the American Philosophical Society; Vol. 88/2), American Philosophical Society, Philadelphia

Fernández Terricabras, I. (2000), *Felipe II y el clero secular: la aplicación del concilio de Trento*, Sociedad Estatal para la Conmemoración de los Centenarios de Felipe II y Carlos V, Madrid.

Feros, A. (1997), 'El viejo monarca y los nuevos favoritos: los discursos sobre la privanza en el reinado de Felipe II', *Studia Historica, Studia Moderna*, Vol. 17, pp. 11-36.

—— (1999), 'Images of Evil, Images of Kings: The Contrasting Faces of the Royal Favourite and the Prime Minister in Early Modern European Political Literature, c. 1580-c. 1650', in J.H. Elliott and L. Brockliss (eds), *The World of the Favourite*, Yale University Press, New Haven and London, pp. 223-38.

—— (2000), *Kingship and Favouritism in the Spain of Philip III, 1598-1621* (Cambridge Studies in Early Modern History), Cambridge University Press, Cambridge.

Ferraro, D. (1989), *Tradizione e Ragione in Juan de Mariana* (Filosofia e scienza nel Cinquecento e nel Seicento; Serie I, Studi; Vol. 32), F. Angeli, Milan.

Figgis, J.N. (1907), *Studies in Political Thought from Gerson to Grotius: 1414-1625*, 2nd edn, Cambridge University Press, Cambridge.

Fontana, B. (1993), 'Tacitus on Empire and Republic', *History of Political Thought*, Vol. 14, pp. 27-40.

Fortea Pérez, J. (1991), 'The Cortes of Castile and Philip II's Fiscal Policy', *Parliaments, Estates and Representation*, Vol. 11, pp. 117-38.

Franklin, J. (1973), *Jean Bodin and the Rise of Absolutist Theory* (Cambridge Studies in the History and Theory of Politics), Cambridge University Press, Cambridge.

Fuente Cobos, C. de la (1995), 'La documentacion sobre patronato eclesiástico de Castilla', *Hispania Sacra*, Vol. 47, pp. 625-79.

Fumaroli, M. (1980), *L'Age de L'Eloquence, Rhétorique et "res literaria" de la Renaissance au seuil de l'époque classique* (Hautes Études Médiévales et Modernes; 43), Droz, Geneva.

García Oro, J. (1981), *Cisneros y la Universidad de Salamanca* (Humanismo, reforma y teologia; Vol. 29), Consejo Superior de Investigaciones Constitucionales - Instituto Francisco Suárez, Madrid.

García Vilar, J.A. (1981), 'El Maquiavelismo en las relaciones internacionales: la anexión de Portugal a España en 1580', *Revista de estudios internacionales*, Vol. 2, pp. 599-643.

Garver, E. (1987), *Machiavelli and the History of Prudence*, University of Wisconsin Press, Madison.

Gierke, O. (1934), *Natural Law and the Theory of Society, 1500-1800*, trans. E. Barker, 2 vols, Oxford University Press, Oxford.

Giesey, R.E. (1961), 'The Juristic Basis of Dynastic Rights to the French Throne', *Transactions of the American Philosophical Society*, Vol. 51, pp. 3-47.

_____ (1968), *If not, not: The Oath of the Aragonese and the Legendary Laws of Sobrarbe*, Princeton University Press, Princeton.

Gil, X. (1993), 'Crown and Cortes in Early Modern Aragon: Reassessing Revisionism', *Parliaments, Estates and Representation*, Vol. 13, pp. 109-22.

_____ (1995), 'Aragonese Constitutionalism and Habsburg Rule: the varying Means of Liberty', in R.L Kagan and G. Parker (eds), *Spain, Europe and the Atlantic World*, Essays in honour of John H. Elliott, Cambridge University Press, Cambridge, pp. 160-87.

_____ (1996), 'Visión europea de la monarquía española como monarquía compuesta', in C. Russel and J. Andrés Gallego (eds), *Las monarquías del antiguo regimen. ¿Monarquías compuestas?*, Editorial Complutense, Madrid, pp. 65-95.

_____ (2000), 'La razón de estado en la España de la Contrareforma. Usos y razones de la política', in S. Rus Rufino et al. (eds), *La rázon de estado en la España moderna*, Real Sociedad Económica de Amigos del País, Valencia, pp. 37-58.

_____ (2004), 'Las fuerzas del Rey. La generación que leyó a Botero', in M. Rizzo et al. (eds), *La forze del principe. Recursos instrumentos y límites en la práctica del poder soberano en los territorios de la monarquía hispánica*, Universidad de Murcia, Murcia, pp. 969-1022.

Gonzalez de la Calle, P.U. (1918-1919), 'Algunas notas complementarias acerca de las ideas morales del Padre Juan de Mariana', *Revista de Archivos, Bibliotecas y Museos*, Vol. 39, pp. 267-87; Vol. 40, pp. 130-40, pp. 231-47, pp. 418-30, pp. 536-51.

Gray, H.H. (1968), 'Renaissance Humanism: The Pursuit of Eloquence', *Journal of the History of Ideas*, Vol. 24, pp. 199-216.

Gschnitzer, F. (1992), 'Volk, Nation, Nationalismus, Masse', II.1: 'Völker als politische Verbände', in O. Brunner, W. Conze and R. Koselleck (eds), *Geschichtliche Grundbegriffe, Historisches Lexikon der politisch-sozialen Sprache in Deutschland*, Vol. 7, Klett-Cotta, Stuttgart, pp. 151-55.

Günther, H. (1982), art. 'Herrschaft [*dominium*]', III.1: 'Herrschaft von der frühen Neuzeit bis zur Französischen Revolution', in O. Brunner, W. Conze and R. Koselleck (eds), *Geschichtliche Grundbegriffe, Historisches Lexikon der politisch-sozialen Sprache in Deutschland*, Vol. 3, Klett-Cotta, Stuttgart, pp. 14-33.

Guillaume-Alonso, A. (1995), *Una institución del antiguo regimen: la Santa Hermandad Vieja de Talavera de la Reina, siglos XVI y XVII*, Ayuntamiento de Talavera de la Reina, Talavera de la Reina.

Gutiérrez, D. (1970), 'Los estudios de la Orden agustiniana desde la edad media hasta la contemporánea', *Analecta Augustiniana*, Vol. 33, pp. 75-149.

Gutiérrez Nieto, J.I. (1990), 'El reformismo social de Olivares: El problema de la limpieza de sangre y la creación de nobleza de mérito', in J.H. Elliott and A. García Sanz (eds), *La España del Conde Duque de Olivares, Encuentro Internacional sobra la España del Conde Duque de Olivares celebrado en Toro los Dios 15-18 Septiembre 1987* (Historia y Sociedad; 14), Universidad de Valladolid, Valladolid, pp. 418-41.

Haliczer, S. (1981), *The Comuneros of Castile: The Forging of a Revolution, 1475-1521*, University of Wisconsin Press, Madison, Wisc.

Hamilton, B. (1963), *Political Thought in Sixteenth-Century Spain, A study of the political ideas of Vitoria, De Soto, Suárez, and Molina*, Oxford University Press, Oxford.

Hampton, T. (1990), *Writing from History. The Rhetoric of Exemplarity in Renaissance Literature*, Cornell University Press, Ithaca and London.

Henshall, N. (1992), *The Myth of Absolutism: Change and Continuity in Early Modern European Monarchy*, Longman, London.

Hermann, C. (1974), 'L'Eglise selon les Cortes de Castille: 1476-1598', *Hispania Sacra*, Vol. 27, pp. 1-35.

—— (1988), *L'Eglise d'Espagne sous le Patronage Royal (1476-1834), Essai d'ecclésiologie politique* (Bibliothèque de la Casa de Velázquez; Vol. 3), Casa de Velázquez, Madrid.

—— (1989), *Le Premier âge de l'Etat en Espagne: 1450-1700* (Collection de la Maison des pays ibériques; Vol. 41), Éditions du Centre national de la Recherche scientifique, Paris.

—— (1994), 'Settlements: Spain's National Catholicism', in T.A. Brady, H. Oberman and J.D. Tracy (eds), *Handbook of European History, 1400-1600, Late Middle Ages, Renaissance, and Reformation*, Vol. 2, *Visions, Programs, and Outcomes*, Leiden, pp. 491-522.

—— (1995), 'La fiscalité monarchique sur l'Eglise de'Espagne' in Association des Historiens Modernistes des Universites (ed.), *Les Eglises et l'argent: Actes du Colloque de 1988* (Bulletin no. 13), Presses de l'Université Paris-Sorbonne, Paris, pp. 9-19.

Höpfl, H. (1982), *The Christian Polity of Jean Calvin*, Cambridge University Press, Cambridge.

—— (2002), 'Orthodoxy and Reason of State', *History of Political Thought*, Vol. 23, pp. 211-37.

—— (2004), *Jesuit Political Thought. The Society of Jesus and the State, c. 1540-1630* (Ideas in Context), Cambridge University Press, Cambridge.

Höpfl, H. and Thompson, M.P. (1979), 'The History of Contract as a Motif in Political Thought', *The American Historical Review*, Vol. 84, pp. 919-44.

Honnefelder, L. (1994), 'Naturrecht und Normwandel bei Thomas von Aquin und Johannes Duns Scotus', in J. Miethke and K. Schreiner (eds), *Sozialer Wandel im*

Mittelalter, Wahrnehmungsformen, Erklärungsmuster, Regelungsmechanismen, Thorbecke, Sigmaringen, pp. 195-213.

Hudon, W.V. (1992), *Marcello Cervini and Ecclesiastical Government in Tridentine Italy*, Northern Illinois University Press, DeKalb.

Ilting, K.-H. (1978), 'Naturrecht', in O. Brunner, W. Conze and R. Koselleck (eds), *Geschichtliche Grundbegriffe, Historisches Lexikon der politisch-sozialen Sprache in Deutschland*, Vol. 4, Klett-Cotta, Stuttgart, pp. 245-313.

Jago, C. (1981), 'Habsburg Absolutism and the Cortes of Castile', *American Historical Review*, Vol. 86, pp. 307-26.

—— (1992), 'Review Essay: Crown and Cortes in Early Modern Spain', *Parliaments, Estates and Representation*, Vol. 12, pp. 177-92.

—— (1995), 'Taxation and Political Culture in Castile, 1590-1640', in R.L. Kagan and G. Parker (eds), *Spain, Europe and the Atlantic World*, Essays in honour of John H. Elliott, Cambridge University Press, Cambridge, pp. 48-72.

Janz, D. (1983), *Luther and Late Medieval Thomism: a Study in Theological Anthropology*, Wilfried Laurier University Press, Waterloo, Ont.

Jardine, L. (1988), 'Humanistic Logic', in C.B. Schmitt, Q. Skinner, E. Kessler and J. Kraye (eds), *The Cambridge History of Renaissance Philosophy*, Cambridge University Press, Cambridge, pp. 173-98.

Jiménez Guijarro, P. (1997), *Juan de Mariana (1535-1624)*, Ediciones del Orto, Madrid.

Joachimsen, P. (1970), 'Loci communes. Eine Untersuchung zur Geistesgeschichte des Humanismus und der Reformation', in –, *Gesammelte Aufsätze, Beiträge zu Renaissance, Humanismus und Reformation; zur Historiographie und zum Deutschen Staatsgedanken*, selected and with an introd. by Notker Hammerstein, 2 vols, Scientia Verlag, Aalen, Vol. 1, pp. 387-442.

Jolowicz, H.F. (1954), *Historical Introduction to the Study of Roman Law*, 2nd edn, Cambridge University Press, Cambridge.

Kagan, R.L. (1974), *Students and Society in Early Modern Spain*, Johns Hopkins University Press, Baltimore and London.

—— (1981), *Lawsuits and Litigants in Castile, 1500-1700*, University of North Carolina Press, Chapel Hill.

—— (1995), 'Clio and the Crown: Writing History in Hapsburg Spain', in R.L. Kagan and G. Parker (eds), *Spain, Europe and the Atlantic World*, Essays in honour of J.H. Elliott, Cambridge University Press, Cambridge, pp. 73-99.

Kahn, V. (1985), *Rhetoric, Prudence, and Skepticism in the Renaissance*, Cornell University Press, Ithaca and London

—— (1994), *Machiavellian Rhetoric: From Counter-Reformation to Milton*, Princeton University Press, Princeton.

Kamen, H. (1993), 'A Crisis of Conscience in Golden Age Spain: the Inquisition against *Limpieza de Sangre*', in –, *Crisis and Change in Early Modern Spain* (Variorum Collected Studies Series; CS 415), VII, pp. 1-29 [a revised English version of 'Una crisis de conciencia en la Edad de Oro en Espana: Inquisicion contra *Limpieza de Sangre*', *Bulletin Hispanique*, Vol. 88, pp. 321-56].

—— (1997), *The Spanish Inquisition, An Historical Revision*, Weidenfeld & Nicolson, London.

Kantorowicz, E.H. (1957), *The King's Two Bodies. A Study in Medieval Political Theology*, Yale University Press, New Haven and London.

Kelley, D.R. (1970), *Foundations of Modern Historical Scholarship: Language, Law and History in the French Renaissance*, Columbia University Press, London and New York.

—— (1970), 'The Rise of Legal History in the Renaissance', *History and Theory*, Vol. 9, pp. 174-94.

—— (1990), 'Second Nature: The Idea of Custom in European Law, Society, and Culture', in A. Grafton and A. Blair (eds), *The Transmission of Culture in Early Modern Europe*, University of Pennsylvania Press, Philadelphia, pp. 131-72.

—— (1991), 'Law', in J.H. Burns (ed.), *The Cambridge History of Political Thought, 1450-1700*, Cambridge University Press, Cambridge, pp. 66-94.

Kempshall, M.S. (1999), *The Common Good in Late Medieval Political Thought: Moral Goodness and Material Benefit*, Clarendon Press, Oxford.

Kersting, W. (1990), art. 'Vertrag, Gesellschaftsvertrag, Herrschaftsvertrag', in O. Brunner, W. Conze and R. Koselleck (eds), *Geschichtliche Grundbegriffe, Historisches Lexikon der politisch-sozialen Sprache in Deutschland*, Vol. 6, Klett-Cotta, Stuttgart, pp. 901-54.

Kingdom, R. (1991), 'Calvinism and resistance theory, 1550-1580', in J.H. Burns, *Cambridge History of Political Thought, 1450-1700*, Cambridge University Press, Cambridge, pp. 193-218.

Koenigsberger, H.G. (1975), 'Spain', in O. Ranum (ed.), *National Consciousness, History, and Political Culture in Early-Modern Europe*, Johns Hopkins University Press, Baltimore and London, pp. 144-172.

—— (1977), '"Dominium regale" or "dominium politicum et regale"? Monarchies and Parliaments in Early Modern Europe', in K. Bosl (ed.), *Der Moderne Parlamentarismus und seine Grundlagen in der Ständischen Repräsentation*, Duncker und Humblot, Berlin, pp. 43-68.

—— (1997), 'Republicanism, monarchism and liberty', in R. Oresko, G.C. Gibbs and H.M. Scott (eds), *Royal and Republican Sovereignty in Early Modern Europe*, Essays in memory of Ragnhild Hatton, Cambridge University Press, Cambridge, pp. 43-74.

Köster, H.M. (1979), *Urstand, Fall und Erbsünde: in der Scholastik* (Handbuch der Dogmengeschichte; Bd.2, Faszikel 3b), Herder, Freiburg.

Konetzke, R. (1973), 'Territoriale Grundherrschaft und Landesherrschaft im spanischen Spätmittelalter, Ein Forschungsproblem zur Geschichte des spanischen Partikularismus', in *Histoire économique du monde méditerranéen 1450-1650, Melanges en l'honneur de Fernand Braudel*, n.p., Toulouse, pp. 299-310.

Koselleck, R. (1985), *Futures Past: on the Semantics of Historical Time* (Studies in contemporary German Social Thought), MIT Press, Cambridge, Mass. [transl. of R. Koselleck (1979), *Vergangene Zukunft: zur Semantik geschichtlicher Zeiten*, Suhrkamp, Frankfurt].

Krebs, R. (1890), *Politische Publizistik der Jesuiten und ihrer Gegner in den letzten Jahrzehnten vor dem Ausbruch des Dreissigjährigen Krieges*, n.p., Halle.

Kristeller, P.O. (1988), 'Humanism', in C.B. Schmitt and Q. Skinner (eds), *The Cambridge History of Renaissance Philosophy*, Cambridge University Press, Cambridge, pp. 113-37.

Láinez Alcalá, R. (1958), *Don Bernardo de Sandoval y Rojas: protector de Cervantes (1546-1618)*, n.p., Salamanca.

Laures, J. SJ (1928), *The Political Economy of Juan de Mariana*, Fordham University Press, New York.

Lewy, G. (1960), *Constitutionalism and Statecraft during the Golden Age of Spain, A Study of the Philosophy of Juan de Mariana, S.J* (Travaux d'Humanisme et Renaissance), Droz, Geneva.

Linehan, P. (1971), *The Spanish Church and the Papacy in the Thirteenth Century* (Cambridge Studies in Medieval Life & Thought, Third Series; Vol. 4), Cambridge University Press, Cambridge.

—— (1993), *History and the Historians of Medieval Spain*, Clarendon Press, Oxford.

Lloyd, H.A. (1991), 'Constitutionalism', in J.H. Burns (ed.), *The Cambridge History of Political Thought, 1450-1700*, Cambridge University Press, Cambridge, pp. 254-97.

Lovejoy, A.O. and G. Boas (1935), *Primitivism and Related Ideas in Antiquity*, Johns Hopkins University Press, Baltimore and London.

Lovett, A.W. (1977), *Philip II and Mateo Vázquez de Leca: the Government of Spain (1572-1592)* (Travaux d'Humanisme et Renaissance; Vol. 155), Droz, Geneva.

Lynch, J. (1991), *Spain 1516-1598, From Nation State to World Empire*, Oxford University Press, Oxford.

Lynn Martin, A. (1973), *Henry III and the Jesuit Politicians*, Droz, Geneva.

Lyons, J.D. (1989), *Exemplum, The Rhetoric of Example in Early Modern France and Italy*, Princeton University Press, Princeton.

Macedo de Steffens, D. (1959), 'La doctrina del tiranicidio: Juan de Salisbury (1115-80) y Juan de Mariana (1535-1624)', *Anales de historia antigua y medieval*, Vol. 35, pp. 123-33.

Maclean, I. (1993), *From Prudence to Policy: Some Notes on the Prehistory of Policy Sciences*, University of Nijmegen, Nijmegen.

Mallet, M. (1990), 'The theory and practice of warfare in Machiavelli's republic', in G. Bock, Q. Skinner and M. Viroli (eds), *Machiavelli and Republicanism*, Cambridge University Press, Cambridge, pp. 173-80.

Marañon, G. (1954), *Antonio Pérez*, Espasa-Calpe, Madrid.

Maravall, J.A. (1956), *Pensamiento político, política internacional y religiosa de Fernando el Católico*, Institución 'Fernando el Católico', Zaragoza [reprint: (1984), *Estudios de historia del pensamiento español*, Vol. 2: *La epoca del renacimiento*, Ediciones Cultura Hispánica, Madrid, xii, pp. 343-61].

—— (1975), *Estudios de historia del pensamiento español*, Vol. 3: *siglo XVII*, 2nd edn, Ediciones Cultura Hispánica, Madrid.

Markus, R.A. (1970), *Saeculum: History and Society in the Theology of St. Augustine*, Cambridge University Press, Cambridge.

Márquez de la Plata, V.M. and Valero de Barnabe, L. (1991), *Nobiliaria española: origen, evolución, instituciones y probanzas* (Colección Persevante Heráldica Borgoña; Vol. 1), Prensa y Ediciones Iberoamericanas, Madrid.

Mayer, T.F. (1989), *Thomas Starkey and the Commonweal: Humanist Politics and Religion in the Reign of Henry VIII*, Cambridge University Press, Cambridge.

—— (2000), *Reginald Pole, Prince and Prophet*, Cambridge University Press, Cambridge.

McGrath, A.E. (1981), '"Augustinianism"? A Critical Assessment of the so-called "Medieval Augustinian Tradition" on Justification', *Augustiniana*, Vol. 31, pp. 247-67.

Mechoulan, H. (1986), 'Le travail du temps dans l'oeuvre politique de Mariana', *Archives de Philosophie*, Vol. 49, pp. 545-59.

Mellor, R. (1993), *Tacitus*, Routledge, New York.

Menéndez Pelayo, M. (1956), *Historio de los heterodoxos españoles*, Vol. 2, Biblioteca de Autores Cristianos, Madrid.

Mercken, H.P.F. (1998), 'Scotus Interpretation of the *Lex Naturae* in the Perspective of Western Philosophical Ethics', in E.P. Bos (ed.), *John Duns Scotus (1265/6-1308): Renewal of Philosoph*, Rodopi, Amsterdam, pp. 171-82.

Mesa, C.E. (1986), 'Tres clasicos españoles de la historia', in *Boletín de Historia y Antigüedades*, Vol. 73, pp. 833-64.

Mesnard, P. (1952), *L'Essor de la philosophie politique au XVIe siecle*, J. Vrin, Paris.

Möhle, H. (2003), 'Scotus' Theory of Natural Law', in T. Williams (ed.), *The Cambridge Companion to Duns Scotus*, Cambridge University Press, Cambridge, pp. 312-33.

Momigliano, A. (1947), 'The First Political Commentary on Tacitus', *Journal of Roman Studies*, Vol. 37, pp. 91-101 [reprinted: –??(1977), *Essays in Ancient and Modern Historiography*, Oxford University Press, Oxford, pp. 205-29].

Moos, Peter von (1998), 'Die Begriffe öffentlich und privat in der Geschichte und bei den Historikern', *Saeculum*, Vol. 49, pp. 161-92.

Moraes, J.Q. de (1993), *A justificacao do tiranicidio no pensamento proto-liberal de Juan de Mariana*, Cadernos IFCH, Campinas.

Moraw, P. (1982), 'Herrschaft [*dominium*]', II.1: 'Herrschaft im Mittelalter', in O. Brunner, W. Conze and R. Koselleck (eds), *Geschichtliche Grundbegriffe, Historisches Lexikon der politisch-sozialen Sprache in Deutschland*, Vol. 3, Klett-Cotta, Stuttgart, pp. 5-13.

Moss, A. (1999), *Printed Commonplace-Books and the Structuring of Renaissance Thought*, Oxford University Press, Oxford.

Mousnier, R. (1964), *L'assassinat d'Henri IV, 14 mai 1610 (Trente journées qui ont fait la France)*; Vol. 13, Gallimard, Paris.

Mühleisen, H.-O. and Stammen, T. (eds) (1990), *Politische Tugendlehre und Regierungskunst, Studien zum Fürstenspiegel der Frühen Neuzeit* (Studia Augustana; Vol. 2), M. Niemeyer, Tübingen.

Münkler, H. (1987), *Im Namen des Staates: Die Begründung der Staatsraison in der Frühen Neuzeit*, S. Fischer Verlag, Frankfurt.

Muldoon, J. (1994), *The Americas in the Spanish World Order, The Justification for Conquest in the Seventeenth Century*, University of Pennsylvania Press, Philadelphia.

Munitiz, J.A. (2004), 'Francisco Suárez and the Exclusion of Men of Jewish or Moorish Descent from the Society of Jesus', *Archivum Historicum Societas Iesu*, Vol. 73, pp. 327-40.

Murphy, M. (1999), 'A Jacobite Antiquary in Grub Street: Captain John Stevens (c. 1662-1726)', *Recusant History*, Vol. 24, pp. 437-54.

Murray, J.C. (1948), 'St. Robert Bellarmine on the Indirect Power', *Theological Studies*, Vol. 9, pp. 491-535.

Nader, H. (1990), *Liberty in Absolutist Spain, The Habsburg Sale of Towns, 1516-1700*, Johns Hopkins University Press, Baltimore and London.

Nelson, E. (2005), *The Jesuits and the Monarchy, Catholic Reform and Political Authority in France (1590-1615)*, Ashgate, Aldershot.

Nicolas, J., Baruque, J.V. and Vilfan, S. (1997), 'The Right of Representation: The Resistance Movements, 2.1: Spain', in P. Blickle (ed.), *Resistance, Representation, and Community* (European Science Foundation series: W. Blockmans and J.P. Genet (eds), *The Origins of the Modern State in Europe, 13th to 18th Centuries*), Oxford University Press, Oxford, pp. 72-76.

Nieto Soría, J.M. (1988), *Fundamentos ideológicos del poder real en Castilla, siglos XII-XVI* (Publicaciones del gobierno de Castilla y Leon), Eudema, Madrid.

—— (1998), 'Propaganda and Legitimation in Castile: Religion and Church, 1250-1500', in A. Ellenius (ed.), *Iconography, Propaganda and Legitimation* (European Science Foundation series: W. Blockmans and J.P. Genet (eds), *The Origins of the Modern State in Europe, 13th to 18th Centuries*), Oxford University Press, Oxford, pp. 105-19.

Noreña, C.G. (1970), *Juan Luis Vives* (International Archives of the History of Ideas; Vol. 34), Nijhoff, The Hague.

—— (1975), *Studies in Spanish Renaissance Thought* (International Archives of the History of Ideas; Vol. 82), Nijhoff, The Hague.

Norris, F.I. (1977), 'Mariana and the Classical Tradition of Statecraft', *Kentucky Romance Quarterly*, Vol. 24, pp. 389-97.

Oakley, F. (1984), *Natural Law, Conciliarism and Consent in the Late Middle Ages*, Ashgate, London.

—— (1991), 'Christian Obedience and Authority, 1520-1550', in J.H. Burns (ed.), *Cambridge History of Political Thought, 1450-1700*, Cambridge University Press, Cambridge, pp. 159-92.

—— (1996), '"Anxieties of Influence": Skinner, Figgis, Conciliarism and Early Modern Constitutionalism', *Past and Present*, Vol. 151, pp. 60-110.

—— (2003), *The Conciliarist Tradition. Constitutionalism in the Catholic Church, 1300-1870*, Oxford University Press, Oxford.

Oberman, H.A. (1963), *The Harvest of Medieval Theology: Gabriel Biel and late medieval Nominalism*, Harvard University Press, Cambridge, Mass.

Oestreich, G. (1982), *Neostoicism and the Early-Modern State*, ed. B. Oestreich and H.G. Koenigsberger, transl. D. McLintock, Cambridge University Press, Cambridge, pp. 135-54 [a translation of G. Oestreich (1969), *Geist und Gestalt des frühmodernen Staates, Ausgewählte Aufsätze*, Duncker und Humblot, Berlin].

—— (1989), *Antiker Geist und moderner Staat bei Justus Lipsius (1547-1606), Der Neustoizismus als politische Bewegung*, ed. N. Mout (Schriftenreihe der Historischen Kommission bei der Bayerischen Akademie der Wissenschaften; Vol. 38), Vandenhoeck and Ruprecht, Göttingen.

O'Keohane, N. (1980), *Philosophy and the State in France, The Renaissance to the Enlightenment*, Princeton University Press, Princeton.

O'Malley, J.W. (1990), 'Renaissance Humanism and the Religious Culture of the First Jesuits', *Heythrop Journal*, Vol. 31, pp. 471-87 [reprinted:– (1993), *Religious Culture in the Sixteenth Century* (Variorum Collected Studies Series, Vol. 404), Ashgate, Aldershot, X].

—— (1993), *The First Jesuits*, Harvard University Press, Harvard.

Overfield, J.H. (1984), *Humanism and Scholasticism in Late Medieval Germany*, Princeton University Press, Princeton.

Pagden, A. (1981), 'The "School of Salamanca" and the "Affair of the Indies"' in C.B. Schmitt (ed.), *History of Universities*, Vol. 1: *Continuity and Change in Early Modern Universities*, Amersham, Avebury.

—— (1982), *The Fall of Natural Man: The American Indian and the Origins of Comparative Ethnology*, Cambridge University Press, Cambridge.

—— (1995), *Lords of all the World, Ideologies of Empire in Spain, Britain and France c. 1500 – c. 1800*, Yale University Press, New Haven and London.

Palomo, F. (1995), 'La autoridad de los prelados postridentinos', *Hispania Sacra*, Vol. 47, pp. 587-624.

Panier, L. (1996), *Le péché originel: naissance de l'homme sauvé*, Éditions du Cerf, Paris.

Paradisi, B. (1983), 'Il pensiero politico dei giuristi medievali', in L. Firpo (ed.), *Storia delle idee politiche, economiche e sociali*, Vol. 2, Unione Tipografico, Turin, pp. 211-366.

Paravicini, W. (2004), 'Der Fall des Günstlings. Hofparteien in Europa vom 13. bis zum 17. Jahrhundert', in J. Hirschbiegel and W. Paravicini (eds), *Der Fall des Günstlings. Hofparteien in Europa vom 13. bis zum 17. Jahrhundert* (Residenzenforschung; Vol. 17), Thorbecke, Ostfildern, pp. 13-22.

Parker, G. (1972), *The Army of Flanders and the Spanish Road, 1567-1659*, Cambridge University Press, Cambridge.

Pennington, K. (1993), *The Prince and the Law, 1200-1600: Sovereignty and Rights in the Western Legal Tradition*, University of California Press, Berkeley.

Perreiah, A. (1982), 'Humanist Critiques of Scholastic Dialectic', *Sixteenth Century Journal*, Vol. 13, pp. 3-22.

Pí y Margall, F. (1888), *Juan de Mariana, breves apuntos sobre su vida y sus escritos*, n.p., Madrid.

Pizarro Lorente, H. (1994), 'El control de la conciencia regia. El confesor real Fray Bernardo de Fresneda', in F.J. Bouza Álvarez (ed.), *La corte de Felipe II*, Alianza Editorial, Madrid.

Plans, J.B. (2000), *La Escuela de Salamanca y la renovación de la teología en el siglo XVI* (Biblioteca de autores cristianos. Maior, Vol. 63), Biblioteca de Autores Cristianos, Madrid.

Pocock, J.G.A. (1975), *The Machiavellian Moment, Florentine Political Thought and the Atlantic Republican Tradition*, Princeton University Press, Princeton.

—— (1987), 'The Concept of Language and the *métier d'historien*: Some Considerations on Practice', in A. Pagden (ed.), *The Languages of Political Theory in Early-Modern Europe* (Ideas in Context), Cambridge University Press, Cambridge, pp. 19-38.

—— (1993), 'A Discourse on Sovereignty', in N. Phillipson and Q. Skinner (eds), *Political Discourse in Early Modern Britain*, Cambridge University Press, Cambridge, pp. 377-428.

—— (1996), 'Concepts and Discourses: A Difference in Culture? Comments on a paper by Melvin Richter', in: H. Lehmann and M. Richter (eds), *The Meaning of Historical Terms and Concepts. New Studies on Begriffsgeschichte*, German Historical Institute, Washington, D.C., pp. 47-58.

Popkin, R. (1979), *The History of Scepticism from Erasmus to Spinoza*, University of California Press, Berkeley.

Post, G. (1946), 'The Romano-Canonical Maxim "quod omnes tangit" in Bracton', *Traditio*, Vol. 4, pp. 197-252.

Potts, Timothy C. (1982), 'Conscience', in N. Kretzmann, A. Kenny and J. Pinborg (eds), *The Cambridge History of Later Medieval Philosophy*, Cambridge University Press, Cambridge, pp. 687-704.

Prat, M. (1876), *Recherches historiques et critiques sur la Compagnie de Jesus en France du temps du Pére Coton, 1564-1626*, Briday, Lyon.

Puigdoménech, H. (1988), *Maquiavelo en España, Presencia de sus obras en los siglos XVI y XVII*, Fundación Universitaria España, Madrid.

Quaglioni, D. (1983), *Politica e diritto nel Trecento italiano. Il 'De tyranno' di Bartolo di Sassoferrato (1314-57). Con l'edizione critica dei trattati 'De Guelphis et Gebellinis', 'De regimine civitatis' e 'De tyranno'* (Il pensiero politica biblioteca; 11), Olschki, Florence.

Quintá de Kaúl, M.C. (1989), 'Consideraciones sobre el Barroco y el derecho de resistencia en Juan de Mariana', *Revista de Historia Universal*, Vol. 2, pp. 191-215.

Ramos y Loscertales, J.M. (1961), *Reino de Aragon bajo la dinastía pamplonesa*, ed. J.M. Lacarra de Miguel (Acta Salmanticensia; Serie de filosofía y letras; Vol. 15/2), Universidad de Salamanca, Salamanca.

Ranke, L. von (1923), *Die römischen Päpste in den letzten vier Jahrhunderten*, 12th edn, Duncker und Humblot, Munich.

Reinhard, W. (1982), 'Confessionalizzazione forzata? Prolegomeni ad una teoria dell'età confessionale', *Annali dell'Istituto Storico Italo-Germanico in Trento*, Vol. 8, pp. 13-37.

Reulos, M. (1973), 'Les sources juridiques de Bodin', in H. Denzer (ed.), *Jean Bodin, Verhandlungen der internationalen Bodin-Tagung in Muenchen*, Beck, Munich, pp. 187-94.

Reusch, F.H. (1970), *Die Indices librorum prohibitorum des sechzehnten Jahrhunderts*, Graaf, Nieukoop.

Révah, I.S. (1971), 'La controverse sur les statuts de pureté de sang: un document inédit. "Relación y consulta del Cardenal Guevara sobre el negocio de Fray Agustín Saluzio" (Madrid, 13 aout 1600)', *Bulletin Hispanique*, Vol. 73, pp. 263-316.

Richter, M. (1996), 'Opening a Dialogue and Recognizing an Achievement', *Archiv für Begriffsgeschichte*, Vol. 39, pp. 19-26.

Robles, L. (1979), *El estudio de la 'Etica' en España (del siglo XIII al XX)*, Instituto de Historia de la Teología Espanola, Salamanca.

Rondet, H. (1967), *Le Péché originel dans la tradition patristique et théologique*, Fayard, Paris.

Rouco-Varela, A.M. (1965), *Staat und Kirche im Spanien des XVI. Jahrhunderts*, Hueber, Munich.

Rubiés, J.-P. (1995), 'Reason of State and Constitutional Thought in the Crown of Aragon, 1580-1640', *Historical Journal*. Vol. 38, pp. 1-28.

—— (1996), 'La idea del gobierno mixto y su significado en la crisis de la monarquía hispanica', *Historia Social*, Vol. 24, pp. 57-81.

—— (1998), 'El Constitucionalisme Català en una Perspective Europea: Conceptes I Trajectòries, Segles XV-XVIII', *Pedralbes*, Vol. 18, pp. 453-74.

Rubinstein, N. (1987), 'The History of the Word *politicus* in Early-Modern Europe', in A. Pagden (ed.), *The Languages of Political Theory in Early-Modern Europe*, Cambridge University Press, Cambridge, pp. 41-56.

Rummel, E. (1995), *The Humanist-Scholastic Debate in the Renaissance and Reformation* (Harvard Historical Studies; 120), Harvard University Press, Cambridge, Mass. and London.

Russel, P. (1967), 'Arms versus Letters: Towards a Definition of Spanish Fifteenth-Century Humanism', in A.R. Lewis (ed.), *Aspects of the Renaissance: A Symposium*, University of Texas Press, Austin, pp. 47-58.

Ryan, M. (2000), 'Bartolus of Sassoferrato and Free Cities (The Alexander Prize Lecture)', *Transactions of the Royal Historical Society*, Vol. 10 (Sixth Series), pp. 65-90.

Salmon, J.H.H. (1959), *The French Religious Wars in English Political Thought*, Clarendon Press, Oxford.

—— (1973), 'Bodin and the Monarchomachs', in H. Denzer (ed.), *Verhandlungen der internationalen Bodin Tagung*, Beck, Munich, pp. 359-78 [now in: J.H.M. Salmon (1987), *Renaissance and Revolt, Essays in the intellectual and social history of early modern France* (Cambridge Studies in Early Modern History), Cambridge University Press, Cambridge, pp. 119-35].

—— (1980), 'Cicero and Tacitus in Sixteenth-Century France', in *American Historical Review*, Vol. 85 , pp. 307-31 [now in: as above, pp. 27-53].

—— (1982), 'An alternative Theory of Popular Resistance: Buchanan, Rossaeus and Locke', in B. Paradisi (ed.), *Diritto e potere nella storia europea*, Leo S. Olschki Editore, Florence, pp. 823-49 [now in: as above, pp. 136-54].

—— (1991), 'Catholic Resistance Theory, Ultramontanism, and the Royalist Response, 1580-1620', in J.H. Burns (ed.), *The Cambridge History of Political Thought 1450-1700*, Cambridge University Press, Cambridge, pp. 219-53.

Sánchez-Albornoz, C. (1924), 'Las Behetrías. La encomendación en Asturias, León y Castilla', *Anuario de historia del derecho español*, Vol. 1, pp. 158-336.

Sanmartí-Boncompte, F. (1951), *Tácito en España*, Ariel, Barcelona.

Schellhase, K. (1976), *Tacitus in Renaissance Political Thought*, University of Chicago Press, Chicago and London.

Schiffman, Z.S. (1991), *On the Threshold of Modernity, Relativism in the French Renaissance*, Johns Hopkins University Press, Baltimore and London.

Schilling, H. (1998), 'Confessionalisation in Europe: Causes and Effects for Church, State, Society, and Culture', in K. Bussmann and H. Schilling (eds), *1648: War and Peace in Europe*, Vol.1, Veranstaltungsgesellschaft, Münster, pp. 219-28.

Schmidt, T. (1989), *Der Bonifaz-Prozeß, Verfahren der Papstanklage in der Zeit Bonifaz VIII. und Clemens V*, Böhlau, Cologne and Vienna.

Schmitt, C.B. (1972), *Cicero Scepticus: A Study of the Influence of the Academica in the Renaissance* (International Archives of the History of Ideas; Vol. 52), Nijhoff, The Hague.

—— (1983), 'The Rediscovery of Ancient Skepticism in Modern Times', in M. Burnyeat (ed.), *The Skeptical Tradition*, University of California Press, Berkeley and Los Angeles, pp. 225-51.

Schüssler, R. (2002), *Moral im Zweifel*, Vol. 1, Mentis Verlag, Paderborn.

Seigel, J.E. (1968), *Rhetoric and Philosophy in Renaissance Humanism. The Union of Eloquence and Wisdom, Petrarch to Valla*, Princeton University Press, Princeton.

Segoloni, D. (ed.) (1962), *Bartolo da Sassoferrato. Studi e documenti per il VI centenario*, Giuffrè, Milan.

Shapiro, B.J. (1983), *Probability and Certainty in Seventeenth Century England*, Princeton University Press, Princeton.

Sigmund, P.E. (1993), 'Law and Politics', in N. Kretzmann and E. Stump (eds), *The Cambridge Companion to Aquinas*, Cambridge University Press, Cambridge, pp. 217-31.

Skinner, Q. (1969), 'Meaning and Understanding in the History of Ideas', *History and Theory*, Vol. 8, pp. 3-53

—— (1978), *The Foundations of Modern Political Thought*, 2 vols., Cambridge University Press, Cambridge.

—— (1988), 'Political Philosophy', in C.B. Schmitt, Q. Skinner and E. Kessler (eds), *The Cambridge History of Renaissance Philosophy*, Cambridge University Press, Cambridge, pp. 389-452.

—— (1989), 'Language and political change', in T. Ball, J. Farr and R.L. Hanson (eds), *Political Innovation and Conceptual Change*, Cambridge University Press, Cambridge, pp. 6-23.

—— (1996), *Reason and Rhetoric in the Philosophy of Hobbes*, Cambridge University Press, Cambridge.

Solana, M. (1940), *Historia de la filosofía Española*, Vol. 3: *época del Renacimiento (siglo XVI)*, Real Academia de Ciencias Exactas, Fisicas y Naturales, Madrid.

Soll, J. (2003), 'Empirical History and the Transformation of Political Criticism in France from Bodin to Bayle', *Journal of the History of Ideas*, Vol. 64, pp. 297-316

Sommerville, J. (1982), 'From Suárez to Filmer', *Historical Journal*, Vol. 25, pp. 525-40.

—— (1988), 'The "New Art of Lying": Equivocation, Mental Reservation, and Casuistry', in E. Leites (ed.), *Conscience and Casuistry in Early Modern Europe*, Cambridge University Press, Cambridge, pp. 159-84.

Springborg, P. (1995), 'Thomas Hobbes and Cardinal Bellarmine: Leviathan and the Ghost of the Roman Empire', in *History of Political Thought*, Vol. 16, pp. 503-31.

Stackelberg, J. von (1960), *Tacitus in der Romania*, Niemeyer, Tübingen.

Stolleis, M. (1983), *Pecunia Nervus Rerum: Zur Staatsfinanzierung der frühen Neuzeit*, Vittorio Klostermann, Frankfurt.

Stone, M.F.W. (2003), 'Scrupulosity and Conscience: Probabilism in Early Modern Scholastic Ethics', in H. Braun and E. Vallance (eds), *Contexts of Conscience in Early Modern Europe, 1500-1700*, Palgrave, Basingstoke and New York, pp. 1-16.

—— (2006), 'Truth, Deception, and Lies. Lessons from the Casuistical Tradition', *Tijdschrift voor Filosofie*, Vol. 68, pp. 101-31.

Stradling, R.A. (1981), *Europe and the Decline of Spain, A study of the Spanish System, 1580-1720*, Allen and Unwin, London.

—— (1994), 'Seventeenth Century Spain: Decline or Survival?', in –, *Spain's Struggle for Europe 1598-1668*, Hambledon Press, London, pp. 3-32.

Thomas, J.A.C. (1975), *The Institutes of Justinian, Text, Translation and Commentary*, North-Holland Publishing Company, Amsterdam and Oxford.

Thompson, I.A.A. (1976), *War and Government in Habsburg Spain, 1560-1620*, Athlone Press, London.

—— (1982), 'Crown and Cortes in Castile, 1590-1665', *Parliaments, Estates and Representation*, Vol. 2, pp. 29-45.

—— (1984), 'The Rule of the Law in Early Modern Castile', *European History Quarterly*, Vol. 14, pp. 221-34.

—— (1990), 'Castile', in J. Miller (ed), *Absolutism in Seventeenth-Century Europe*, Macmillan, Basingstoke, pp. 69-98.

—— (1994), 'Castile: Polity, Fiscality and Fiscal Crisis'; in P.T. Hoffmann and K. Norberg (eds), *Fiscal Crises, Liberty and Representative Government, 1450-1789*, Stanford University Press, Stanford, pp. 140-80.

—— (1994), 'Castile: Absolutism, Constitutionalism and Liberty', in [as above], pp. 181-225.

—— (1995), 'Castile, Spain and the Monarchy: The Political Community from *patria natural* to *patria nacional*', in R.L. Kagan and G. Parker (eds), *Spain, Europe and the Atlantic World*, Essays in honour of John H. Elliott, Cambridge University Press, Cambridge, pp. 125-59.

—— (1997), 'Oposición política y juicio del gobierno en los Cortes de 1592-1598', *Studia Historica, Studia Moderna*, Vol. 17, pp. 37-62.

—— (1999), 'The Institutional Background to the Rise of the Minister-Favourite', in J.H. Elliott and L. Brockliss (eds), *The World of the Favourite*, Yale University Press, New Haven and London, pp. 13-25.

Tierney, B. (1963), 'The Prince is Not Bound by the Laws: Accursius and the Origins of the Modern State', *Comparative Studies in Society and History*, Vol. 5, pp. 379-400 [reprint: – (1979), *Church Law and Constitutional Thought* (CSS; 90), Ashgate, Aldershot, III].

—— (1998), *Foundations of the Conciliar Theory: the Contribution of the Medieval Canonists from Gratian to the Great Schism*, new, enlarged edn (Studies in the History of Christian Thought; Vol. 81), Brill, Leiden [originally published: (1955), Cambridge University Press, Cambridge].

Tierno Galvan, E. (1971), 'El tacitismo en las doctrinas políticas del siglo de oro español', in –, *Escritos*, Tecnos, Madrid, pp. 11-93 [originally published: (1947/48), Publicaciones de la Universidad de Murcia, Murcia].

Tomás y Valiente, F. (1979), *Manual de Historia del Derecho Español*, Tecnos, Madrid.

Toulmin, S. and Goodfield, J. (1965), *The Discovery of Time*, Harper and Row, New York.

Trentman, J.A. (1982), 'Scholasticism in the Seventeenth Century', in N. Kretzmann, A. Kenny and J. Pinborg (eds), *Cambridge History of Later Medieval Philosophy*, Cambridge University Press, Cambridge, pp. 818-37.

Trinkaus, C. (1970), *In our Image and Likeness: Humanity and Divinity in Italian Humanist Thought*, Vol. 1, Constable, London.

Truman, R. (1999), *Spanish Treatises on Government, Society and Religion in the Time of Philip II, The 'de regimine principum' and associated Traditions*, Brill, Leiden.

Tuck, R. (1979/81), *Natural Rights Theories. Their Origin and Development*, Cambridge University Press, Cambridge.

—— (1993), *Philosophy and Government 1572-1651* (Ideas in Context), Cambridge University Press, Cambridge.

Tully, J. (ed.) (1987), *Meaning and Context: Quentin Skinner and his Critics*, Polity Press, Cambridge.

Turchetti, M. (2001), *Tyrannie et tyrannicide de l'antiquité à nos jours*, Presses Universitaires de France, Paris.

Urriza, J. (1941), *La Praeclara Facultad de Arte y Filosofía de la Universidad de Alcalá de Henares en el Siglo de Oro, 1509-1621*, Consejo Superior de Investigaciones Científicas – Instituto Jeronimo Zurita, Madrid.

Valdeavellano, L.G. de (1968), *Curso de historia de las instituciones españolas, De los orígenes al final de la Edad Media*, Alianza Editorial, Madrid.

Vázquez, I. (1968), 'La Enseñanza del Escotismo en España', in *De Doctrina Ioannis Duns Scoti, Acta Congressus Scotistici Internationalis Oxonii et Edimburgi 11-17 sept. 1966 celebrati*, 4 vols., Vol. 4: *Scotismus Decursu Saeculorum*, Cura Commissionis Scotisticae, Rome, pp. 191-220.

Vilar, J. (1968), 'Intellectuels et Noblesse: Le *Docteur* Eugenio de Narbona (Une admiration politique de Lope de Vega)', *Études Iberique*, Vol. 3, pp. 7-28.

—— (1970), 'Docteurs et marchands: l'école de Tolede' (Communication to the Fifth International Congress of Economic History), n.p., Moscow.

—— (1973), *Literatura y enconomía: la figura satírica del arbitrista en el Siglo de Oro*, Revista de Occidente, Madrid.

Viroli, M. (1998), *Machiavelli* (Founders of Modern Political and Social Thought), Oxford University Press, Oxford.

Warmelo, P. van (1976), *An Introduction to the Principles of Roman Civil Law*, Juta, Cape Town.

Watt, J.A. (1988), 'Spiritual and Temporal Powers', in J.H. Burns (ed.), *The Cambridge History of Medieval Political Thought*, Cambridge University Press, Cambridge, pp. 367-423.

Weil, R. (1977), 'Aristotle's View of History', in J. Barnes, M. Schofield and R. Sorabji (eds), *Articles on Aristotle*, Vol. 2: *Ethics and Politics*, Duckworth, London, pp. 202-17.

Werner, K. (1887), *Die Scholastik des späteren Mittelalters*, Vol. 4(2): *Der Übergang der Scholastik in ihr nachtridentinisches Entwicklungsstadium*, Braumüller, Vienna.

Westerman, P.C. (1997), *The Disintegration of Natural Law Theory. Aquinas to Finnis* (Brill's Studies in Intellectual History; Vol. 84), Brill, Leiden.

Wilks, M. (1963), *The Problem of Sovereignty in the Later Middle Ages, The Papal Monarchy with Augustinus Triumphus and the Publicists*, Cambridge University Press, Cambridge.

Woolf, C.N.S. (1913), *Bartolus of Sassoferrato: His position in the History of Medieval Political Thought*, Cambridge University Press, Cambridge.

Wright, A.D. (1991), *Catholicism and Spanish Society under the reign of Philip II and Philip III*, The Edwin Mellen Press, Lewiston.

—— (2005), *The Counter-Reformation. Catholic Europe and the Non-Christian World*, Ashgate, Aldershot.

Wyduckel, D. (1979), *Princeps legibus solutus, Eine Untersuchung zur frühmodernen Rechts- und Staatslehre* (Schriften zur Verfassungsgeschichte; Vol. 30), Duncker und Humblot, Berlin.

Zagorin, P. (1990), 'Ways of Lying: Dissimulation, Persecution, and Conformity in Early Modern Europe', Harvard University Press, Cambridge (Mass.) and London.

Index

BIRKBECK COLLEGE

1912585473

Malet Street, London WC1E 7HX
020-7631 6239
Items should be returned or renewed by the latest date stamped below.
Please pick up a Library guide or visit the Library website
http://www.bbk.ac.uk/lib/
for information about online renewals.